The Annals of Fulda

Manchester Medieval Sources series

series adviser Janet L. Nelson

This series aims to meet a growing need amongst students and teachers of medieval history for translations of key sources that are directly useable in students' own work. The series will provide texts central to medieval studies courses and will focus upon the diverse cultural, social as well as political conditions that affected the functioning of all levels of medieval society. The basic premise of the new series is that translation must be accompanied by sufficient introductory and explanatory material and each volume will therefore include a comprehensive guide to the sources' interpretation, including discussion of critical linguistic problems and an assessment of the most recent research on the topics being covered.

already published in the series

Janet L. Nelson *The Annals of St-Bertin: ninth-century histories, volume I*

forthcoming titles in the series will include

Donald Bullough *The Vikings in Paris*

John Edwards *The Jews in western Europe, 1400–1600*

Chris Given-Wilson *Chronicles of the Revolution, 1397–1400*

Rosemary Horrox *The aftermath of the Black Death*

Simon Lloyd *The impact of the crusades: the experience of England, 1095–1274*

Richard Smith *Sources for the population history of England, 1000–1540*

Robert Swanson *Catholic England: religion, faith and observance before the Reformation*

J. A. Watt *The origins of anti-semitism in Europe*

THE ANNALS OF FULDA

NINTH-CENTURY HISTORIES, VOLUME II

translated and annotated by Timothy Reuter

Manchester University Press
Manchester and New York

distributed exclusively in the USA and Canada by St. Martin's Press

Copyright © Timothy Reuter 1992

Published by Manchester University Press
Oxford Road, Manchester M13 9PL, England
and Room 400, 175 Fifth Avenue, New York, NY 10010, USA

Distributed exclusively in the USA and Canada
by St. Martin's Press, Inc., 175 Fifth Avenue, New York, NY 10010, USA

British Library Cataloguing-in-Publication Data
A catalogue record for this book is available from the British Library

Library of Congress cataloging in publication data applied for

Reprinted 1994

ISBN 0 7190 3458 2 *paperback*

Typeset in Monotype Bell
by Koinonia Ltd, Manchester
Printed in Great Britain
by Bell & Bain Ltd, Glasgow

CONTENTS

FOREWORD

This translation of the *Annals of Fulda* complements the *Annals of St-Bertin*, published last year as the first of the new MUP series of translated medieval sources. Both volumes of *Ninth-century histories* continue the story told in earlier Frankish historical writings. The eastern and western Carolingian successor-kingdoms were continuations of Charlemagne's Empire, variations on a theme. It seems entirely appropriate that the *Annals of Fulda* should appear in English in 1992: as diverse Western European countries move closer to political unity, their common starting-point in a world dominated by the heirs of Charlemagne needs, more than ever, to be appreciated. It is equally appropriate that the translator should be a historian who in the past decade or so has done more than anyone to make medieval German history, and its modern German historiography, accessible to English-speaking students. Tim Reuter's translation of the *Annals of Fulda* takes its place alongside, most recently, his brilliant account of *Germany in the Early Middle Ages* (Longman, 1991). If in that book he showed how Germany was created, he presents in this one some of the basic materials from which the creation was put together. That story has its analogue in the making of France. Between them, the two volumes of *Ninth-century histories* will allow readers to form their own assessments of the distinctive variety, as well as the unity, of early medieval Europe.

Janet L. Nelson

PREFACE

This translation has its origins in a meeting with Jinty Nelson at a conference at Leeds in 1978; at that time she had already completed a draft of her translation of the *Annals of St-Bertin*, and we both felt that it would be desirable to produce translations of the two works at the same time, though in the end it has proved impracticable to publish both in a single volume. We embarked on the joint project with enthusiasm, but inevitably we have taken far longer over it than the year or two which we initially envisaged. Over the years we have exchanged and criticised each other's translations and commentaries, and I owe a great deal to her friendship and support and to her guidance on ninth-century matters. The errors in this translation and commentary are not hers; but a lot else is. In particular I have drawn on her translation of the *Annals of St-Bertin* both for information and as a model of how to organise this book. As by the time I had finished the translation I had ceased for the time being to teach in an English-speaking environment it has not had the baptism of fire in practical use which hers has had, and although I trust there are no horrible blunders in it, some infelicities and obscurities may still remain which using the text to teach from might have revealed.

I have also profited from discussions with a number of friends and colleagues in Germany and Britain over the last ten years – Gerd Althoff, Eckhard Freise, Johannes Fried, Wilfried Hartmann, Rudolf Schieffer, Martina Stratmann, Chris Wickham and Ian Wood – all of whom have given me the benefit of their expertise and insights. Franz Fuchs gave me valuable information about the manuscript transmission when I was writing the introduction and has helped me to clarify in my own mind some of the complex issues involved. Again, the errors and omissions which remain are mine, not theirs; but I am grateful for their help.

I hope that this translation, together with Jinty Nelson's translation of the *Annals of St-Bertin*, will help to show students and their teachers that the history of the Frankish kingdoms after the death of Charles the Great in 814 and the division of the Frankish empire in 843 is interesting in its own right and is not simply a story of chaos and decay. The world east of the Rhine is a strange one to most

Anglo-Saxon medievalists, who have on the whole preferred to study the history of the Romance-speaking countries if they have crossed the Channel at all, and it is time that it became more familiar.

Monumenta Germaniae Historica, Munich
December 1991

LIST OF ABBREVIATIONS

AA — *Annales Alamannici*

AB — *Annales Bertiniani*

AC — *Annales Corbeienses*

AF — *Annales Fuldenses*

AfD — *Archiv für Diplomatik*

AH — *Annales Hildesheimenses*

AKG — *Archiv für Kulturgeschichte*

ARF — *Annales regni Francorum*

AS — *Annals of Salzburg (Annales Iuvavenses)*

ASC — *Anglo-Saxon Chronicle*

AV — *Annales Vedastini*

AX — *Annales Xantenses*

BM — J. F. Böhmer, *Regesta Imperii 1. Die Regesten des Karolingerreichs*, 2nd edn by E. Mühlbacher *et al.* (Innsbruck 1908)

D, DD — Diploma(ta). By convention this refers by number to the diploma(ta) as edited by the *MGH*; the rulers are distinguished by an abbreviation (LG = Louis the German, LY = Louis the Younger, Lo I = Lothar I, C III = Charles III, A = Arnulf). Thus D A 78 is no. 78 in the edition of Arnulf's diplomata (Kehr 1940)

DA — *Deutsches Archiv für Erforschung des Mittelalters*

FMS — *Frühmittelalterliche Studien*

HJb — *Historisches Jahrbuch*

HZ — *Historische Zeitschrift*

JE/JL — P. Jaffé, *Regesta Pontificum Romanorum ab condita ecclesia ad annum post Christum natum MCXCVIII*, 2nd edn by W. Wattenbach, S. Löwenfeld, F. Kaltenbrunner and P. Ewald, 2 vols. (Leipzig 1885-88); cited as JE and number (for papal letters up to 882) or JL and number (for papal letters after 882)

JEccH — *Journal of Ecclesiastical History*

MGH — *Monumenta Germaniae Historica*, with subdivisions:

Capit. — *Capitularia regum Francorum*

Conc. — *Concilia*

Epp. — *Epistolae in quarto*

SRG — *Scriptores rerum Germanicarum in usum scholarum separatim editi*

SRG NS — *Scriptores rerum Germanicarum, nova series*

SRL — *Scriptores rerum Langobardicarum*

SS — *Scriptores*

MIÖG — *Mitteilungen des Instituts für österreichische Geschichtsforschung*

NA — *Neues Archiv der Gesellschaft für ältere Geschichtskunde*

PL — *Patrologia Latina*

QFIAB — *Quellen und Forschung aus ital·enischen Archiven und Bibliotheken*

Regino — Regino of Prüm, *Chronicon*

Settimane — *Settimane di Studi sull' alto medioevo*

ZRGGA — *Zeitschrift der Savigny-Stiftung für Rechtsgeschichte, germanistische Abteilung*

Map I   The world of the *Annals of Fulda*

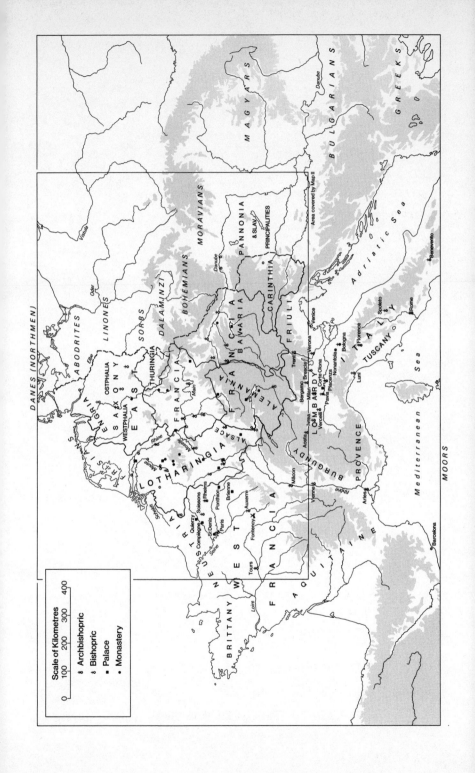

Map II   The east Frankish kingdom and Lotharingia

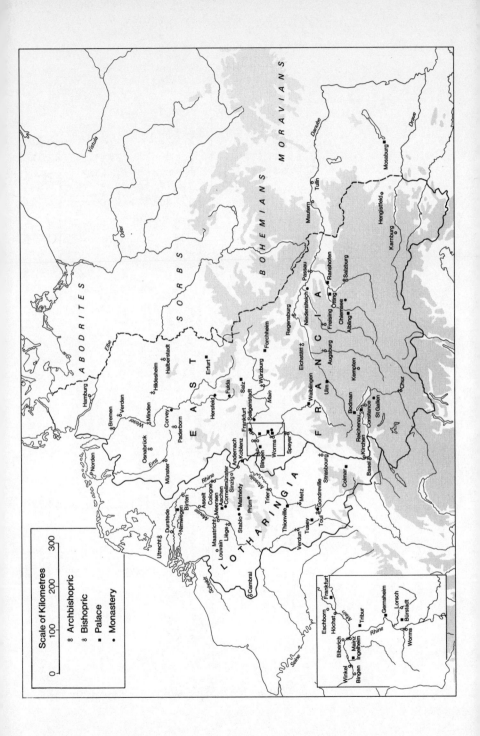

Genealogy I The descendants of Louis the Pious

Child of marriage ‖ Child of mistress

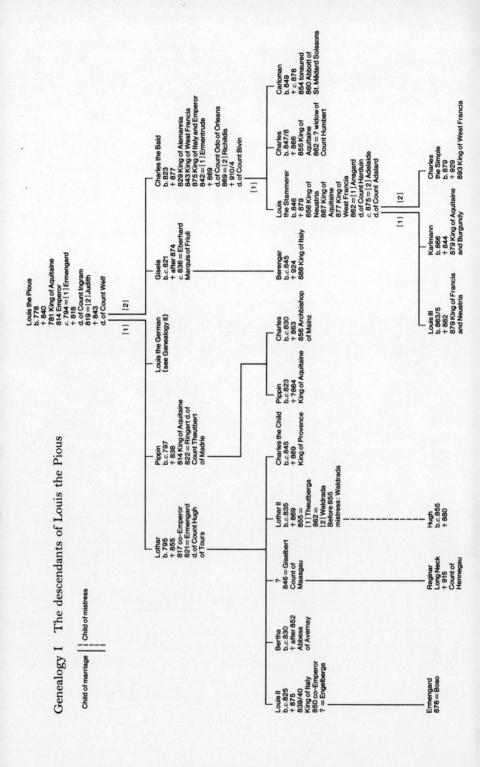

Genealogy II The descendants of Louis the German

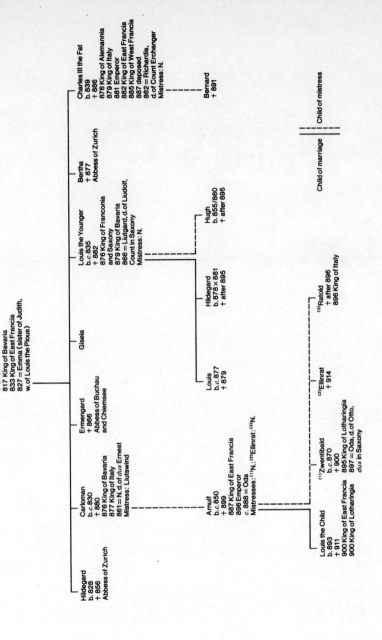

INTRODUCTION

The *Annals of Fulda* and their authorship

By the ninth century annals were one of the major vehicles for historical writing within the Frankish empire.[1] The earliest annals were probably no more than brief marginal notes on the tables used for calculating the date of Easter, but it was soon discovered that an account of events organised year by year could be not simply an *aide-mémoire* of this kind but coherent historical narrative which both recorded events and commented on them and attempted to explain them. By the time of Charles the Great substantial works were being produced in this form: the *Annals of Lorsch*, the *Royal Frankish Annals*, the *Older Metz Annals*.[2] The works themselves are almost all without contemporary titles or ascriptions of authorship: the titles used in manuscripts, which are mostly not original, are general ones like *Gesta Francorum* or *Historia Francorum*, and those used in scholarly literature often reflect no more than the place in which a manuscript came to rest, which is not necessarily the centre in which the work was composed, or else a scholarly theory about the origins of the work.[3] Most of the smaller works are monastic in origin; the larger works, including those mentioned earlier, were often produced in association with members of court circles, though none should be read without qualification as an 'official' account of events. Textual similarities have made it possible to show how the authors of annals borrowed from one another and compiled from older works, and the presence of common material in independent works shows that some annals which we now do not possess must once have existed.[4] What we have are in effect the

1 See McCormick 1975 and Nelson 1991: 2-5 for the origins of medieval annalistic writing.

2 *MGH SS* 1: 20-39; Kurze 1895; von Simson 1905.

3 See for example Nelson 1991: 2 on the name of the *Annals of St-Bertin*. The *Royal Frankish Annals*, so called because of their seemingly 'official' nature, were originally known as the *Greater Lorsch Annals*, and so illustrate both tendencies; Levison and Löwe 1953: 247.

4 Hoffmann 1958 is a good sceptical guide to the elaborate theories of nineteenth-century scholarship about the existence of 'lost' annals.

fossilised remains of debates and discussions about the Frankish political world which we can reconstruct only in part, and in reading these texts it is important to listen to their silences and note their emphases. The seemingly disinterested objectivity of the genre, found over long stretches even of the *Annals of Fulda* (henceforth *AF*), whose authors were by no means dispassionate observers of events, can be very deceptive.

AF – so called since Marquard Freher's edition at the beginning of the seventeenth century because a section of them has been ascribed to the monk and hagiographer Rudolf of Fulda and because they were thought to have made use of Fulda materials – offer the major narrative account of the east Frankish kingdom from the death of Louis the Pious down to the end of the ninth century, one which has crucially shaped our view of events. In this respect they are the equivalent of the companion text translated in this series, the *Annals of St-Bertin*, which play a similar role for the history of the west Frankish kingdom. The *Annals of St-Bertin* have a comparatively straightforward make-up: they are a continuation of the *Royal Frankish Annals* by two identifiable authors, Prudentius of Troyes and Hincmar of Rheims, about whom a good deal is otherwise known.[5] The *AF*, which are translated here from 838 onwards, have had several of their sections ascribed to authors, but their genesis appears to have been more complex, and it is also perhaps more typical of annalistic works of the early and high Middle Ages. It must be examined before we can turn to the text and its outlook.

The surviving manuscripts are only an echo of what must once have been a much more extensive transmission, to judge by the use made of *AF* by a number of later annalists and compilers.[6] There are three groups of manuscripts. Group 1 is represented by a manuscript now in Sélestadt in Alsace, and by another manuscript, now lost, which was in the cathedral library at Worms at the end of the fifteenth century and at the beginning of the sixteenth and of which three copies have survived.[7] The manuscripts contain annals from 714 to the middle of

---

5 See Nelson 1991: 6-13.

6 *AF* were used by, among other authors, Hermann the Lame, Adam of Bremen, the Annalista Saxo and Gobelinus Person; see Kurze 1892: 104-7, Hellmann 1909: 63-5 and Löwe 1990: 672 n. 66, 674 n. 69, 683 n. 91 for details.

7 Kurze's ms. '1' is Sélestat, Stadtbibliothek 11, an eleventh-century manuscript (not early tenth as Bresslau and Kurze thought). The Worms manuscript is represented by three copies: Munich, Staatsbibliothek, clm 1226 (made by the Bavarian lawyer Dietrich Reysach in 1511, not, as stated by Kurze 1891: IX,

882, where they break off. The text of group 1 occasionally diverges substantially from that of the other manuscripts, as well as showing a large number of minor stylistic revisions compared with the texts found in groups 2 and 3. Next to the entry for 838 ms. '1' has the note 'Thus far Enhard'; before the entry for 864 it has the note 'Thus far Rudolf'. The single manuscript of the second group[8] extends to 887, but omits a number of episodes between 838 and 870; where groups 1 and 3 diverge it sometimes has the readings of group 1 and sometimes of group 3.[9] Group 3, with the Bavarian continuation from 882, has the greatest number of manuscripts. The oldest may even be an autograph for the last years of the annals.[10] Later manuscripts in this group come from much further west and testify to the diffusion of *AF* in this form.[11]

in 1540), Kurze's '1a'; Copenhagen, Royal Library, ms. Arne-Magnaeanus 830 (written in 1496 in Kirschgarten near Worms), Kurze's '1b'; and Munich, Staatsbibliothek, clm 28511 (late fifteenth-century; unknown to Kurze). Kurze thought that the Worms manuscript was a copy of the Sélestat manuscript, but this needs looking at again. They were evidently closely related, but may have been derived from a common ancestor rather than lying in direct descent. I am grateful to Franz Fuchs of Mannheim for calling my attention to clm 28511 and for discussing the manuscripts of *AF* with me.

8 Vienna, Nationalbibliothek, lat. 615, Kurze's ms. '2', eleventh century, of unknown provenance, though there are hints that it may have come from Saint-Trond in Lotharingia (Kurze 1891: XI).

9 The omitted episodes are in the entries for 847, 850, 859, 866, 867, 868 and 870 (below: 26-7, 31-2, 34-5, 56, 57, 58, 63-4). For the divergences (of substance, not due simply to scribal errors), see the entries for 848, 856, 863, 864, 865, 870 (below: 28, 38, 49-51, 51-2, 52-4, 63). Only very occasionally does '2' offer a text against the common witness of the other two groups: in 853 it has a sentence taken from Regino of Prüm; for 861 it has an additional name 'Gerold' among the list of those proscribed by Louis the German (below: 47); and in 880 the accounts of Poppo's expedition against the Slavs (below: 89) show slight differences between all three groups.

10 Leipzig, Stadtbibliothek II 129a (late ninth-century, from Niederalteich), Kurze's ms. '3'. It now lacks a number of leaves and quires, but originally contained the text from 714 to 901. A copy of this, made for the early sixteenth-century Bavarian antiquary Johannes Aventinus at a time when it was in a more complete state, is Munich, Staatsbibliothek clm 966, ms. '3f' in Kurze's edition. Aventin's copy has marginal notes which show that he had access to a copy of the lost Worms manuscript, probably that made by Reysach (clm 1226); it ended where the other manuscripts of group 1 do, as is shown by a marginal note on f. 42r of clm 966. A further copy was made for Marquard Freher for his edition of 1600 (see below). Kurze thought '3' autograph (in the sense that the manuscript shows by gaps and compression of the writing that it was being composed as it was written, rather than being copied from an existing exemplar) perhaps from 894 onwards, certainly from 897 (Kurze 1891: 95-7, 154), and this view was also taken by Bischoff 1980: 7-8; cf. Löwe 1990: 673 n. 67 on the question.

11 Munich, Staatsbibliothek clm 15121 (later 29088), from Rebdorf, and Bern, Bürgerbibliothek 746 (Kurze's '3a' and '3b') are small fragments of no great

So far as we can judge it was also manuscripts of group 3 on which most later users of *AF* drew.[12] Its text extends in the complete manuscripts from 714 to 901, but from mid-882[13] it offers a completely different version of events from that given in group 2, and it has additional material for the years 863 to 865, including in particular some duplicate entries and also two texts (also found in the *Annals of St-Bertin*) relating to the dispute between Pope Nicholas I and the archbishops Gunther of Cologne and Theodgaud of Trier, which are referred to in the text offered by groups 1 and 2 as being available in a number of archives and hence not needing repetition in the work itself.[14]

This brief description of the manuscript tradition must be amplified by looking at the content of the annals. For the years 714 to 830 the work is undoubtedly a compilation which draws on earlier annals, in particular on the *Royal Frankish Annals* and the *Lorsch Frankish Chronicle*, with occasional use of other smaller sets of annals and saints' lives.[15] From 830 onwards the compilation consists largely of information and phrases not found in its known sources, though it is possible that these are drawn from a now lost set of annals. By the time of the marginal note referring to Enhard (meaning Einhard) in ms. '1' the narrative has definitely become independent of other known sources. Until about 869 some passages seem to have been composed close in time to the events they record, but there are a number of distortions of chronology which suggest composition rather later.[16] From 869 onwards the

importance for establishing the text. Vienna, Nationalbibliothek, lat. 451 (eleventh-century, perhaps from St Eucharius in Trier; cf. Hellmann 1909: 34 and Märtl 1986: 122) and Brussels, Biblioth/que Nationale, ms. 7503-7518 (twelfth-century, perhaps from Mainz) are mss. '3c' and '3e' respectively in Kurze's edition and textually closely related. Vatican City, Bibliotheca Apostolica Vaticana, ms. Reg. Lat. 633 is an eleventh-century manuscript from Fécamp in Normandy, Kurze's ms. '3d', which breaks off in 883.

12 See the references given in n. 6 .

13 The point at which groups 2 and 3 diverge comes slightly after that at which group 1 ends.

14 Below: 51 with n. 15.

15 Löwe 1990: 677-8 summarises the present state of scholarship on the sources of the first section of *AF* (which is not translated here).

16 The theft from Fulda recorded in 853 (below: 35 with n. 6) seems to have been recorded soon after the event, as perhaps was the account of Gundachar's treachery in 863 (below: 49-50 with n. 5). For distortions which may be the result of later reworking cf. for example the dating of events in 843 and 844 (below: 12), the entries on Aquitaine under 851 (below: 32), the account of the Slav campaigns of 858 (below: 41 with n. 9), the misdating of the meeting at Tusey in 865 (below: 52 with n. 5) and some entries in 867-68 (below: 57 n. 4, 58 n. 6), though these last errors are also explicable on the assumption that

text was evidently composed very close in time to the events it records.[17] This seems to be true also of the Bavarian continuation from 882 to 901.[18]

The facts outlined above have allowed widely differing views on the origins and authorship of *AF*. The last person to provide a scholarly edition, Friedrich Kurze, relied heavily on the 'thus far' notes for 838 and 863 in ms '1'.[19] For him, the annals up to 838 were compiled by Einhard (the author of the Life of Charlemagne). From 838 to 863 they were continued by Rudolf of Fulda, a distinguished scholar and hagiographer, whose death is recorded in *AF* under 865;[20] the confusion in the annals for 863, 864 and 865 was taken by Kurze to show that Rudolf had not had time to revise them properly before his death. From 865 onwards the annals were continued by Rudolf's pupil Meginhard, an identification suggested by the state of another work left unfinished by Rudolf on his death, the *Translatio Sancti Alexandri*, which Meginhard is known to have completed.[21] A first version of the work extended to 882, and is represented by group 1, and also by group 3 in its text up to 863; group 2 contains a 'second edition' with a text extending to 887. Kurze also thought that the text of group 3 from 882 onwards was not all due to the same author; he saw the annals from 882 to 896 as having been written in Regensburg, and the remainder as a further continuation written in Niederalteich, the home of the oldest manuscript of group 3.

This account of the origins of *AF* was heavily criticised by Siegmund Hellmann in a number of articles written some fifteen years after the

work on a text up to 863-65 was resumed only in 869 and the author needed to fill in the gap.

17 Note especially the comments on Charles the Bald under 875 and 876 (below: 77 with n. 10 and 82 with n. 16).

18 See the account of the Pannonian feud 884(II) (below: 110 n. 8).

19 He set out his views, which owed much to Rethfeld 1886, in Kurze 1892 and defended them in Kurze 1911 and Kurze 1912.

20 Below: 52-3; on Rudolf as teacher (Ermanrich of Ellwangen was among his pupils) and author of a number of hagiographical works including the *Vita Leobae*, *Translatio Sancti Alexandri* and the *Miracula sanctorum inFuldenses ecclesias translatorum*, possibly also of a letter collection, see Finsterwalder 1922 and Löwe 1990: 680-7, 709-14.

21 Krusch 1933. Meginhard and Rudolf are referred to explicitly in the *Translatio*; another reason for supposing that Rudolf was responsible for the text of *AF* from 838 to 863 is that both the *Translatio* and *AF* (below: 31) refer to Tacitus's *De Germania*, a work which seems to have survived only at Fulda and at Hersfeld in the Middle Ages and apart from these citations does not seem to have been known until its rediscovery in the Renaissance.

appearance of Kurze's edition in 1891.[22] Hellmann rightly criticised the inaccuracies of Kurze's edition, which was not based on a complete collation of all the manuscripts.[23] From Kurze's edition and his own additional collations Hellmann put together a rather different account. The references to Einhard and Rudolf in ms. '1' he saw as a red herring and the theories about Meginhard's continuation of Rudolf's work as unsubstantiated. After careful examination of the manuscripts he constructed a stemma of the manuscripts in which there were two classes, one represented by the manuscripts of groups 1 and 2, and the other represented by the manuscripts of group 3. Both groups 1 and 2 showed in different ways signs of having had their texts reworked and were demonstrably further from the archetype than the oldest manuscript of group 3.[24] Group 1 was also not to be taken as representing an early recension to 882, for the texts of groups 2 and 3 do not diverge until after the text in 1 has already broken off; 1 is, like some other manuscripts in group 3, simply an incomplete text.[25] The work was put together between the 870s and 887 by an author who drew on two older compilations. Hellmann thought that the Bavarian continuation from 882 found in group 3 was written after 887 as a deliberate replacement for the highly tendentious account of Charles III's reign found in ms. '2', and he disputed Kurze's theory that ms. '3' was at any point an autograph, since it contains errors not found in '3c' and '3e'; the theory of a separate continuation after 896 thus collapsed.[26] Hellmann also pointed to use of materials in later annalistic works referring to the period after 901 which in his view probably came from the Bavarian continuation of *AF*. This was a final demonstration that ms. '3' was not an autograph, since the lost 'original' evidently went beyond 901.[27]

Although many of Hellmann's points have not been refuted either by

22 Hellmann 1908, 1909; Hellmann 1912 is a rejoinder to Kurze 1911, Hellmann 1913 a reply to Janssen 1912.

23 Hellmann 1908: 701-3. In fairness to Kurze it should be said that this was normal practice in nineteenth-century scholarly editions; one collated what seemed to be the key manuscripts as far as possible and asked librarians or paid collators to check critical passages in the remaining manuscripts.

24 Hellmann 1908: 705-17.

25 Hellmann 1908: 706, citing Wibel 1902: 254.

26 Hellmann 1909 deals with the manuscripts of group 3. Kurze in his edition unfortunately did not give the readings for the other manuscripts of this group for those sections where ms. '3' survives intact.

27 Löwe 1990: 684 n. 95, discusses this question and concludes that there is no firm evidence for the existence of a text of *AF* which went beyond 901.

Kurze or later, subsequent scholarship has by and large accepted Kurze's account, and in particular his ascription to Rudolf of Fulda of the section between 838 and 863.[28] The unsatisfactory nature of Kurze's text means that no definitive account of the origins and composition of the work can be offered at present. There is no doubt as to the essential wording or meaning of the text, but neither Kurze's edition nor the corrections offered by Hellmann are enough for the kind of close textual argument needed to sort out the relations of the manuscripts to one another. What is needed is a new edition based on a full collation of all the available manuscripts. It is clear, however, that the controversy between Hellmann and Kurze created in many ways more heat than light, and the manner in which it was conducted obscured much that was common to the two accounts as well as some points overlooked by both scholars.[29] Both Kurze and Hellmann assumed in effect that the archetype of *AF* was a finished literary manuscript; but there are hints, in the disorganisation of the entries for the years 863 to 865 and elsewhere,[30] that much of the 'original' was more like a bundle of loose notes and jottings. Moreover, there is not all that much difference between the view that a later author made use of earlier compilations and the view that the work was continued successively by three named authors; the practical consequences are not great for our understanding of the text, especially as the ascription of the first part of the work to Einhard rests on very shaky ground[31] and we know virtually nothing about Meginhard except that he completed Rudolf's *Translatio Sancti Alexandri.*

28 Janssen 1912, Stengel 1914 and Finsterwalder 1922 all defended the ascription of the second part to Rudolf, accepted also in Eggert 1973:17-18 and with slight modifications by Löwe 1990: 687-714. A study of the problem announced by Rexroth 1978: 307 n. 71 in support of the theses of Rethfeld and Kurze has not yet appeared.

29 Each side took extreme positions; thus Hellmann's stemma (Hellmann 1909: 49) requires there to be no fewer than four lost manuscripts between the lost archetype and ms. '3', which even Hellmann admitted to be from the late ninth or early tenth century, while Kurze's theories (1892: 96-7) about how the text of '3' drew on Rudolf's text as well as on the supposed 'second edition' by Meginhard seem equally improbable.

30 In particular the duplicate entries for 864 and 865 in the manuscripts of group 3 (below: 51-2 and 52-4). Note also the missing letters of 857 and 884 (below: 39, 96), the changes made in the text in the references to the elections at Mainz in 856 and 863 (below: 38, 50), the missing name of the river in 863 (below: 50) and the gap left for the date and place of Louis II of Italy's death in 875 (below: 50).

31 Löwe 1990: 676-8.

Most seriously, however, the two inscriptions of 838 and 863[32] have drawn attention away from more substantial breaks in continuity. From 830, as we have noted, *AF* cease to be dependent on other known sources and give an independent account of events, though their entries for the period from 830 to 838 are fairly thin and uninteresting and for that reason have not been translated here. From about 869 through to 887 (in the text of group 2) the character of the text changes again; it becomes much fuller, and there are no further errors in chronology or entries which must have been written rather later than the events they record, as there are in many of the annals between 838 and 869. There are also changes of vocabulary at the same time; for example, from 870 onwards Bavaria and the Bavarians are often called *Noricum* and *Norici* respectively, words not used in the text up until then.[33] It must remain open for the time being whether the author or authors of this text made substantial revisions to the earlier text, in particular to the annals for the period 830-68, or whether they took them over intact. Much play was made in the debate between Kurze and Hellmann of the similarities in phraseology between the supposedly 'different parts' of the annals.[34] They can be explained both as imitation of the earlier compilations by the later writer and as reworking of the earlier sources by the later writer in his style, but the latter seems a more natural assumption. Further work needs to be done here, though it would need to take the manuscripts into account. At all events the text from the 840s onwards shows close links with Mainz,[35] and in particular with Archbishop Liutbert (863-89). Liutbert was archchancellor under Louis the German and Louis the Younger, but lost office to Liutward of Vercelli when the east Frankish kingdom

---

32 Löwe 1990: 676 n. 74 has suggested that these might have originated in marks made by manuscript copyists rather than marginal notes denoting authorship or supposed authorship, that is, 'Thus far Einhard' might mean 'Einhard has copied up to here' or 'Einhard is to copy up to here'. He also notes (1990: 674 n. 69) that later authors who used *AF* do not all place the note for 838 in the same position in their accounts, showing that it was not a fixed part of the text but a marginal note (as in ms. '1').

33 *Norici* is also used in an entry in the first part of *AF* (Kurze 1891: 2) for 723 which appears here to diverge from *AF*'s known sources.

34 Cf. Hellmann 1908: 722-7; Kurze 1911: 357-64; Hellmann 1912: 59-62; Janssen 1912; Hellmann 1913. Löwe 1990: 680 summarises the controversies. There are studies of the language of *AF* in Schlachter 1914 and Beeson 1926, but these, though interesting, do not allow us to solve the problem.

35 Note the references to the archiepiscopal elections in 847, 856 and 863, to the councils held there in 847, 848, 852 and 857, to Hrabanus and the famine of 851 and to the priest Probus in 859. A hagiographical work written at Mainz in the late 850s also cited the first compilatory part of *AF*; Löwe 1990: 678 and n. 81.

was reunited under Charles III, returning only in the final months of Charles's reign.[36] It might thus be supposed that *AF* are a product of the east Frankish royal chapel,[37] were it not for their account of the years 882 to 887, which is extremely hostile to Charles III and his current advisers until the very end of Charles III's reign, when Liutbert returned to royal favour and to the archchancellorship, and emphasises Liutbert's activities. They thus seem to represent the work of Liutbert and his circle rather than of the royal chapel as such, though their interest in the deeds of kings and their justifications show that so long as Liutbert was in power it is not easy to separate the two things.

The possibility that a text of the annals to 882 remained available to members of the royal chapel is suggested by the Bavarian continuation, though one would have expected a chapel work produced under Charles III to have an Alemannic rather than a Bavarian slant on affairs. At all events the Bavarian continuation gives a favourable account of Charles III's reign. Hellmann, who was concerned to show that there had never been an independent version of *AF* which went only up to 882, argued that this was a deliberate rewriting of the text written in Liutbert's circle, but the differences between the texts do not force us to assume this, as may be seen by comparing the two, and the account of the Pannonian feud under 884 appears to be contemporary.[38] Although the most recent studies of ms. '3' have tended to confirm Kurze's view that this is an autograph at the end,[39] this does not mean that the work was written in the monastery of Niederalteich (the subsequent home of the manuscript) from 897 onwards as Kurze thought; there is no discernible change of style or emphasis between 896 and 897.

The world of the *AF*

Neither the original *AF* nor their Bavarian continuation were concerned to record everything important that occurred. This is of course

---

36 Fleckenstein 1959: 182-6, 189-91, Keller 1966: 336-41 .

37 This is the view taken by Löwe 1990: 682-7 at the end of his very thoughtful and balanced survey of the problem, to which I am much indebted in the account given above. Löwe also argues that the section ascribed to Rudolf of Fulda by Kurze and others may have been written under his direction by a number of authors with links with the chapel, rather than as a piece by Rudolf himself.

38 Hellmann 1909: 20-30; but see the entry in 884(II) (below: 110 n. 8).

39 See above, n.10.

to some extent true of all annalistic works, but the *AF* are particularly noteworthy for the way they select some episodes for extended treatment and omit other matters entirely. The long accounts of Louis the German's invasion of West Francia in 858, the trenchant commentaries on Carolingian politics especially but not only for the years from 873 to 877, the descriptions in both texts of the end of Charles III's reign and in the Bavarian continuation of the Pannonian feud as well as of Arnulf's campaigns in 891, 894 and 896, all show that the authors were doing something rather different from simply recording what happened when. The interest taken in the miraculous and in natural disasters point in the same direction, though it is worth noting that group 2 omits a number of the extended narratives not concerned with political matters.[40] The outlook is a court one rather than a clerical one; only rarely do we find signs of a specifically ecclesiastical viewpoint, as in the remarks about the episcopal elections at Mainz in 856 and at Passau in 899.[41] There is no sign of Hincmar's disapproval of warrior bishops, and the authors take a well-informed interest in military matters, offering a great number of detailed accounts of battles and campaigns. Even the interest in the miraculous should not be seen as specifically clerical. What is evident is the desire to write literature within an annalistic form, though perhaps not with such complex intentions as have been suggested for Hincmar of Rheims;[42] the extended narratives in *AF* seem more like rhetorical set pieces.

The outlook of *AF* has been characterised as 'eminently east Frankish',[43] but this becomes true only gradually. The period of brotherly rule between 843 and Lothar's death in 855 is reflected in the *AF*'s interest in west Frankish and Lotharingian events, perhaps also in a certain distance towards Louis the German's rule. However, the *AF* tell us notably less about west Frankish politics than the *Annals of St-Bertin* do about east Frankish ones, and the emphasis from the 860s is undoubtedly east Frankish. Italian affairs are given prominence only from the mid-870s onwards, coinciding with east Frankish ambitions for the Italian kingdom. Here especially *AF* are often discreetly silent about events which the author or authors must have known about, such as Louis the German's manoeuvrings for the succession to his nephew Louis II of Italy, and their information is often fragmentary

40 See above, n. 10.
41 Below: 38 and 139-40.
42 Cf. Meyer-Gebel 1987; Nelson 1988; Nelson 1990a; Nelson 1991: 13-15.
43 Fried 1976: 202.

and not supported by other sources. The doings of the Slavs and Northmen on the open borders to the east and north were recorded, but here again it is often difficult to make sense of the information we are given. Partly this is because the authors were writing for an audience which had far more background knowledge than we do, but it is likely also that the deficiencies of *AF* here reflect deficiencies in the authors' own knowledge. This should be borne in mind when considering east Frankish 'policy' towards the Slavs and Northmen. It should also be noted that the interest taken by the authors of the Bavarian continuation in events on the south-east frontier was not shared by the authors of the original text, who kept an eye on the Moravians and Bohemians, but were much less interested in the east Bavarian aristocracy or the Bulgars.

Where the annals are not recounting the miraculous or indulging in extended and detailed narrative they offer a version of events which is distinctly king-centred, more so than that of the *Annals of St-Bertin*. Lay leading men are mentioned only comparatively rarely before the 880s. The authors of the Mainz account of Charles III's reign continue king-centred in their outlook, in spite of their hostility to Charles, though they do make some attempt to treat the doings of Archbishop Liutbert and the Babenberger Henry almost as if these two were rulers, no doubt because they were the chief advisers of the deceased king Louis the Younger. The Bavarian continuation has a new tone: a fair number of Bavarian leading men are mentioned in the accounts of the 880s and 890s, though the king is still at the centre of the political world. The author or authors also show an emotional commitment to a particular region – Pannonia, the eastern march of Bavaria – of a kind rare in Frankish historical writing. Here too, as in the shifting emphases on Slav and Italian affairs, the annalists were probably reflecting real changes in the world they were depicting: a world which was slowly becoming more regionalised and in which the gap between rulers and their leading men was closing.

Earlier editions and translations

The text was published twice in the early modern era, by Pierre Pithou,[44] who used the incomplete ms. '3d', and by Marquard Freher,[45]

---

44 Pithou 1588.
45 Freher 1600: 1-55.

who used a copy made from ms. '3' when it was in a more complete state than it is now and is thus an additional witness to the manuscript transmission. A number of scholars in the seventeenth and eighteenth centuries published additional material from newly discovered manuscripts,[46] but the first scholarly edition drawing on a range of materials was published by Pertz in 1826.[47] This was superseded, though as we have seen not definitively, by Friedrich Kurze's edition.[48] A German translation of Pertz's text by C. Rehdantz was published in the *Geschichtsschreiber der deutschen Vorzeit* and in a revised edition by Wilhelm Wattenbach;[49] Reinhold Rau published a text based on Kurze with a facing translation based on Rehdantz and a brief introduction and commentary in the *Freiherr-von-Stein-Gedchtnis-Ausgabe.*[50]

This translation

The text translated here is based on Kurze's edition, though it is a 'mixed text' which does not follow any one manuscript group consistently; in view of the nature of Kurze's edition that would in any case hardly have been possible. The more significant differences between the various groups of manuscripts are indicated in the notes. The division into paragraphs, which owes much to Kurze's edition, is intended to help understanding; it is not a feature of any of the original manuscripts. The *AF* present the usual difficulties associated with translating medieval Latin texts. The manuscripts are not in the least consistent about their spelling of personal and place-names; theoretically one could reproduce this inconsistency in the text and standardise in the notes and the index, but the effect on a reader unfamiliar with the period is likely to be confusing. I have thus standardised the translations of Frankish names as far as possible: generally a modern English form has been used where there was one available, but not where this seemed too different from the original to be recognisable; where there is no common English form a medieval spelling has been preferred to a modern French or German form. Thus Lothar (not Lothair or Lothaire) II's wife is Waldrada, not Waldtraut; the king of

46 Hellmann 1908: 697-8 gives a helpful summary of this.

47 *MGH SS* 1: 337-415. Pertz did not have access to ms. '3', which was not rediscovered until 1840, and had to use Freher's edition as a substitute.

48 Kurze 1891.

49 Rehdantz 1852; Wattenbach 1889.

50 Rau 1960: 20-177.

west Francia from 888 to 898 is Odo, not Eudes or Otto. Slav and Scandinavian names have been given in a form more like that found in *AF*; thus no distinction is made between the Moravian ruler generally known in modern scholarly literature as Sviatopulk and the illegitimate son of Arnulf of Carinthia, both of whom are here called Zwentibald.

More difficult is the question of consistency and neutrality in translating technical terms (and in deciding when a writer is using a word in a technical sense and when not). Terms like *populus, fideles, optimates, villa, honores, beneficia* and so on are difficult, because any translation is also an interpretation. The translation generally avoids the feudal vocabulary of the high Middle Ages (fealty, fief, etc.), and uses neutral renderings where possible: 'leading men' for *optimates* or *principes* rather than 'nobles' or 'aristocrats'; 'faithful men' for *fideles* rather than 'subjects' or 'vassals'. Almost certainly complete consistency has not been achieved, and it is doubtful whether this is possible – no translation can be a complete substitute for the original. I have left the term *dux* (plural *duces*) untranslated, since 'duke' has misleading overtones for the ninth century, and *villa*, which can mean 'estate', 'estate centre', 'settlement', and so on, has also been left in its Latin form.

The commentary is intended to aid the understanding of the text, but it is not and could not be the full scholarly commentary which a new edition of the *AF* would require. I have noted some points of interest which might not immediately strike the attention of a reader unfamiliar with the period, though to have done this systematically would have impossibly overloaded the commentary. Difficulties of translation are noted, as are references to the same events in other sources; where appropriate, excerpts from these, in particular from Regino of Prüm's *Chronicon*, have been translated in the notes. The information given by *AF* on the movements of rulers has been supplemented by that revealed in the dating-clauses of royal diplomata, though the reign of Louis the German in particular is characterised by long periods, sometimes as much as a whole year, from which no diplomata have survived. I have generally kept references to the secondary literature to the minimum necessary to show where I have drawn my information from and to inform the user where she or he may turn for a more detailed account. Inevitably much of the literature cited is in German, and more would be in Czech, Hungarian and the Scandinavian languages if I read them. Much of what is cited is now very old, but that is because most of the spade-work of sorting out what happened when was done in the great age of nineteenth-century positivism and has needed little correction since then; those of us who now look disparagingly on positivism can do so the more easily because the positivists have done our work for us. Additions in square brackets in the texts themselves are also part of the commentary: they have been used for giving precise dates to movable feasts like Easter (in the case of Lent the beginning only is given), and for giving fuller identifications of persons, mostly bishops and abbots, mentioned only by their Christian names. Following conventional practice, names of places which are not certainly identifiable or no longer extant are given in italics. To avoid confusion, cross-references to the account for the years 882 to 887 in the Bavarian continuation are given in the form '882(II)', etc.

838

On the evening of January 18 there was an earthquake in Lorsch and the region around Worms, Speyer and Ladenburg.

Ships were built against the Northmen.[1]

The best part of the kingdom of the Franks was given to the young Charles.[2] Lothar and Louis had a meeting in the Tridentino before mid-Lent [March 24].[3] The emperor, however, having held a general assembly at Nimwegen in the month of June, followed the advice of certain of the leading Franks and in a written judgement deprived Louis his son of the kingdom of the eastern Franks, which he had previously held with his approval.[4] Louis, realising that this judgement resulted from the enviousness of the emperor's advisers, ignored the edict and came to Frankfurt with his men on November 29.[5] The emperor came against him with an army, as if against a rebel, to Mainz, where he celebrated Christmas.

Pippin also, his son, king of the Aquitanians, died in November of the same year.[6]

---

1 This notice perhaps belongs to 837; cf. *AB* 837 with *AB* 838 (Nelson 1991: 37, 39).

2 This notice also belongs in 837; for Charles's portion see *AB* 837 (Nelson 1991: 38).

3 As a reaction to the new *divisio*; see Nithard I, 6 (Scholz 1972: 136-8). After this entry ms. '1' of *AF* has the marginal note 'thus far Einhard'; see introduction, 3-7.

4 The annalist here conceals Louis the German's visit and submission to his father at Easter 838 and his presence in Nimwegen in June: *AB* 838 (Nelson 1991: 38-9). See also Nithard I, 6 (Scholz 1972: 136-8) and Astronomer, c. 59 (*MGH SS* 2: 644). The lands he was deprived of – Saxony, Thuringia, east Francia and Alemannia – were regions he had had *de facto* control over since Louis the Pious's deposition in 833, a control which had not been affected by the restoration of 834; Zatschek 1935: 198-216; Ewig 1981: 247-51. The 'leading men of the Franks' who opposed Louis the German certainly included Count Adalbert of Metz and Archbishop Otgar of Mainz (see 847 n. 5), and probably also the counts Poppo, Gebhard and Hatto (see 839 n. 2).

5 Frankfurt lay within the lands of which he had just been 'deprived', hence by going there he was publicly ignoring Louis the Pious's decision.

6 More accurately on December 13; see *AB* 838 (Nelson 1991: 40).

839

The emperor, after the feasts of Christmas and of the Epiphany [January 6] had been celebrated, crossed the Rhine by ship with his army on January 7.[1] Here he met the Saxons, who had come partly in response to threats, partly by the persuasions of Count Adalbert [of Metz].[2] When he learnt this, Louis, knowing that it was wicked for a son to fight his father and judging it the moment to fall back, retreated into Bavaria. The emperor came to Frankfurt and, remaining there, began the fast of Lent [February 19]. Then, passing into Alemannia, he celebrated Easter [April 6] by Lake Constance.[3] After Easter he went to Worms in May, and was reconciled with his son Lothar, who had returned from Italy and into his fidelity.[4] He divided up the kingdom of the Franks between Lothar and his small son Charles. To Lothar, as the eldest, he gave the dignity of his title and the capital of the kingdom.[5] To Louis, his younger son, he allowed only the province of the Bavarians, because he had offended him. After July 1, when Lothar had returned to Italy, the emperor, taking Charles with him, set off for the West to deal with the affairs of Aquitaine.[6]

In the same year a comet appeared in the sign of Aries and other portents were seen in the sky. For the clear sky turned red at night and for several nights many small fireballs like stars were seen shooting through the air.

---

1 The annalist here passes over the negotiations between Louis and his son, and the fact that Louis the German had attempted to deny his father passage over the Rhine; see *AB* 839 (Nelson 1991: 41).

2 Adalbert's brother, Banzleib, was margrave in Saxony; Dümmler 1887a: 128 n. 2. Other east Frankish nobles, including Poppo, count in the Grabfeld, and Gebhard, count in the Lahngau, as well as Adalbert's brother Hatto, also supported Louis the Pious, according to a letter of about this time from Einhard to an unnamed count (*MGH Epp.* 5: 130 no. 41).

3 In the palace of Bodman; cf. *AB* 839 (Nelson 1991: 41).

4 On Louis the Pious's reconciliation with Lothar and the details of the new *divisio* see *AB* 839 (Nelson 1991: 45).

5 the capital of the kingdom' = *sedem regni:* either Aachen or more generally rule/ overlordship, cf. 858 with n. 20.

6 To drive out Pippin II, the son of Pippin I, who had established himself as king in Aquitaine; see *AB* 839 (Nelson 1991: 46 and n. 11).

840

Louis [the German], the son of the emperor, claimed the part of the kingdom across the Rhine[1] as if due to him by right; he made a journey through Alemannia and came to Frankfurt,[2] having won over many of the eastern Franks to him by a careful plan. Learning of this, the emperor was forced to return from Aquitaine with his business there[3] unfinished, and sent ahead the archchaplain Drogo[4] and Count Adalbert with many others to guard the west bank of the Rhine. He himself followed, and celebrated Easter [March 28] in Aachen.

At this time an exceptional reddening of the sky appeared from the south-east for several nights; another appeared from the north-west until they met in a cone and gave the appearance of a clot of blood in the heavens directly overhead.

After Easter the emperor, having gathered an army, pursued his son through Thuringia as far as the frontiers of the barbarians, drove him out of the kingdom, and compelled him to make his way back through the lands of the Slavs to Bavaria with great difficulty.[5] He himself, having dealt with affairs in these parts, returned to the royal *villa* of Salz and there celebrated Ascension and the period leading up to it.[6] On the eve of Ascension, that is on May 12 [really May 5], there was so great an eclipse of the sun around the seventh and eighth hour of the day that even the stars could be seen because of the veiling of the sun, and terrestrial objects changed colour.[7] In these days the emperor was stricken by a sickness and became seriously ill. He went by boat along the Main to Frankfurt, and was brought from there after a few

1 See 838 n. 4.

2 Note that Louis here followed his father's itinerary of the previous year in the reverse direction; according to Astronomer c. 62 (*MGH SS* 2, 646) he was joined by Saxons and Thuringians. There are no diplomata to put a precise chronology on these events, but they probably took place between Christmas and Easter of 840; cf. Nithard I, 8 (Scholz 1972: 139-40).

3 See above, 839 n. 6.

4 Louis the Pious's illegitimate half-brother. He was bishop of Metz, 823-55 and head of the imperial chapel under Louis the Pious (834-40) and Lothar I (840x844-55); Fleckenstein 1959: 83-4, 119-20.

5 Note that Louis the German could apparently count on the support of the Slavs and that Louis the Pious did not contest his possession of Bavaria.

6 According to Nithard I, 8 (Scholz 1972: 140) and Astronomer, c. 62 (*MGH SS* 2: 646), Louis the Pious summoned Lothar and his faithful men to an assembly at Worms for July 1, at which counsel was to be taken about Louis the German.

7 Taken by several contemporary writers to be a portent of Louis the Pious's death; von Simson 1876: 226.

days to a certain island in the Rhine near Ingelheim. His sickness increased and he died on June 29. His body was brought to the city of Metz and buried with ceremony in the church of the holy Arnulf the Confessor.[8]

The Franks chose Lothar, who came too late from Italy,[9] to rule over them for the future in his father's place. They say that the dying emperor designated him as the one who should take the government of the kingdom, sending him the royal insignia, that is, the sceptre and crown of the empire.[10] His brothers did not agree to this, and prepared to rise up against him. First his brother Louis came with a strong force of the eastern Franks to defend the part of the kingdom east of the Rhine and met him as he came with an army outside the walls of Mainz.[11] An agreement was made and judgement[12] deferred until another time. Lothar set out to the west against Charles. Louis bound the eastern Franks, Alemans, Saxons and Thuringians to him with oaths of fidelity.[13]

841

Meanwhile, as Louis was setting garrisons in the places near the Rhine and preparing the defence of the eastern bank against invasion by the westerners, Lothar, worried by rumours brought by messengers of this, gave up pursuing Charles and returned in April, crossing the

---

8 Bishop of Metz 614–29, d. around 640. He was one of the ancestors of the Carolingian family: on Metz and the Carolingians see Oexle 1967.

9 'too late' = *sero*. According to Nithard II, 1 (Scholz 1972: 141), Lothar advanced cautiously from Italy, wishing to see how the land lay, but since he was in Italy at the time of his father's death and issued diplomata at Strasbourg at the end of July the delay cannot have been all that great: D Lo I 44, dated July 24, is falsified but its date is confirmed by the genuine D Lo I 45 of July 25.

10 This is confirmed by Astronomer, c. 63 (*MGH SS* 2: 647), which adds that Louis specified that Charles should keep the part of the kingdom allowed him by the agreement made at Worms in 839. Lothar was received as his father's successor in August 840, at a meeting at Ingelheim which wasattended by a large number of secular and ecclesiastical magnates from the whole of the Frankish empire; Dümmler 1887a: 139–43.

11 On the meeting see Nithard II, 1 (Scholz 1972: 142); it is to be dated around August, since Lothar issued a diploma at Mainz on August 13 (D Lo I 46).

12 ... *dilato in aliud tempus placito*: *placitum* is a judicial term, though it may also be used of a battle.

13 For Louis's hold on these regions see above, 838 with n. 4, and compare *AB* 841 (Nelson 1991: 49). Louis was in Westfalia in October (DD LG 26–8).

Rhine secretly with his army near Worms.[1] He compelled Louis, who was betrayed by some of his followers and almost surrounded, to retreat into Bavaria.[2] After he [Lothar] had set guards whom he thought faithful to him over those parts, he turned his plans and his forces once again to fighting Charles, who had already begun to pitch his camp beyond the Meuse. Meanwhile Louis, whom Charles had summoned to his aid by messengers, passed through Alemannia. Here those counts whom Lothar had left as guards met him with an army in the Ries.[3] A battle took place, and Count Adalbert, the instigator of these disputes,[4] was killed, and with him an uncountable number of men, on May 13. Louis, the victor in the battle, crossed the Rhine and came into Gaul to bring help to his brother Charles. When the three brothers met in the Auxerrois near the *villa* of Fontenoy they could not agree about the division of the kingdom because Lothar claimed supreme rule for himself.[5] They decided that the issue should be determined by the sword and subjected to God's judgement. On June 25 a great battle was fought between them, and there was such slaughter on both sides that no one can recall a greater loss among the Frankish people in the present age.[6] Lothar indeed began to withdraw to the palace of Aachen of the same day; Louis and Charles overran his camp, gathered up and buried the bodies of their followers, and parted from each other. Charles remained in the west; Louis came to the royal

1 *AB* 841 (Nelson 1991: 49) say that this campaign took place in Lent, and confirm *AF*'s statements about treachery.

2 Note once again the role of Bavaria as Louis the German's stronghold.

3 The Ries is a district to the west of the Danube in the region of Nördlingen and Oettingen (cf. Kudorfer 1970), so that the battle took place just beyond the Bavarian borders.

4 On him see above, 839 and 840, with notes. It is not clear why he is called the 'instigator', though it may be a reference to his role in the judgement against Louis the German of 838. His death was widely noted; Dümmler 1887a: 151 and notes.

5 On these negotiations see Nithard II, 10 (Scholz 1972: 152-3) and *AB* 841 (Nelson 1991: 50). Louis and Charles offered Lothar parts of their 'kingdoms' (i.e. the areas they already controlled or claimed by virtue of one of the divisions of Louis the Pious's reign); failing that, they were prepared to have a new division of the Frankish empire drawn up and let him have first choice. Lothar negotiated for a time but broke off talks after he had been joined by Pippin II of Aquitaine.

6 Similar comments are found in other contemporary accounts of the battle of Fontenoy. The number killed was probably not very high in absolute terms, but as a proportion of the trained fighters of the Frankish empire considerable, so that the comment by Regino 841 (Kurze 1890: 75) that from this point 'not only could the Franks no longer extend their frontiers, but they could not even defend their own lands' is understandable.

villa of Salz around the middle of August.[7] Lothar, having again collected his men from all sides, came to Mainz and ordered the Saxons to come to him at Speyer with his little son Lothar.[8] He himself, crossing the Rhine as if to drive his brother Louis into exile among the peoples beyond the frontiers,[9] broke off the pursuit and returned to Worms. There he celebrated the wedding of his daughter[10] and again set off into Gaul against Charles. He spent the whole of the winter in wasted effort and returned to Aachen.

On December 25 a comet appeared in the sign of Aquarius.

842

Louis, seeing now that Lothar remained obstinate in his original intention and would still not give up although defeated, collected a fair-sized army of the easterners and crossed the Rhine. He received the surrender of the cities on the western bank of the Rhine, who supported Lothar.[1] Charles met him at the town of Argentoratum, which is now called Strasbourg. From there they set out with a common purpose[2] and forced Lothar, deserted by his men, in whom he had placed much trust, to flee from the *villa* of Sinzig, where he was staying, on March 19.[3] They supposed that he was making for Italy, having given up hope as it was rumoured, and so divided the part of

---

7 He is found at Heilbronn on August 18 (D LG 30).

8 Lothar was at Mainz on August 20 (D Lo I 61). Even after Fontenoy he still had considerable support among the east Frankish magnates; cf. Nithard III, 3 (Scholz 1972: 159), *AB* 841 (Nelson 1991: 51) and the opening of *AF*'s annal for 842. He had also been in contact with the leaders of the *Stellinga* uprising in Saxony, promising them his support in return for theirs; see 842 n. 6 for references.

9 A repetition of his tactics and those of his father; the attack, confirmed by *AB* 841 (Nelson 1991: 51), cannot have been much more than a feint, however, as by September 1 Lothar was in Thionville heading west (D Lo I 62).

10 Her name and that of her husband are not known; for speculation see Dümmler 1887a: 167 n. 2.

1 The cities (and their surrounding territories) of Mainz, Worms and Speyer, which finally came to Louis by the Treaty of Verdun in 843.

2 A reference to the Strasburg Oaths taken by Charles the Bald, Louis the German and their followers; see Nithard III, 4-5 (Scholz 1972: 161-3) and also *AB* 842 (Nelson 1991: 52).

3 We have no details about who it was who deserted Lothar; compare *AB* 842 (Nelson 1991: 53). The date of March 19 is a conjectural emendation of the manuscript tradition, which has March 15 or 16, when the two brothers were still at Mainz, cf. Nithard III, 7 (Scholz 1972: 164).

the kingdom which he had held up to now between them. But Lothar, having gathered a very trustworthy army, took up a position near the Gallic town of Mâcon.[4] His brothers pursued him there, and as they saw that he was now more ready to make peace with them, preferred to make a treaty rather than to go on for a long time in savage fighting. They made the condition, however, that forty of the leading men from each side should be chosen to come together and draw up a uniform inventory of the kingdom, so that it might later be easier to divide it amongst them equally.[5] When these things had been done, Louis returned from Mâcon and held a general assembly in the month of August in the *villa* called Salz. Then he set out for Saxony, where there was a very serious conspiracy of freedmen seeking to oppress their lawful lords.[6] He crushed this ruthlessly by sentencing the ringleaders to death. Towards autumn he met his brother Charles in Worms, while Lothar remained in the *villa* of Thionville. When their representatives, meeting in the castle of Koblenz, were unable to agree on the partition of the kingdom, they put off the judgement until another time[7] and each returned to his own kingdom.

In the same year there was an eclipse of the moon on March 30, the fifth day of the week before Easter, in the tenth hour of the night.

4 In early June; cf. *AB* 842 (Nelson 1991: 53) and Nithard IV, 4 (Scholz 1972: 169).

5 On the way in which the various proposed divisions culminating in the Treaty of Verdun were drawn up see Nithard IV, 4 (Scholz 1972: 170-1), *AB* 842 and 843 (Nelson 1991: 53-4 and 56) and Ganshof 1971: 289-302.

6 The *Stellinga* uprising in Saxony between 841 and 845 is one of the very rare examples of a popular revolt in early medieval Europe. The Saxons seem to have been divided into three castes (excluding slaves): nobles, freemen and freedmen. The conquest of Saxony by Charles the Great was achieved to a large extent by winning over the Saxon nobility. The consequence was a depression of the status of the freemen, and a tendency for both freemen and freedmen to become dependent peasants, whereas previously they had enjoyed considerable political rights; Reuter 1991: 66-7. According to Nithard IV, 2 (Scholz 1972: 166-7), Lothar had promised the rebels the rights their forefathers had had when they were still heathens, and both Nithard and *AB* 842 (Nelson 1991: 54) imply that their revolt was combined with an anti-Christian reaction. A com-parable revolt by the Slav Liutizi against Saxon domination in 983 following Otto II's defeat in southern Italy shows a similar mixture of politico-economic and religious motivation. The *Stellinga* – the name means 'companions, comrades' (Wagner 1980: 131-3) – was taken very seriously, and the penalties handed out were brutal; compare the similar treatment of the peasants' self-defence league in the Seine basin reported in *AB* 859 (Nelson 1991: 89). A final uprising in 843 was crushed by the Saxon nobility themselves; Nithard IV, 6 (Scholz 1972: 173). On the whole subject see Müller-Mertens 1972.

7 On the reasons for the delay see Nithard IV, 4-5 (Scholz 1972: 169-72).

843

After the kingdom had been surveyed by the leading men and divided
into three parts, the three kings met in the month of August at
Verdun, a city in Gaul, and divided it amongst themselves. Louis
received the eastern part; Charles held the western part; Lothar, who
was the oldest, obtained the part which lay in between.[1] After peace
had been made between them and confirmed by oath, each set off to
govern and defend the lands of his own kingdom.[2] Charles, who
claimed Aquitaine as if belonging to his portion of the kingdom by
right, made difficulties for his nephew Pippin [II of Aquitaine] by
frequent attacks; but often his own army suffered severe loss.[3]

Pope Gregory died, and in his place Sergius was chosen.[4]

The Moors occupied Benevento.[5]

844

Charles killed Bernard, *dux* of Barcelona, who was taken unawares and
did not expect any enmity from him.[1]

Pippin's *duces* defeated Charles's army on June 7. In this battle fell
Hugh the Abbot, Charles's maternal uncle, Abbot Rihboto, Hrabanus
the standard-bearer, with many others of the nobility.[2]

Louis crushed the Abodrites in battle, who had been preparing to
defect from his allegiance; as their king Goztomuizli had been killed,
he had the land and people which God had brought under his yoke

1 For the details of the division see *AB* 843 (Nelson 1991: 56).

2 Louis was at Hersfeld at the end of October (DD LG 32-3).

3 Some at least of these attacks took place in the period before the Treaty of
Verdun (Lot and Halphen 1909: 84 n. 3). Charles's difficulty lay in the nature
of the division reached at Verdun. Each of the three rulers was deemed to have
a 'core' kingdom: Bavaria, Italy and Aquitaine, to each of which a portion of the
regnum Francorum proper was added. But whereas Louis and Lothar actually
controlled their 'cores', Charles did not, since Aquitaine was *de facto* controlled
by Pippin II, as *AF* in effect point out.

4 Gregory IV died on January 25 844; his successor Sergius II was elected
shortly afterwards.

5 Early in 843; compare Nithard IV, 6 (Scholz 1972: 173), and the report in *AB*
843 (Nelson 1991: 56), that the Moors had been driven out of Benevento.

1 See *AB* 844 (Nelson 1991: 57).

2 See *AB* 844 (Nelson 1991: 58-9).

ruled by *duces*.[3]

Hrabanus,[4] a learned man and second to none of the poets of his time, sent the book which he had composed on the praises of the Holy Cross of Christ, full of a variety of figures and written in a remarkable and difficult verse-form, to Pope Sergius by Aschrich and Hruobert, monks of the monastery of Fulda, to be offered to St Peter.[5]

845

The Northmen ravaged Charles's kingdom, came by boat up the Seine as far as Paris and, having received a great sum of money both from him and from the inhabitants of the region, departed in peace. In Frisia they also fought three battles. in the first they were indeed defeated, but in the remaining two they were victorious and killed a great number of men. They also destroyed a castle in Saxony, called Hamburg, and returned, not without punishment.[1]

3 *AB* 844 (Nelson 1991: 59) as well as *AX* 844 (von Simson 1909: 13-14), AC 844 (Prinz 1982: 103) and *AH* 844 (Waitz 1878a: 17) refer to a number of kings of the Abodrites of whom Goztomuizli was one; the *AF* here imply that Goztomiuzli was *the* king, i.e. a high king or overlord. The report here that the Abodrites were henceforth ruled by dukes (*duces* = leaders appointed by Louis, as opposed to a *rex* or *reges*, kings who ruled in their own right) corresponds to the usual Frankish technique in conquered territories: compare Einhard's account of Charles the Great's subjugation of Bavaria after 788, *Vita Karoli*, c.11 (Holder-Egger 1911: 14), though the terminology used is different, and the warning by Hellmann 1973 against interpreting such terminology too strictly should be noted. However, the arrangements made here did not last; the Abodrites threatened rebellion again the following year (see 845 with n. 4), rebelled in 858 (see 858 with n. 7), and are again found under a single leader in 862 (862 with n. 3): cf. Friedmann 1986: 116-18, 142-80 on the political development of the Abodrites in the ninth century. When all this took place is unclear; Louis's diplomata from April 844 to March 845 are all issued from Regensburg (DD LG 35-40), but there are plenty of gaps for an expedition to the north-eastern frontier.

4 Abbot of Fulda and later archbishop of Mainz; on his career see below, 847 n. 6.

5 The work (prefatory verses *MGH Poetae* 2: 159-61; complete Migne, *PL* 107: 133-294) was actually dedicated to Pope Gregory IV, so that this notice is probably a sign of later revision – the revisor had noted thesuccession of Sergius to Gregory IV, and hence made the work to be dedicated to the `current' pope.

1 For these attacks compare the account in *AB* 845 (Nelson 1991: 61); the 'Slav city' in Prudentius's account may be identified with Hamburg, but this is not certain, and Kahl 1971: 126-33 has suggested Schwerin. One result of this attack on Saxony – the last major one until 880, though see *AB* 858, 862, 863 (Nelson 1991: 87, 102, 104) for lesser ones – was that the missionary bishop and papal legate Ansgar, who had previously directed the Danish mission from

Charles fought the Bretons and after great loss to his army barely managed to escape with a few of his men.[2]

Louis received fourteen of the *duces* of the Bohemians with their men, who wished to become Christians; he had them baptised on the octave of Epiphany [January 13].[3] In the autumn he held a general assembly in Saxony at Paderborn, where he received ambassadors from his brothers and from the Northmen, Slavs and Bulgars;[4] he heard them and allowed them to depart.

Lothar received the surrender of Folcrat, *dux* of Arles, and the other counts of those parts who were planning rebellion, and arranged affairs in Provence as he wished.[5]

846

Gislebert, a vassal of Charles, kidnapped a daughter of the Emperor Lothar and made for Aquitaine, where he took her to wife. Louis set

Hamburg, was forced to withdraw to Bremen, and the Danish mission suffered a severe setback; *Vita Anskarii* c. 16 (Waitz 1884: 37-8); Wood 1987: 47-8.

2 See *AB* 845 (Nelson 1991: 62); the reference is to the Battle of Ballon in November.

3 This probably took place in Regensburg, where Louis is found in October 844 and March 845. For *duces*, meaning something like 'leading men', see Graus 1980: 194-5 and Hellmann 1973; whereas in 805 only one *dux* was mentioned, here and subsequently (see below, 856, 872, 895, 897) there are always several. The baptism may possibly be seen as the result of missionary work by the bishops of Regensburg in Bohemia, of which there are some traces in the ninth century; possibly also it was a response to the increasing threat from the expanding Moravian Empire. In any case it affected only some of the Bohemians, and it did not imply permanent subordination of the Bohemians to the east Frankish kingdom; we hear repeatedly in the following years of wars between the Franks and Bohemians. The real beginnings of Christianity in Bohemia are to be placed in the 870s and 880s, and the initiative then came largely from the Church in Moravia itself. See Dvornik 1970: 206-8; Vlasto 1970: 86-8.

4 The Slavs referred to were the Abodrites, who had threatened to rebel against the settlement of the previous year. Louis's presence in Saxony (with a large army) caused them to send legates to make peace; cf. *AX* 845 (von Simson 1909: 14-15). This source says that the ambassadors of the Northmen were also offering peace coupled with a general release of Christian captives. The purpose of the legations from Lothar and Charles is unknown, but it was perhaps connected with Norse attacks on their kingdoms. The assembly must have been after September 3, when Louis was still at Regensburg (D LG 44).

5 Compare *AB* 845 (Nelson 1991: 61, 62). The title of *dux* here given to Folcrat is an indication that he held high military command over the other counts of the region. He seems to have been reconciled with Lothar, since he is found holding office in a list of 846; Poupardin 1901: 3-4.

off for the west, where he had a meeting with Charles in March. At this each of them declared publicly that it had not been by their will that Gislebert had married Lothar's daughter, so that Lothar might be more easily pacified after hearing this.[1] From here Louis returned and celebrated Easter by Lake Constance on April 4. After this he spoke with Lothar, wishing to reconcile him to Charles. When he was unable to do this, he set off around the middle of August with an army against the Moravian Slavs, who were planning to defect. There he arranged and settled matters as he wished, and set Rastiz, a nephew of Moimar, as a *dux* over them.[2] From there he returned through the lands of the Bohemians with great difficulty and serious loss to his army.

At this time the Moors came to Rome with an army, and after they had failed to break into the city they destroyed the church of St Peter.[3]

1 Gislebert is generally identified with the Gislebert, count of the Maasgau, mentioned as a supporter of Charles (but a vassal of Lothar's) by Nithard III, 3 (Scholz 1972: 158) and thought to have been an ancestor of the tenth-century Reginarid dukes of Lotharingia (Parisot 1899: 36-40; Werner 1967: 449-50 and table). The whole episode is puzzling. It is clear that the Carolingians exercised close control over the marriage of their daughters, so that Lothar's anger is understandable; what is not clear is why Lothar should have felt that Charles was responsible, particularly since Gislebert himself took refuge with Pippin II of Aquitaine and so presumably did not feel sure of Charles's support. There are no diplomata for this year which give precision to the annalist's account of Louis's itinerary.

2 The Moravians are first mentioned in *ARF* 822 (Scholz 1972: 112); we know from the *Conversion of the Bavarians and Carinthians* that they were expanding their territory and influence under their leader Moimar I from the end of the 820s at the latest (Wolfram 1987: 359-62). Rastiz ruled until 870 (see the account of his end that year below) but was no more reliable than Moimar, in spite of having come to power with Frankish help. *AX* 846 (von Simson 1909: 15) talk of an expedition against the Bohemians at this point. The location and extent of the Moravian empire is disputed; Sós 1973: 29-65 gives a number of different mappings of its extent, all of which see the core of the empire as having been in present-day Moravia around the River Maraha, as does Wolfram 1987: 359-60. Boba 1971, Boba 1976 and Bowlus 1987 offer the 'revisionist' view that the core lay much further south along the Danube with a centre near Sirmium. Neither side has as yet really come to terms with the arguments which can be put for the opposite case.

3 On August 27; see *AB* 846 (Nelson 1991: 63). The event was widely-reported and led to a major campaign against the Saracens; cf. Zielinski 1991.

847

This year was free of wars,[1] and Lothar and Louis spent it in each other's company. For each of them was invited to the home of the other and was honoured with feasts and royal gifts.[2] Louis was not, however, able to reconcile Lothar and Charles as he wished, for Lothar refused to forgive the injury done him by Gislebert, Charles's vassal, in carrying off his daughter.[3]

The Northmen burned and laid waste Dorestad.[4]

Otgar, bishop of Mainz, died on April 21.[5] In his place Hrabanus[6] was consecrated on June 26; at King Louis's order he held a synod at Mainz around October 1.[7] At this time a certain woman from Alemannia called Thiota, a false prophetess, came to Mainz; she had disturbed the diocese of Bishop Salomon [I of Constance] not a little with her prophecies. For she said that she knew a definite date for the ending of the world, and other things known only to God, as if they had been

1 A biblical reminiscence, cf. Joshua 11:23: *quievitque terra a proeliis.* Carolingian annalists normally noted the (rare) occasions when a year passed without fighting; cf. e.g. *ARF* 790 (Scholz 1972: 69). However, *AB* (Nelson 1991: 65) record a campaign by Louis the German's forces against the Slavs in this year.

2 For these public demonstrations of 'brotherhood' see Althoff 1990: 99-100; Schneider 1964; and for Louis and Charles in 842 Nithard III, 6 (Scholz 1972: 163-4). The itineraries as revealed in the diplomata of Louis and Lothar neither confirm nor deny the account given here.

3 On Gislebert see above, 846 with n. 1. The annalist here passes over the meeting of the three brothers at Meersen in February 847 (*MGH Capit.* 2: 68-71 no. 244) at which Louis was able to persuade Lothar to forbid his men to attack Charles's lands (cf. II c. 4, p. 70).

4 An *emporium* in Frisia; on its fate see Nelson 1991: 104 n. 1.

5 Otgar was archbishop from 826 to 847; he had been a strong supporter of Lothar in the civil war of 840-43, as seen in his attempt to prevent Louis from meeting Charles in early 842 recorded by Nithard III, 4 (Scholz 1972: 161), and his death marked an important step for Louis in consolidating his hold on the east Frankish kingdom.

6 Hrabanus (or Rhabanus) Maurus, archbishop of Mainz from 847 to 856, had previously been abbot of Fulda from 823 to 842. He had been a strong supporter of Louis the Pious and then of Lothar in the 830s, and resigned his office after Lothar's defeat at Fontenoy had left his supporters in the lands east of the Rhine in a precarious position. Some time between then and 847 he was reconciled with Louis the German; cf. *MGH Epp.* 5: 465-7 no. 33 and 467-70 nos. 34-5. On Hrabanus see Sandmann 1980; Kottje and Zimmermann 1982; Kottje 1982/3.

7 The canons of this council (Hartmann 1984: 150-77), preceded by a letter from Hrabanus to Louis, have survived; they repeat provisions of the council held at Mainz in 813, which evidently served as a model, and from Hrabanus's own penitential; Hartmann 1989: 222-6.

divinely revealed to her; she predicted that the world would see its last day that same year. As a result many of the common people of both sexes were struck by fear; they came to her with gifts and commended themselves to her prayers. Still worse, men in holy orders, ignoring the teaching of the Church, followed her as a teacher sent from heaven. She was brought into the presence of the bishops at St Alban's [Mainz]. After she had been carefully questioned about her claims, she admitted that a certain priest had coached her in them and that she had made them in hope of gain. For this she was publicly flogged by the judgement of the synod and ignominiously stripped of the ministry of preaching which she had unreasonably taken up and presumed to claim against the custom of the church; thus shamed, she finally put an end to her prophesyings.[8]

848

Lothar and Louis had a meeting in the castle of Koblenz in February.[1] It was rumoured that Lothar's party was mainly concerned to see that Louis should put aside his friendship with Charles and ally himself with Lothar as their brotherhood demanded.[2] Louis, however, remembering the treaty which he had long ago made with Charles and confirmed by an oath in God's name,[3] cleverly avoided their skilled persuasion, and returned to his own kingdom. Around the middle of August he sent an expedition under his son Louis against the Bohemians, who were planning rebellion, and crushed them, forcing them to send ambassadors to sue for peace and to give hostages.[4] Around October 1 he held a general assembly at Mainz, where he

8 See Nelson 1990b: 73-4 on this episode, though it seems unlikely that the objection was to Thiota's having done something 'unreasonably' which she might in principle have done 'reasonably'; the tone of the passage suggests that the unreasonableness lay in her having done it at all. The whole account is missing in ms. '2'.

1 Louis was at Frankfurt in mid-January (D LG 47) and at Regensburg in early March (D LG 48), but the dating of both diplomata is not quite certain, and there would in any case have been enough time for a meeting at Koblenz in between.

2 Lothar and Louis the German were sons of Louis the Pious by his first wife Ermengard, and so full brothers; Charles was the son of Louis's second wife Judith, and so only their half-brother.

3 A reference to the oaths of Strasbourg; see above, 842 with n. 2.

4 According to AB 848 (Nelson 1991: 65) the Bohemians had not only planned rebellion but actually attacked. AX, usually well-informed on the eastern frontier, have nothing.

received, heard and dismissed ambassadors from his brothers and from
the Northmen and Slavs.[5] He also reconciled the men of [Arch]bishop
Hrabanus [of Mainz], who had been publicly proved to have conspired
against their lord, to him. He sent his own ambassadors to his brother
Lothar in Thionville, where he was holding an assembly, to intercede
for Gislebert, who had returned to his allegiance that same year.[6]

A certain priest called Gottschalk, who held wicked opinions about
divine predestination, namely that the good were predestined by God
to life and the evil to eternal death, was condemned at an episcopal
synod, reasonably as it seemed to many. He was sent to Hincmar, his
own bishop, at Rheims, but first took an oath that he would never
return to the kingdom of Louis.[7]

849

The Bohemians in their usual fashion denied their loyalty and planned
to rebel against the Franks. Ernest, the *dux* of those parts and chief
among the king's friends, was sent with not a few counts and abbots
and a large army to crush these treacherous moves.[1] The heathen,

5 Nothing specific is known about the purpose of these embassies. Horic king of
  Denmark was concerned to keep on good terms with the Carolingians – see
  above, 845 n. 4 and *Vita Anskarii*, c. 24 (Waitz 1884: 51-3); the Slavs are
  probably the Bohemians and Moravians, but could be Abodrites.

6 Gislebert had probably fled from Aquitaine to Louis himself after Charles's
  seizure of power there, on which see *AB* 848 (Nelson 1991: 66) and below under
  851, though the Latin implies if anything that Gislebert had already done
  homage to Lothar. It would seem from a letter of Pope Nicholas I (JE 2722 =
  MGH Epp. 6: 370 no. 60) on the similar case of Baldwin and Charles the Bald's
  daughter Judith that Lothar and Gislebert were indeed reconciled; this was no
  doubt a preliminary to the reconciliation between Lothar and Charles at the
  beginning of the following year reported in *AB* 849 (Nelson 1991: 66-7).

7 Instead of this paragraph ms. '1' has the following entry: 'Gottschalk, who was
  called a heretic, was condemned at Mainz by Archbishop Hrabanus and many
  other bishops, rightly, as it seemed to many, though he persisted afterwards in
  his opinion.' On Gottschalk and his heresy compare *AB* for 849 and 861
  (Nelson 1991: 67, 94), *AX* for 848 (von Simson 1909: 16), and see further
  Hartmann 1989: 226-7 (on the council at Mainz in 848) and 260-72 (on the
  later west Frankish councils on predestination); Nineham 1989; Ganz 1990;
  Marenbon 1990.

1 Ernest, whose description here as *dux illarum partium* is probably to be
  construed as a military command over the other Bavarian counts (compare
  Folcrat of Arles, above, 845 with n. 5), was until his fall in 861 (see under that
  year) one of the most powerful men in the east Frankish kingdom. Count
  Gebhard of the Lahngau was probably his brother-in-law, and his daughter
  was married to Carloman, Louis the German's oldest son (Mitterauer 1963:
  132-7).

however, promised through legates sent to Thachulf that they would give hostages for their peace and safety and would do as they were commanded. They trusted him above all others as one who was knowledgeable in the laws and customs of the Slavic people, for he was *dux* of the Sorbian March;[2] but he had already been severely wounded in the expedition. For on the previous day, as the army broke through an enemy fortification with great force and the enemy resisted, many on both sides were wounded without respect of persons. He was struck by an arrow in his left knee. However, he spoke with the legates who had been sent to him, sitting on a horse as if in good health, so that they might not discover his weakness. When he sent messengers to some of the leading Franks to report the terms offered by the legates, some of them were angry with him, because they thought he wanted to be set above the others and to take over the supreme command. With a hurried onslaught, without consulting the others,[3] they renewed the attack on an enemy seeking peace, and immediately learnt what the power and boldness of the quarrelsome can do without the fear of God. For the enemy were victorious and pursued them with slaughter to their camps, and removed the arms of the dead undisturbed before their eyes, frightening them so much that they thought they were absolutely without hope of escape. They were forced by this to give hostages to those from whom they had scorned to receive them, so that they might return unharmed straight down the main road to their home country. So that there might be still more confusion for the proud and for those over-confident in their own strength, it happened in the same year after a short time in the *villa* of Höchst in the territory of Mainz that an evil spirit announced through the mouth of a possessed man that he had been in charge of the Bohemian war and his allies had been the spirit of pride and discord through whose treacherous machinations the Franks had fled from the Bohemians.[4]

2 That is, he had a military command like that of Ernest over the counts bordering on the Sorbs. For his later career see 858 with n. 8, 873 with n. 19.

3 For similar examples of jealousies within an army and a badly-prepared attack which led to disaster compare below 872 or *ARF* 782 (Scholz 1972: 60-1); it was a permanent problem in early medieval armies and examples could easily be multiplied.

4 See the shorter account of this campaign in *AB* 849 (Nelson 1991: 68) where it is explained that Louis was ill and could not command in person, an explanation also hinted at in *AX* 849 (von Simson 1909: 16). The reference to internal disputes in Louis's army in *AB* 846 (Nelson 1991: 63) may belong here. *AF* do not mention the meeting between Louis and Charles; *AB* 849 (Nelson 1991: 67).

850

Roric the Northman held the *vicus* Dorestad as a benefice with his brother Heriald in the time of the emperor Louis. After the deaths of the emperor and his own brother he was denounced as a traitor – falsely as it is said – to Lothar, who had succeeded his father in the kingdom, and was captured and imprisoned. He escaped and became the man of Louis, king of the eastern Franks. After he had stayed there for some years, living among the Saxons, who are neighbours of the Northmen, he collected a not insubstantial force of Danes and began a career of piracy, attacking places near the northern coast of Lothar's kingdom by the North Sea.[1] He came through the mouth of the river Rhine to Durestad, seized and held it. Because the emperor Lothar was unable to drive him out without danger to his own men, Roric was received back into fealty on the advice of his [Lothar's] counsellors and through mediators on condition that he would faithfully handle the taxes and other matters pertaining to the royal fisc, and would resist the piratical attacks of the Danes.[2]

The Northmen under their *dux* Godafrid came up the Seine and plundered Charles's kingdom. Lothar was called to help with their expulsion, and thought that he was to come with his men to fight; but Charles changed his plan secretly, received Godafrid with his men into the alliance of his kingdom and gave them land to live on. Lothar, seeing that his coming was pointless, returned to his own lands.[3]

1 I.e. Frisia, which had fallen to Lothar under the terms of the treaty of Verdun; for attacks by the Northmen there see above, 845, 847 with n. 4; *AX* 845, 846, 847, 848 (von Simson 1909: 14–16); *AB* 850 (Nelson 1991: 69).

2 The rather condensed account given here of Roric's past history is difficult to verify, as the references to Roric and Harald/Heriald in the different sets of Frankish annals do not match up. It is not certain whether Roric was Harald's brother, as claimed here and in *AX* (von Simson 1909: 17) or his nephew, as in *AB* 850 (Nelson 1991: 69), perhaps meaning simply 'relative'. It is also not clear whether this Heriald was the same person as the man referred to in the *ARF* between 814 and 826, who was baptised at Louis the Pious's court in 826 and given land in Frisia; probably not. Nor is it certain whether they were related to the Harald mentioned in the annal for 852. The essential texts are *AB* 841 and 850 (Nelson 1991: 51 and 69), the present annal, and *ARF* 811-14, 819, 821, 823, 826-8 (Scholz 1972: 93-9, 106, 110, 114, 119, 122-3). Vogel 1906: 100ff., 128ff., 402-12 provides a good discussion of the issue and of the conflicting information we have on Danish royal genealogy in the ninth century; see also Wood 1987: 42-5. The uncertainty is not difficult to explain: it was useful for the Franks to support exiled members of the royal or ducal families of the Danes and Slavs, but they did not need to concern themselves closely with the genealogies of these families: royalty was sufficient.

3 The events referred to here belong to 852 and 853; compare *AB* 852 and 853

In the same year a severe famine struck the German people, especially those living along the Rhine. At Mainz, one bushel of corn was sold for ten shekels of silver.[4] At that time Archbishop Hrabanus [of Mainz] was staying in a *villa* in his diocese, called Winkel,[5] and receiving poor men from all over the place daily fed more than three hundred, quite apart from those who regularly dined in his presence.[6] There came also a certain woman almost dead of starvation with a small child among the others seeking help. Before she could cross the threshold she collapsed from weakness and died. The child tried to pull the breast of his dead mother out from her clothes and suckle, which caused many of those who saw this to groan and weep.At that time also a certain man from the Grabfeld[7] set out for Thuringia with his wife and small son to see if they could find some relief from hunger. On the journey he said to his wife as they were going through a wood: 'Surely it would be better to kill the boy and eat him than that we should all die of hunger?' She refused to allow so great a crime to be committed, but he, driven by hunger, at length seized the son from her arms by force and would have carried out his intention, if God in his mercy had not prevented him. For as he afterwards told to many when he came to Thuringia, when he had drawn his sword to kill his son, and had, vacillating, put off the murder, he saw at a distance two wolves standing on a deer and tearing its flesh. At once he spared his son and hurried to the corpse of the deer, where he drove off the wolves and took away some of the flesh which they had begun to eat, and then returned to his wife with their son unharmed. For before, when he had taken the boy away from his mother's hands, he had gone off a little way, so that she would not see or hear the dying boy. She, on her husband's return, seeing fresh meat dripping with blood, thought that the boy had been

(Nelson 1991: 75). The statement that Charles gave Godafrid land is probably confirmed by the more cautious wording of *AB*, and by the provisions of an assembly held by Charles at Soissons in 853 (*MGH Capit.* 2: 267 no. 259, c. 1), where his *missi* were ordered to draw up a list (*inbrevient*) of what had been given to the Northmen 'by our commendation'; *inbreviare* is more likely to refer to land than to tribute. See Vogel 1906: 135; Dümmler 1887a: 355 n. 1.

4 Shekels are a biblical reminiscence, not a current unit of account; the price was probably 10 *solidi*, i.e. 120 silver pennies, a considerable sum. This whole paragraph is missing in MS 2.

5 On the left bank of the Rhine between Mainz and Bingen.

6 Both the provision for *pauperes* and its extension in times of famine were normal for churchmen in the ninth century, though there was a tendency to institutionalise these by providing *xenodochia* and *hospitalia*; see Boshof 1976.

7 The region south-east of Fulda on the borders between Franconia and Thuringia.

killed and fell almost lifeless. He came to her and comforted her and lifted her up to show her that the boy was still alive. Then she recovered full consciousness and gave thanks to God that she had been allowed to have her son back well; so did he, that God had thought fit to keep him innocent of killing the child. Both, however, were driven by necessity to strengthen themselves by feeding on the meat which the Law prohibits.[8]

851

The Sorbs violated the Frankish border with frequent attacks and incendiary raids. The king, angry at this, proceeded through Thuringia with an army, invaded their territory and oppressed them severely. He tamed them, after they had lost their harvests and so the hope of food, rather through hunger than through fighting.[1]

Pippin, king of Aquitaine, was taken by his own men and handed to King Charles with his kingdom. He was made a cleric and shut away in the monastery of St-Médard at Soissons in monk's habit.[2] Similarly Charles, his younger brother, was captured by King Charles's counts as he set out from Lothar's kingdom to see his brother, and at Charles's orders was tonsured and sent to be guarded in the monastery of Corbie.[3]

852

Heriald the Northman had in earlier years fled the anger of his lord Horic, king of the Danes, and come to King Louis, by whom he was well received. He was baptised and received into the Christian faith, and held in honour among the Franks for many years. At length he became suspect to the leading men[1] of the northern regions and the

8 The law referred to here is that of the Old Testament, which forbids the eating of carrion flesh: see for example Exodus 22:31; Deuteronomy 14:21.

1 The Sorbs were a confederation of Slav tribes to the east of the Thuringians; see Brankačk and Mětšk 1977. This campaign, which cannot be more precisely dated, is also noted in *AB* 851 (Nelson 1991: 73). The rather deprecatory account given here seems strange, as the Sorbs under their *dux* Zistibor are found as Louis's allies until Zistibor's murder in 858/9; see below, 856, 857, 858.

2 In 852: see *AB* 852 (Nelson 1991: 74-5).

3 In June 849: see *AB* 849 (Nelson 1991: 68), in which account Charles's tonsure is represented as voluntary.

1 The Latin is *principibus*, which in the plural has much the same meaning as words like *optimates, priores, maiores natu*, and so on. 'Princes' conveys a sense of independent power which is lacking here.

warders of the Danish march as of doubtful loyalty and a potential traitor, and was therefore killed by them.[2]

By the will of the same most serene prince a synod was held in the city of Mainz, the metropolitan of Germany, under the presidency of Hrabanus, the reverend archbishop of that town, with all the bishops and abbots of eastern Francia, Bavaria and Saxony.[3] While they were holding meetings to settle ecclesiastical matters, the king with the leading men and the prefects of the provinces [counts] was busy with the affairs of the kingdom and with settling disputes. After he had confirmed by his approval the canons of the synod,[4] and had heard and dismissed the embassies of the Bulgars and Slavs,[5] he returned to Bavaria. He arranged and settled what seemed necessary and returned along the Rhine by ship without delay to Cologne. Here he held talks with some of the leading men of Lothar's kingdom,[6] and then set out for Saxony, mainly in order to judge their [the Saxons'] cases, which, so they say, had been neglected by bad and unfaithful judges so that they had been deprived of their rights and suffered long and serious injury through many kinds of delay. There were also other matters which concerned him especially: lands which had come to him by hereditary right from his father and grandfather, which he needed to restore to their rightful owner through lawful claim against wicked usurpers. Therefore he held a general assembly in the place which is called Minden, on the river, which Cornelius Tacitus, author of a book which describes what the Romans did to that people,[7] calls the

2 See 850 with n. 2, for references to the Franks' vassal Northmen; compare Heriald's fate with that of Godafrid in 885 (below 885(I) and (II)). The raid on Frisia mentioned in *AB* 852 (*recte* 851) (Nelson 1991: 74) may belong in this connection.

3 October 1 852; on it see Hartmann 1989: 228-32. The sentence in the text is taken almost verbatim from the preface to the canons of the synod (Hartmann 1984: 235-52).

4 Standard Carolingian practice for conciliar legislation; see most recently Hartmann 1989: 9-10.

5 Nothing more is known about these embassies; for the Bulgarians, who had already sent an embassy in 844 (see above), cf. *AB* 853 (Nelson 1991: 77), which suggest that Charles had bribed them to attack Louis.

6 Nothing more is known about this meeting, but it is presumably to be seen in the context of the growing estrangement between Charles and Louis and correspondingly cordial relations between Charles and Lothar in the years following the meeting of the three brothers at Meersen in 851; cf. *AB* 851, 852, 853, 854 (Nelson 1991: 70, 74, 76, 78).

7 Tacitus's *De Germania*, one of the very few citations of this work between late antiquity and its rediscovery in the Renaissance; on this passage see introduction, 5 n. 21.

Visurgis, but nowadays is called the Weser. Here he not only dealt justly with the cases brought to him by the people but received the possessions belonging to him according to the judgment of men of that people learned in the law. From here he went through the lands of the Angrians, the Harudi, the Suabians and the Hochseegau,[8] halting in individual holdings as opportunity permitted[9] and hearing the people's cases, and came to Thuringia. He held an assembly at Erfurt, and decreed among other things that no count or deputy should take up anyone's case as an advocate within his own county or district, though they might freely do so in the districts of others.[10] Leaving Erfurt, he celebrated Christmas in Regensburg.[11]

853

The Northmen came up the Loire to plunder the city of Tours in Gaul and set fire to the church of St Martin the Confessor among other

8 Engern is the middle and northerly province of Saxony; the Harudi are the inhabitants of the Harzgau around Halberstadt; the Suabians are not the inhabitants of Alemannia but a remnant settled east of the Harzgau by the Franks after their victory over the Thuringians in 531; and the Hassegau lies between the Unstrut and the Saale. Louis thus traversed a great arc to the eastern border before returning through Erfurt to Regensburg.

9 *per mansiones singulas, prout se praebuit oportunitas*, an interesting text on the king's right to claim hospitality.

10 The terms used by the annalist are *prefectus* for count and *questionarius*, which one would normally translate as a torturer or hangman but here almost certainly refers to the *vicarius* or *centenarius*, the count's deputy; Waitz 1885: 410 n. 2. The count and his deputies were responsible for holding public courts within their districts at regular intervals; ecclesiastical establishments were supposed to be represented in cases brought before such courts by an advocate. The edict, the only specific reference to an east Frankish ruler's having issued a capitulary, was obviously intended to prevent conflicts of interest. On the institutions here referred to see Ganshof 1968: 28, 32, 73–81.

11 The journey was a rapid one; between October 1 and December 25 Louis had travelled from Mainz to Bavaria (presumably Regensburg), back to Cologne (probably largely by water), thence to Minden, and thence along the eastern frontier through Thuringia to Regensburg. If his diploma for Herford (D LG 51) is to be dated to 852, then he was still in Herford (in Westfalia) on December 8, but that would hardly leave any time for his judicial tour; a date to 851, however, is equally difficult to fit in to his itinerary. There are otherwise no diplomata between June 852 and January 853 (DD LG 63–4). It is conceivable that there is some error in the annals at this point, perhaps as a result of condensation (see introduction, p. 4 n. 16, for other distortions of chronology in the entries for the 840s and 850s). Reuter 1991: 85–91 offers a commentary on the implications of the annal for east Frankish governmental practice.

buildings, meeting no resistance.[1]

Legates from the Aquitanians made repeated requests to King Louis that he should either take up the kingship over them or send his son to liberate them from the tyranny of King Charles. Lest they should be forced to seek help from foreigners and enemies of the faith with danger to the Christian religion, since they could not obtain it from their orthodox and legitimate lords.[2]

Heimo bishop of Halberstadt departed from this world on March 27, and Hildigrim was consecrated bishop in his place.[3] Reginher the chorbishop died on August 27 and left Folchard as his successor.[4] Also Hadawart bishop of Minden died on September 16 and left his see to Theotric.[5]

On September 1 thieves broke into the church of St Boniface the Martyr [at Fulda] by night and took away part of the treasure. Up to the present day it is still the case that the criminals have not been identified nor has any trace of the treasure been found.[6]

854

Louis, son of King Louis, came to Aquitaine, wishing to see if the promises made by that people's ambassadors to his father were true. When he arrived, however, he was not acknowledged by anyone except by that one kindred whom Charles had greatly offended through the murder of their kinsman Gauzbert which he had ordered.

1 November 8 853; see *AB* 853 (Nelson 1991: 77). Ms. '2' takes its account at this point from Regino 853 (Kurze 1890: 76).

2 Compare *AB* 853 (Nelson 1991: 77); for Louis the Younger's expedition to Aquitaine see below, 854 with n 1.

3 Heimo, 840-53, was a biblical scholar; his successor Hildigrim ruled from 853 to 886.

4 This notice appears to be self-contradictory, since chorbishops were assistant bishops without dioceses, and so could not have successors; in any case both Reginher and Folchard are found as chorbishops at the council of Mainz in 852 (Hartmann 1984: 241). The explanation appears to be that Reginhar acted *de facto* as bishop of Erfurt, a bishopric founded by Boniface in 741 or 742 but soon absorbed into the diocese of Mainz, and was succeeded in this capacity by Folchard (Gottlob 1928: 28-9).

5 For the careers of Hadawart (830/6-53) and Theotric (853-80) of Minden see Weinfurter and Engels 1982: 88-90.

6 It is unclear whether this entry was composed at the time or later; see introduction, p. 4. *AF* do not mention the Bulgar-Slav campaign recorded in *AB* (Nelson 1991: 77).

The rest declined to come to him, and he judged his coming superfluous; after taking counsel with his men he returned to the Frankish kingdom around the autumn.[1]

The Northmen, who for twenty years continuously had cruelly afflicted with fire and slaughter and pillage those places on the borders of Francia which were accessible by ship, came together from the different parts to which they had scattered in their greed for plunder, and returned to their own country. There a civil war had begun between Horic, king of the Danes, and Gudurm, his brother's son, who up till then had been driven by Horic from the country and had lived a piratical existence. The two parties so wore each other down with killing that countless common people were killed, and of the royal family no one remained except one small boy.[2] Thus God revenged the injuries done to his saints and dealt out just rewards to his enemies for their crimes.

855

There are said to have been twenty earth tremors in Mainz. Unusually changeable weather brought loss to many through whirlwinds, storms and hailstorms. Many buildings were burnt by lightning, including the church of St Kilian the Martyr [in Würzburg] on June 5. The clergy were celebrating vespers when the church was suddenly struck by a bolt and caught fire. Miraculously the fire hung around the roof-beams of the church for so long without spreading that the bones of the holy martyr and the whole of the church treasure could be brought to safety without loss. Some of the clergy were also struck by the bolt and were burnt on various parts of the body without their vestments being damaged. They also say that one man in those parts was completely burnt up by lightning, though his clothes remained undamaged. On the eighth day of the following month, at the beginning of the feast-day of that same holy martyr, the walls of the church, which the

---

1 For the events in Aquitaine in 854 see the fuller account in *AB* 854 (Nelson 1991: 78), which says that Louis was driven out of Aquitaine by Charles the Bald. It would appear that Louis the Younger's support dwindled after Pippin II's escape from custody. For Gauzbert see Nelson 1991: 78 n. 3.

2 The survivor was also called Horic: see below, 857. The statement that Gudurm had been driven out by Horic probably indicates the cause of the civil war, as Horic, according to *AB* 850 (Nelson 1991: 69), had divided his kingdom with his two nephews. Saxo Grammaticus (Fisher and Davidson 1979: 276-7, 292-3) gives a vague but identifiable version of these events at the end of his history. See also *AB* 855 (Nelson 1991: 80).

previous lightning had not burnt, collapsed in a terrible storm which blew up suddenly. This disaster was followed by the death of Bishop Gozbald [of Würzburg] in the third month after that, that is on September 20. He was succeeded by his pupil Arn.[1]

King Louis took an army against the Moravians and their *dux*, Rastiz, who was rebelling against him, with little success. He returned without victory, preferring to leave for the time being an enemy defended by strong fortifications, as it was said, rather than risk heavy losses to his own soldiers. However, his army plundered and burnt a great part of the province, and annihilated a not inconsiderable enemy force which attempted to storm the royal camp, but not without retaliation; after the king's return Rastiz and his men followed them and devastated the places near to the border across the Danube.[2]

In October, on the 16th, there were thick showers of tiny fireballs like arrows going westward throughout the night. The Emperor Lothar, renouncing all that he had, went into the monastery of Prüm and became a monk. He died on September 29 and went to eternal life. The princes and leading men[3] of his kingdom wanted his son Lothar to reign over them, and brought him to Louis, king of the eastern Franks and his uncle, in Frankfurt. With Louis's agreement and support they agreed that he should rule them.[4]

Samuel, bishop of Worms died.[5]

---

1 Gozbald was bishop of Würzburg from 842 to 855; he had been Louis's archchancellor up to 833 and was also abbot of Niederalteich, and left a substantial library; cf. Wendehorst 1962: 42-6. Arn's episcopate lasted from 855 to 892: see on him Wendehorst 1962: 46-51 and below 871, 872, 884, 892.

2 It is difficult to give any more precision to this rather vague indication: the Danube was probably the common frontier at this time for the whole of the stretch between Krems and Vác (Sós 1973: 43), and for the location of the Moravian empire see 846 n. 2. For Rastiz' rebellion and the campaigns against him in the 850s see 861 n. 7.

3 *Principes ... et optimates*; but see 852 n. 1.

4 Lothar I had divided his kingdom between his three sons shortly before his death; see *AB* 855 (Nelson 1991: 80-1). Why Lothar II and his magnates should have turned to Louis is not entirely clear (though for earlier contacts between Louis and some of the leading men of the middle kingdom see 852 with n. 6); possibly as a guarantee against Charles the Bald or Lothar II's brother Louis II, on whose claims cf. *AB* 856 (Nelson 1991: 81), or in an attempt to get backing for disinheriting Lothar I's youngest son Charles of Provence (Nelson 1991: 83)?

5 A marginal note in ms. '1'. Samuel had also been abbot of Lorsch, 838-56; cf. Gensicke 1974: 253-5.

856

In February, on the fourth day of that month, Archbishop Hrabanus ofMainz died; he had been bishop for nine years, one month and four days.[1] He was succeeded by Charles, more by the wish of the king and his advisers than by the consent and election of the clergy and people.[2] Hatto, abbot of the monastery of Fulda, also died, on April 12. In his place Thioto, one of the monks of Fulda, was ordained by the election of the monks and the authority of the king.[3]

In August King Louis collected an army, proceeded through the lands of the Sorbs, whose *duces* joined him, and conquered the Daleminzi[4] in battle. He took hostages and made them pay tribute. From there he returned through the lands of the Bohemians, and received the surrender of several of their *duces*. In this expedition Counts Bardo and Erpf and many others were slain.[5]

857

In February King Louis had a meeting at the castle of Koblenz with his nephew Lothar.[1] In Lent [March 3] he held an assembly at

1 This calculation treats Hrabanus as having been archbishop for the whole of 847. The manuscripts diverge in their accounts of the length of Hrabanus's pontificate; the text translated above is in the manuscripts of group 3; ms. '1' lacks it and ms. '2' had at first only 'nine years' before the text was completed by 'and one month'. On the divergences see introduction, 7. Ms. '1' also records the death of an otherwise unknown Abbot Albrich in a marginal note.

2 Mss. '1' and '2' have instead of this sentence the following: 'Charles, the son of King Pippin [I of Aquitaine], who, after escaping from his imprisonment in the monastery of Corbie, had fled to Louis his uncle, succeeded him in the bishopric on March 12, not only by the will of the king, but also by the consent and election of the clergy and people.' See introduction, 7.

3 Abbot 856-69; Sandmann 1978: 187.

4 The Daleminzi were a tribe of Slavs who occupied lands to the east of the Sorbs; it is not clear whether they were independent of the Sorbs, subject to them or part of the Sorbic confederation. They had submitted to Charlemagne in 805, but are not prominent in ninth-century sources, though Henry I undertook several campaigns against them in the early tenth century (Herrmann *et al.* 1972: 8-9, 264, 269, 272-74).

5 These men are not identifiable with certainty. Bardo was perhaps the man whom Louis the German sent to Saxony in 842 according to Nithard III, 7 (Scholz 1972: 164) and who gave land to Corvey (Krüger 1950: 58), and was hence a Saxon count; the name suggests an Ostfalian/Thuringian origin.

1 The meeting was apparently friendly, but did not lead to any agreement; immediately following it Lothar II met Charles the Bald at St-Quentin at the beginning of March and renewed his father's alliance with him. See *AB* 857 (Nelson 1991: 84) and *MGH Capit.* 2: 293-5 no. 268).

Worms.[2]

Roric the Northman, who ruled in Dorestad, took a fleet to the lands of the Danes with the agreement of his lord King Lothar. With the agreement of Horic, king of the Danes, he and his comrades occupied the part of the kingdom which lies between the sea and the Eider.[3]

Bishop Otgar [of Eichsätt],[4] Hruodolt, count of the palace,[5] and Ernest, son of the *dux* Ernest,[6] were sent with their men against the Bohemians and occupied the city of the *dux* Wiztrach, which had been rebellious for many years, first driving out Sclavitag, son of Wiztrach, who ruled unlawfully there at that time. After he had fled to Rastiz, his brother, whom he had driven out of the country and who had taken refuge with Zistibor the Sorb, came in loyalty to the king and was made *dux* in the place of his brother.[7]

Also, a synod was held at Mainz around October 1 under Archbishop Charles.[8] Among other matters of ecclesiastical law which were discussed there, there was read out a letter from Gunther [arch]bishop of Cologne to Bishop Aldfrid [of Hildesheim].[9] This said that there had been a terrible storm at Cologne on September 15, and the whole people had taken refuge in fright in the church of St Peter, and rung

2 This assembly is also noted by *AX* 858 (sic) (von Simson 1909: 18). It may have concerned itself with the relations between the diocese of Bremen and the province of Cologne; Hartmann 1989: 299. Louis issued diplomata at Worms on March 24 and March 27 (DD LG 78, 79).

3 This rather curious expression probably means North Frisia. Roric (on whom see 850 with n. 2) had continued to hold benefices in Frankish Frisia from Lothar II (Vogel 1906: 158).

4 Bishop from before 847 to *c.* 880: Heidingsfelder 1938: 24, 28 nos. 52, 64.

5 Hruodolt was a Suabian count who held office in the Affagau (Borgolte 1986: 225). It is doubtful whether he should be seen as an ancestor of the Erchanger family, prominent in Alemannia in the late ninth and early tenth centuries (so Lintzel 1929: 249, 255). As count of the palace his functions would have been mainly, but not exclusively, judicial (Lintzel 1929: 252-53).

6 On him see 849 with n. 1.

7 The location of Wiztrach's 'city' (on this word see below, 872 n. 7) is uncertain; Slàma 1973 has suggested Zabusany near Brüx/Duchchar. Note the rivalry shown here between the east Frankish kingdom and the Moravian empire for control over Bohemia; this is one of the earliest indications of something which becomes clearer from the 870s onwards: see below, 895 with n. 10. 'who ruled unlawfully' = *tyrannidem ... exercebat*; cf. 879 n. 3 on the Frankish notion of tyranny.

8 The acts of this synod have not survived, but for possible echoes of them see Hartmann 1983 and Hartmann 1989: 299.

9 This has not survived.

the church bells, imploring the mercy of God with one voice. Suddenly a powerful lightning-bolt like a fiery dragon ripped open the church and penetrated inside. Three out of all the men who were there were killed, standing in different places, but by a single stroke. One was a priest, next to the altar of St Peter; another was a deacon by the altar of St Denis; a third was a layman by the altar of St Mary. A further six were so injured by the same bolt that they were carried away half-dead and had barely recovered. They say that other marvels happened at Trier at this time, but I have not described them, as I have no certain report of them.[10]

858

On January 1 a great earthquake was felt in various cities and regions, especially, however, at Mainz, where the old walls were cracked and the church of St Alban the Martyr was so shaken that a piece of wall falling from the top struck the twin-chambered chapel of St Michael on the west side and both roof and walls, levelling it to the ground.

Then in February the king had a conference with certain of his counsellors in Forchheim.[1] From there he fixed a day and named particular counts to meet at a *villa* in Alemannia called Ulm, where he received and gave audience to the legates of his nephew Louis [II], Bishop Noting [of Brescia] and Count Eberhard [of Friuli].[2] After

10 Other annalists report that a dog was seen sitting on the episcopalthrone at Trier; Dümmler 1887a: 411 n. 1, and see *AB* 857 (Nelson 1991: 84). This would have been taken as a portent of some horror or disaster to come. Possibly the strange happenings at Cologne and Trier were taken to foretell the depositions of Archbishops Gunther and Theotgaud in 863. see below and *AB* 863 (Nelson 1991: 106-10).

1 He was still at Regensburg on February 2 (D LG 88).

2 Noting, who between about 830 and his death (858x863) was successively bishop of Vercelli, Verona and Brescia, and Eberhard, margrave of Friuli from 828 or shortly after until his death in 866, had been close to Lothar I and continued as prominent advisers to Louis II of Italy; both had Suabian connections (Schmid 1959: 30-52; Hlawitschka 1960: 169-72). Earlier scholars saw in this embassy and the meeting which took place between Louis the German and Louis II in 857 – cf. *AB* 857 (Nelson 1991: 84) and below, n. 4 – essentially high diplomacy, the counterpart to the contemporary rapprochement between Lothar II and Charles the Bald; *AB* 857 (Nelson 1991: 84). More recently it has been suggested that the principal reason for the visit was to settle the details of the foundation of the monastery of Rheinau, which is recorded as having been given to Louis in a notice of February 19 (858). Noting at least was related to the founding clan, and Rheinau had lands in Italy (Schmid 1957: 276-82). The two explanations are of course not mutually exclusive.

mid-Lent [March 13] he went to Frankfurt[3] and there he celebrated Easter [April 3]. Meanwhile, the legates whom he had sent to Lothar his nephew came to him and announced that Lothar would meet the king as agreed in the castle of Koblenz. The king believed his promises and came before Rogation Days [May 9-11] to the agreed place at the agreed time, but Lothar was false to his promise and did not come, nor would he send any of his men. For he had made a treaty with Charles against the king, which each side confirmed with an oath.[4] Louis, seeing himself deceived, returned to Frankfurt,[5] and, after he had discussed and dealt with many things of importance for the kingdom with his men, decided that three armies should be sent to different frontiers of his kingdom.[6] The first, under Carloman his eldest son, he sent against the Moravian Slavs and Rastiz; a second under Louis, his younger son, against the Abodrites and Linones;[7] the third was sent under Thachulf against the Sorbs who refused to obey his commands.[8] This was done that he might more easily order the affairs of his kingdom, once the external threats to it had been suppressed.

In July, after the armies had been gathered together and formed up and were about to set out,[9] suddenly[10] the king was burdened with a great weight of troubles. For messengers came from the west, Abbot

---

3 DD 89-92 are all dated from Frankfurt between March 18 and April 29.

4 This seems to be a reference to the alliance of 857 rather than to any new agreement.

5 D LG 93 was issued there on June 13.

6 Note that Louis was now powerful enough, as Charles the Great had been at the height of his power, to deploy several armies at once (cf. also the campaigns of 869 and 870).

7 The Linones were a Slav tribe inhabiting land beyond the Elbe, south of the territory inhabited by the Abodrites. They formed a separate tribe, but are often found under Abodrite control or influence (Fritze 1960: 208-9).

8 Commander of the Sorbian march; see 849 with n. 2.

9 'And were about to set out' translates *ireque profectis*: the army under Louis the Younger certainly did campaign (Dümmler 1887a: 427 n. 3) and that under Carloman probably did so, as we have a report of Carloman's defeating Rastiz and then making peace with him about this time (see 861 n.). Whether Thachulf's army set out is more doubtful: there is a report of a Sorb rebellion at the end of the year which implies that there had not previously been any trouble in that quarter, and there may be some confusion in *AF* (see also n. 19).

10 The manuscripts in group 3 have after *subito*: *die media*, which is not translated here because its meaning is uncertain: the middle day of the month? at midday? in broad daylight (i.e. publicly and not just privately)?. Hellmann 1908: 717 n. 2 and Kurze 1911: 354 n. 1 discuss the meaning polemically and inconclusively.

Adalhard and Count Odo,[11] asking him to comfort with his presence a
people sore pressed and in peril. If he did not do this swiftly and they
were denied hope of liberation at his hands, they would have to seek
protection from the pagans with great danger to the Christian
religion, since they could not get it from their lawful and orthodox
lords.[12] They declared that they could no longer bear the tyranny of
Charles. Anything that was left to them, after the pagans from outside
had plundered, enslaved, killed and sold them off without even a show
of resistance being made to them, the king destroyed from within with
his evil savagery. There was now no one left in the whole people who
still believed his promises or oaths, and all despaired of his good faith.
Hearing these things, the king was very disturbed, and found himself
in a dilemma. If he acceded to the request of the people, he would have
to move against his brother, which would be wicked.[13] If, however, he
spared his brother, he would have to turn back from liberating the
people in danger, which would be equally wicked. Besides this there
was the not negligible consideration that the people in general would
suspect that all that was being done in this matter was not done out
of concern for the people's well-being but simply out of a desire to
extend his kingdom, although the matter was quite different from the
vulgar opinion, as all those who knew of the king's plans truly testify.
Thus placed beneath a weight of cares, he at length agreed to the
advice of his wise men and relied on the purity of his conscience,
preferring to act for the good of many rather than in agreement with
the obstinacy of one man. He yielded to the prayers of the legates and
promised according to the people's wishes that with God's help he
would come to those who longed for his presence.

In the middle of August he set out from Worms with the escort he
had gathered through Alsace to Gaul to a royal *villa* in Charles's
kingdom called Ponthion,[14] where he was met by almost all the great
men of those regions except for those whom Charles had with him in

11 Adalhard was abbot of St-Bertin; Odo was count of Troyes; both belonged by
   politics and family connection to the group of west Frankish nobles around
   Queen Ermentrude which also included Robert the Strong (Werner 1959:
   153-6). They do not appear to have been long-standing members of the
   opposition to Charles, though *AB* 858 (Nelson 1991: 88 and n. 13) say they
   were. For earlier invitations to Louis see above, 854, and *AB* 856 (Nelson 1991:
   82).

12 Compare the wording of the Aquitanians' appeal to Louis in the annal for 853.

13 Not just from considerations of family piety, but because of the mutual oaths
   taken at Strasbourg in 842.

14 September 1; see *AB* 858 (Nelson 1991: 88).

his army at the time fighting the Northmen on the River Loire.[15] Charles, when he heard that Louis was within the borders of his kingdom, broke off the siege and came against him at a place called Brienne; there, seeing the number of easterners and of his own men who had sworn to resist his tyranny, he realised that his forces were inferior and that he could not join battle with his brother's army without great peril to his own men. However, he drew up his forces in battle line as if to fight, and then slipped away secretly with a few men.[16] His army, which he left on the field of battle, went over to Louis once it realised that its leader had deserted it. He calmed the wish of the people to pursue Charles and turned his attention to dealing with the affairs of the kingdom as if he had a free hand.[17] First, with a careless sense of security, he sent home the whole army which he had brought with him from the east, relying – vainly – on those who had deserted and betrayed their own lord. By their advice he decided to spend the winter there, unaware of the danger threatening him on all sides which Charles was preparing for him. He, wanting to avenge himself for the injuries done him, had stirred up the sons of Count Conrad,[18] who informed him that Louis felt safe and had only a few men with him. Louis had sent Conrad's sons as if they were his faithful men to spy and report back on Charles's activities, but they betrayed their faith and went over to Charles, plotting how Louis might be attacked unawares with a large army. Meanwhile it was reported to him that the Sorbian march in the east was troubled, because the Sorbs, having treacherously killed their *dux* Zistibor, his most faithful man, were planning to rebel.[19] On this news he returned to his own

15 For details see *AB* 858 (Nelson 1991: 88 and notes).

16 November 12; see *AB* 858 (Nelson 1991: 88).

17 Louis appears to have begun ruling in west Francia without any special initiation rites; compare the account in *AB* (Nelson 1991: 88-90). A diploma dated from Attigny on December 7 858 (D LG 94) is dated 'in the first year of our rule in western Francia'; the episode of his rule did not last long enough for us to be able to say when he regarded this first year as having begun.

18 Conrad was count in a number of counties around Lake Constance, but also lay abbot of St-Germain in Auxerre. His sons were Conrad 'the Younger', count of Auxerre, and Hugh 'the Abbot'; his sister was Judith, Charles the Bald's mother. This family (the Welfs) was at the centre of an aristocratic party in opposition to the group around the family of Queen Ermentrude (see above, n. 11). They seem to have supported Louis at first, then gone over to Charles in early January in the (justified) expectation that they would be richly rewarded (Fleckenstein 1957; 119-24; Tellenbach 1957b: 339; Dümmler 1887a: 444-5).

19 It is not clear whether Zistibor's death did in fact occur at this point rather than earlier (an expedition against the Sorbs was planned for the summer of 858); possibly the annalist is here trying to conceal the fact that Louis was in effect driven out of west Francia.

kingdom with what speed he could to crush the rebellion. After his departure Charles retook the capital[20] of his kingdom with no opposition or difficulty.

There[21] is a certain *villa* [Kempten] not far from the town of Bingen, called 'Caput Montium' because the mountains along the valley of the Rhine begin here (though the common people corrupt the name to 'Chamund'). Here an evil spirit gave an open sign of his wickedness. First, by throwing stones and banging on the walls as if with a hammer, he made a nuisance of himself to the people living there. Then he spoke openly and revealed what had been stolen from certain people, and then caused disputes among the inhabitants of the place. Finally he stirred up everyone's hatred against one man, as if it were for his sins that everyone had to suffer such things; and so that he might be the more hated, the evil spirit caused every house which the man entered to catch fire. As a result the man was forced to live outside the *villa* in the fields with his wife and children, as all his kin feared to take him in. But he was not even allowed to remain there in safety, for when he had gathered in and stacked his crops, the evil spirit came unexpectedly and burnt them. To try to appease the feelings of the inhabitants, who wished to kill him, he took the ordeal of hot iron and proved himself innocent of the crimes which were alleged against him. Priests and deacons were therefore sent from the town of Mainz with relics and crosses to expel the wicked spirit from that place. As they were saying the litany and sprinkling holy water in a house where he had been particularly active, the old enemy threw stones at men coming there from the *villa* and wounded them. After the clerics who had been sent there had departed, the same devil made lamentable speeches in the hearing of many. He named a certain priest and said that he had stood underneath his cope at the time when the holy water was being spread around the building. Then, as men crossed themselves in fear, he said of the same priest, 'He is my servant. For anyone who is conquered by someone is his servant; and lately at my persuasion he slept with the daughter of the bailiff of this *villa*.' This crime had not before been known to anyone except those who had committed it. It is clear that as the Word of Truth says, 'nothing is hidden which will not be revealed' [Matt. 10:26]. With these and similar deeds the apostate spirit was a burden to the

---

20 'The capital of his kingdom' = *sedem regni sui*; *sedes* may refer to Paris, but might also simply mean 'possession' – for a similar ambiguity see 839 with n. 5.

21 This paragraph is missing in ms. '2'.

above-mentioned place for the course of three whole years, and he did not desist until he had destroyed almost all the buildings with fire.

859

King Louis came back from Gaul around the beginning of spring to Worms.[1] He sent repeated embassies to reconcile his brother and his nephew to him, and received their replies from their ambassadors.[2] At length, each came at an agreed time with the same number of nobles nominated by the other by ship to a certain island in the Rhine by the castle of Andernach, while the rest of their followings remained on the shores on each side.[3] After they had held lengthy and inconclusive discussions both about what had been done in the past and about what should be done, they agreed to meet again in the autumn at Basle, and each returned home with his men. Louis, however, was unable to secure for those men who had broken with Charles the previous year and done homage to him [Louis], that they should receive their offices[4] back; the matter was put off until a future assembly.

Meanwhile he talked with his own advisers and sent Thioto, abbot of Fulda, to Louis his nephew, the emperor of Italy,[5] and to Pope Nicholas

1 He issued diplomata at Frankfurt in April and May 859 (DD LG 95-7).

2 Lothar II, who in the account given in *AB* 858-59 (Nelson 1991: 88-9) seems to have wavered between his two uncles, played a major part in reconciling Charles with Louis. Lothar and Charles met as early as February 12, immediately after Louis's departure for east Francia (Dümmler 1887a: 446). The meeting at Andernach was prededed by synods held jointly by the bishops of Lothar's and Charles's kingdom at Metz (May 28; Hartmann 1984: 434-44) and Savonnières (June 14: 447-89); in between these an embassy led by Hincmar of Rheims negotiated with Louis the German at Worms (June 4: for the letter of the embassy to the synod of Metz see Hartmann 1984: 443-4). Hartmann 1989: 274-85 gives a succinct account of the dispute and the councils called to deal with it and matters arising from it.

3 It was characteristic of such 'summit meetings' in the early and high Middle Ages that they took place on 'neutral' ground such as islands, bridges or ships anchored in rivers; cf. Schneider 1977 and Voss 1987: 38-9. This provided both security and equality; inferiors have to go to their superiors' territories to meet them.

4 'offices' = *honores*, which could also simply mean benefices. It was not just Charles who was reluctant on this point, as the annalist implies; the Welfs – Count Conrad and his sons (see 858 with n. 18) – also lost the *honores* they had held from Louis the German (Fleckenstein 1957: 124-6). See 860 with n. 1.

5 On this title for Louis II, also found in *AB*, see Zimmermann 1974, who shows that its use by writers north of the Alps was not normally intended to be a polemical hint at the gap between claim and reality; it probably derived from the dating-clauses of the diplomata of the 'Italian emperors' themselves.

in Rome to explain his actions and if possible to bring back their replies to the meeting agreed on.[6] He was received honorably by them, and was able to clear the king's name by giving a reasoned explanation of what had happened the previous year. He returned with a letter[7] from the pope and met the king by Lake Constance on his return from the royal conference; neither of the kings had turned up at the agreed place and time.[8] When he had satisfied the king about his embassy in all things he received leave to depart and returned to his monastery.

The[9] town of Mainz and the places near by it were troubled the whole year by strong earth tremors. Probus, a devout priest, whose chaste way of life and zeal for doctrine had given lustre to the church of Mainz, died on June 25. It would be a long story to relate how he worked without shirking day and night in the above church with great profit, or how he was all things to all men, that he might win all for Christ [1 Cor. 9:22]. At least some of his virtues may be committed here to memory in two verses, so that the reader may grasp from these the other things which God worked through him:

How learned, humble, patient and chaste he was
Neither speech nor writing can fully relate.[10]

860

The winter was very hard and longer than usual and there was much damage to trees and crops. It was found that blood-red snow had fallen in many places. Even the Ionian [Adriatic] Sea was so affected by the extreme cold that the merchants, who had never before gone there except by ship, were able to visit Venice with their wares on horses and carts.

King Louis and his brother Charles and their nephew Lothar came

---

6 It was particularly necessary to get Nicholas I's approval (or at least some expression of goodwill towards Louis), as it would appear that Charles and/or his supporters had already appealed to Nicholas to condemn Louis's invasion (Dümmler 1887a: 454).

7 This has not survived.

8 The meeting at Basle had been fixed for October 25; it was called off because Lothar was unable to attend it, perhaps because of a journey to Italy, and as a result Charles turned back. See *AB* 859 (Nelson 1991: 90). There are no diplomata to give a precise date to Louis's visit to Alemannia.

9 This paragraph and the verses following it are omitted in ms. '2'.

10 Probus seems to have been a minor figure in Carolingian literary circles; see *MGH Poetae* 2: 394 l. 12 and n. 3.

together with their leading men in the castle of Koblenz and confirmed peace and mutual faith with an oath, whose wording was as follows:[1]

From now on and as long as I live I will be an aid to this my brother Charles and my nephews Louis and Lothar and Charles with genuine assistance for God's will and for the state of the Holy Church and for our common salvation and honour and for the safety and peace of the Christian people entrusted to us and for the preservation of law and justice and right reason, as far as God gives me knowledge and ability and they hear me and request of me, with true counsel and according to what is reasonable and lawfully possible to me, so that I may help them to keep their kingdoms; nor will I conspire against their life and limb nor their rule; all this provided that they make and keep a similar oath towards me.

861

King Louis held an assembly in Regensburg in the third week [April 20-27] after the holy festival of Easter, in which he deprived Ernest, the chief among all his leading men,[1] of all his public offices as a man who was guilty of infidelity. Similarly he deprived the counts Uto, his brother Berengar,[2] and Sigihard,[3] and Abbot Waldo[4] of their offices,

1 The following oath is taken from the *acta* of the meeting at Koblenz, which are also recorded independently in a number of manuscripts; cf. *MGH Capit.* 2: 152-8, no. 242 and *AB* 860 (Nelson 1991: 93 and n. 5). The decisions reached at the meeting consisted of a number of general provisions about peace and justice within the Frankish empire; a reaffirmation of concord and brotherhood between Louis, Charles and their three nephews; and a promise by Charles that he would restore the family lands of those who had gone over to Louis in 858, provided that they acted peacefully in the future and that Louis would do the same for Charles's supporters who held lands in eastern Francia, and that he (Charles) would also consider restoring their benefices and offices.

1 For Ernest see 849 with n. 1.

2 Uto, Berengar and Waldo were the sons of Count Gebhard of the Lahngau, and so Ernest's nephews; cf. 849 with n. 1.

3 Ms. '2' has 'Sigihard and Gerold'. Neither Sigihard nor Gerold are mentioned in other accounts of this purge; *AB* 861 (Nelson 1991: 94-5), *AH* 861 (Waitz 1878a: 18). Sigihard can plausibly be identified with a Sigihard who was count in the Kraichgau and perhaps married to the sister of Liutswind, Carloman's mistress and mother of Arnulf of Carinthia (Mitterauer 1963: 226). Gerold cannot be identified, but the name suggests a relationship with Gebhard and his sons (Dienemann-Dietrich 1955: 191).

4 Waldo's monastery is not known: the usual suggestion is Schwarzach, where an Abbot Waldo is found in 828, but since Waldo's father Gebhard was still alive in 879 the two Waldos can scarcely have been identical (Parisot 1899: 187 n. 4).

5 Translating *proprietas*; this is a good example of how those who lost favour in

along with some others who were guilty of complicity in his infidelity. Of these, Uto and Berengar with their brother Waldo went to Gaul to King Charles, and the others remained within the kingdom on their hereditary lands.[5]

Carloman, the king's eldest son, also planned a change in government: he drove out the *duces* to whom the Carinthians and the Pannonian march had been entrusted, and put the administration of the border under his own men.[6] This angered the king, who suspected a rebellion, not a little.[7]

862

Carloman came to Regensburg under oaths of peace and safe-conduct, and having given an account of his actions defeated his opponents and was reconciled with his father.[1] He took an oath that he would henceforth not undertake anything in bad faith against his father's legitimate power. So Carloman returned to his own domains with peace. The king, however, set out for Mainz and there met his nephew Lothar, who had come for a conference.[2]

In the same year the king led an army against the Abodrites and

Carolingian kingdoms could be more easily deprived of their benefices and offices (*honores*) than of their allodial lands.

6 See *AB* 861 (Nelson 1991: 94).

7 Our other source of information for these events, apart from *AB* 861 (Nelson 1991: 94), is *AS* (*MGH SS* 30: 744), which have unfortunately survived only in partial copies and later derivations. From them we learn that Radbod, prefect of the eastern march, was deposed for infidelity in 854 and that Rastiz rebelled (cf. above, 855, and Mitterauer 1963: 160). There may be a connection between the two events. Carloman was made prefect in his place in 856. A major campaign by Carloman, probably in 858, forced Rastiz to make peace. At about the same time Carloman replaced Count Rihher of Pannonia by Udalrich; and Gundachar replaced Pabo (of Carinthia), who had conspired with other counts against Carloman. There is obviously a connection between these events and Louis's purge of a group of nobles most of whom were connected to Carloman by marriage (see above); other events, such as Louis's granting of extensive lands in Pannonia to the church of Salzburg in 860, probably fit in here as well. But it is not clear whether Louis's purge provoked or was provoked by Carloman's display of independence, though the latter is more probable. See Bresslau 1923: 46-9; Mitterauer 1963: 160-2, 168 and *passim*; Dopsch 1980: 179-84; Wolfram 1987: 283-7.

1 This meeting probably occurred around Easter [April 19]. On the agreement between Louis and Carloman compare *AB* 862 (Nelson 1991: 99).

2 Louis wanted Lothar's help against the Abodrites; *AB* 862 (Nelson 1991: 102), *AX* 863 (sic) (von Simson 1909: 20).

compelled their *dux* Tabomuizli, who had rebelled, to be obedient and to give his son and others as hostages.[3]

863

Carloman the king's son, who had been set over the Carinthians, was accused before his father in his absence of so many and such great crimes, that he would have been deservedly held guilty of treason, if his accusers had been able to prove the things that were said about him.[1] This so enraged the king that he declared on his own account before a great mass of his people that his son Carloman should, then and henceforth, so long as he himself lived and ruled, never hold public office with his consent.[2] When this became known Carloman was frightened off the journey which he had begun to the court and returned to Carinthia, wishing to remain safely among his own men, whom he thought to be faithful to him, until his father's anger had died down and he himself was able to clear himself of the false accusations through truthful intermediaries.[3] Meanwhile the king had collected an army, ostensibly to subdue Rastiz, the *dux* of the Moravian Slavs, with the help of the Bulgarians who were said to be coming from the east.[4] In fact he moved against the Carinthians to overcome his son. Carloman indeed would have defended himself up to now[5] if he had not

3 To judge by the name, Tabomuizli was probably a relative of the Gostomuizli killed in 844 (see above); like Gostomuizli he appears to have ruled over all the Abodrites (Fritze 1960: 157). According to *AB* 862 (Nelson 1991: 102) this expedition was not very successful; but no more is heard of the Abodrites in *AF* until 889, though there is a brief notice of an expedition against them in *AB* 867 (Nelson 1991: 139).

1 guilty of treason' = *reus maiestatis*, meaning probably an alliance or peace treaty with Rastiz.

2 The language used by the annalist at this point suggests a formal oath by Louis.

3 Note the parallels with Louis the German's own behaviour in 838-40.

4 The mention of the Bulgarians here is slightly puzzling: there had been no known contacts with them since the early 850s – their embassy to Louis recorded above, 852, and the note in *AB* 853 (Nelson 1991: 77). On the other hand *AB* 864 (Nelson 1991: 118) report a meeting between Louis and the Bulgar khan, which is confirmed by a letter from Nicholas I to Louis, JE 2758 (*MGH Epp.* 6: 293 no. 25 [March 30 864]). Possibly the annalist is confusing the campaigns of 863 and 864. On the other hand Rastiz's request to Byzantium for missionaries in 862/3 is normally explained as a response to a Franco-Bulgarian alliance, and such an alliance is certainly not out of the question; Dvornik 1970: 100-1; Vlasto 1970: 26-7.

5 'up to now' = *ad id temporis*; an alternative translation is 'at that time'. It is not clear which point in time is meant or whether the phrase is to be taken as a sign

been taken unawares by the treachery of Gundachar,[6] his count, who had almost the whole of the army with him to defend the crossing of the River Schwarza[7] but who went over to the king with all his troops and was set over the Carinthians, as had secretly been promised to him on condition that he betrayed his lord. And in this way he earned indeed the dignity of a prefect. Carloman however came to his father on the security of oaths of the leading men, unconcerned about the crimes of which he was accused, because he was innocent; and supported by his own clear conscience he showed himself happy and cheerful in all things.[8]

At that time Charles, archbishop of the church of Mainz, died on June 4, and the church remained vacant for the whole of the year;[9] Liutbert was installed in the see on November 30.

In Lothar's kingdom a synod was held at Metz[10] of all his bishops apart from Hungarius of Utrecht, who was ill; this was because Lothar had set aside his lawful wife and taken another.[11] The legates[12] of Pope Nicholas of Rome were also sent there to investigate the case carefully. When the case was discussed in the synod, the king asserted that the action of which he was accused had been done with the advice and on the authority of the bishops. These did not deny it, and produced a number of dubious arguments in support of what had been done; at the suggestion of the papal legates these were set down in writing and

that the annal was written contemporaneously or not; Janssen 1912 argued that it is, Hellmann 1913: 41-3 argued that it is not.

6 Gundachar, who came from a family with local connections, came to power as count in Carinthia and successor to Pabo at the end of the 850s (see 861 n. 7). For his further career see below, 866 with n. 7 and 869; Mitterauer 1963: 168, 175-8.

7 The manuscripts in group 3 have *N.* for the place-name, which means that it was missing, unreadable or unintelligible in their common ancestor. Mss '1' and '2' have *Schwarza*; Gundachar had thus been left in charge of the Semmering Pass which controlled the route from the Danube valley to Styria.

8 According to *AB* 863 and 864 (Nelson 1991: 105-6, 120), Carloman was kept in honourable captivity but escaped the following year; Louis the German had been concerned that Charles the Bald might give him support.

9 This clause, which is to some extent contradicted by the following sentence, is found only in the manuscripts of group 3, and is possibly a vestige of an earlier draft by the annalist. Ms '1' has 'whom Liutbert succeeded in the honour of the bishopric on November 30' instead.

10 In mid-June; cf. *AB* 863 (Nelson 1991: 106); Hartmann 1989: 280-2.

11 The lawful wife was Theotberga; the other lady was Waldrada. See *AB* 857, 862 (Nelson 1991: 84, 102) for details and further references.

12 Radoald of Porto and John of Cervia; Dümmler 1887b: 62.

sent by the hand of Gunther of Cologne and Theotgaud of Trier, the archbishops of Belgian Gaul,[13] to Nicholas, the pontiff of the apostolic see, for approval. He called a council of bishops at the city of Rome[14] and condemned the synod of Metz with anathema and deposed and excommunicated the bishops who had been sent to him: justly indeed and canonically, as his own writings show; unjustly, however, according to what they tried to show in their letters and speeches. If anyone is interested in knowing what was said in the writings of both sides, he can find them in several places in Germany.[15]

864

Gunther,[1] [arch]bishop of Cologne, was moved by penitence and set out for Rome with the intention of reconciliation and making amends, because he had begun a quarrel with the lord pope for an unjust cause. He came to the presence of Pope Nicholas, but he could not obtain any forgiveness.

King Louis crossed the Danube in the month of August with a great army and besieged Rastiz in a certain city, which in the language of that people is called Dowina.[2] Rastiz did not dare to meet the armies of the king in battle, and saw that there was nowhere to which he could flee; of necessity he was forced to give hostages, as many and as high-ranking as the king ordered. Moreover, he swore an oath with all his leading men that he would keep fealty to the king for the rest of his

13 Note the characteristic survival of Roman administrative terminology in ecclesiastical affairs.

14 October 863; see *AB* 863 (Nelson 1991: 106); Hartmann 1989: 282-4.

15 For a similar reference to archives see the reference to the oaths taken by Louis the German's sons in 876 below. At this point ms. 1 has the marginal note: 'thus far Rudolf' (see introduction, 00). In place of the final sentence the manuscripts of group 3 have: 'For this reason I have decided to include the text of the letters written by each side, and leave the reader to judge the truth of the matter'; there then follow the texts of the letters found in *AB* 863 and 864 (Nelson 1991: 107-10, 113-16). The letter from Nicholas I is addressed to the bishops of Louis the German's kingdom, but presents essentially the same text as that found in *AB*, while the text of the archbishops' reply is slightly different, probably because Hincmar edited the text in *AB*; cf. Nelson 1991: 113ff. and notes.

1 This paragraph is found only in the manuscripts of group 3; it duplicates the entry at the end of the annal for 864 which is found in all three groups of manuscripts. See introduction, p. 3-7.

2 The location is uncertain; see Havlík 1966: 98. Louis was back (or still) in Regensburg on August 20 (D LG 113), and in Mattighofen in upper Bavaria on October 2 (D LG 115), so the siege cannot have been a long one.

life, although he did not observe the oath at all.[3]

Louis and Charles, kings and brothers, met in the *villa* of Tusey in the month of September,[4] and made an alliance. They agreed to forgive each other whatever they had done as a result of human frailty or the urgings of their soldiers, thinking that the past should be forgotten. Suitable witnesses and adjudicators for the inviolability for all time of this treaty of alliance were stipulated by both sides. Louis nominated from Charles's side Archbishop Hincmar of Rheims and Count Engilram; Charles nominated from Louis's side Archbishop Liutbert [of Mainz] and Bishop Aldfrid [of Hildesheim], so that if by chance the terms of the treaty were infringed by anyone, these might point it out and recall to mind what had been done before, so that peace could more easily be restored.[5]

Gunther bishop of Cologne repented of having continued to exercise the episcopal office which had been forbidden him by the pope and set out for Rome, but found no opporunity to get himself restored or make satisfaction.

Ernest died.[6]

865[1]

Rudolf, priest and monk of the abbey of Fulda, who was held in almost

3 An indication that this entry was written somewhat after the event. *AF* next record fighting with Rastiz in 869, though there are reports of contacts between him and rebellious east Frankish nobles in 865 and 866. *AB* 864 (Nelson 1991: 118) imply that Louis had sought Bulgarian support for his campaign against Rastiz; cf. 863 n. 4.

4 Tusey near Toul; the meeting in fact took place in mid-February 865, asshown by *AB* 865 (Nelson 1991: 121-2) and the *acta* of the meeting (*MGH Capit.* 2: 165-7, no. 244), which are dated February 19. Ms. '2' of *AF* has 'October'; perhaps we have here an unsuccessful condensing of an originally longer report on the negotiations leading up to the meeting. *AB* add that Louis after this made peace with Carloman.

5 For the career and standing of Engilram, an important adviser of Charles's at this time, see Nelson 1991, index. Such 'minders' played an important role in Carolingian treaty-making; for another example see Nithard III, 3 (Scholz 1972: 158).

6 This note is found only in ms. '1' (though see the opening of 865 for the report of Ernest's death in the manuscripts of group 3). On Ernest see above, 849 with n. 1 and 861.

1 The first three paragraphs of the 865 annal are found in the manuscripts of group 3 only; the third, on Arsenius's legation, is duplicated by the later entry found in all three groups of manuscripts.

all parts of Germany to be a distinguished teacher, a notable historian
and poet, and a most noble practitioner of all the arts, died happily on
March 8.[2]

Count Ernest also died in the same year.[3]

And[4] Bishop Arsenius, the legate of Nicholas, pope of the city of Rome,
was sent to Francia to bring about and renew peace and concord
between Louis and his brother Charles and their nephew Lothar. He
came to the royal *villa* of Frankfurt and was honourably received and
loaded with magnificent gifts. After they had agreed to hold a meeting
at Cologne for the purpose of arranging peace, he set off for King
Charles in Gaul. There he was splendidly received by the king and
loaded with royal gifts, and then came to the agreed meeting at
Cologne, as we have said, where the two brothers, that is Louis and
Charles, met him but not their nephew Lothar who was absent. After
he had well ordered a number of affairs there he returned with peace
to Rome.

Count Werinhar,[5] one of the leading men of the Franks, was accused
before King Louis of having stirred up Rastiz against him and was
deprived of his public offices.

Bishop Arsenius,[6] the legate of Nicholas the Roman pontiff, was sent
into Francia to renew[7] peace and concord between King Louis and his
nephews, Louis, emperor of Italy, and Lothar his brother. He came to
Frankfurt in June and was honourably received by King Louis;[8] with
his leave he went on to Gaul and restored Queen Theotberga, who had
long been put aside by Lothar, to that same king as the pope had
instructed him, and ordered Lothar's concubine Waldrada to be taken
to Italy. He made twelve of Lothar's leading men swear an oath that
Lothar would henceforth treat Theotberga as a king should treat a

---

2 On Rudolf see introduction, 5.

3 See 864 n. 6.

4 For the events recorded in this paragraph see the notes to the common entry
on Arsenius's legation later in the annal for this year.

5 Count in the region between the River Enns and the Wienerwald; he was
related to the group of nobles purged in 861 (Mitterauer 1963: 125-31, 168. See
also below, 866 n. 3). *AF* here pass over Louis the Younger's marriage with the
daughter of Adalard mentioned in *AB* 865 (Nelson 1991: 128), though there
may be a connection; cf. below, 866, for Louis the Younger and Werinhar.

6 Arsenius, bishop of Orte. This account of his legation should be compared with
the somewhat different one given in the text offered by the manuscripts of
group 3 at the start of 865 and with the account in *AB* 865 (Nelson 1991:
123-4).

queen lawfully married to him.[9] Then he went on to Charles's kingdom and after he had well ordered a number of affairs there which he had come to deal with, returned to Rome.[10]

866

Louis, son of King Louis, angered at the fact that the king had taken certain benefices from him and given them to his brother Carloman, rebelled against the king.[1] He sent messages through the whole of

7 Thus ms. '1'; ms. '2' and group 3 do not talk about renewing peace, but merely about making it. The duplicate account of this legation given in the group 3 manuscripts at the beginning of 865 describes the purpose of the legation as making peace between Louis, Charles and Lothar. Both descriptions have some point: relations between the three transalpine rulers were strained because of Lothar's marital affairs, but Louis II was also involved, both because he too was interested in the Lotharingian succession question, and because Charles and Louis were on sufficiently bad terms with him at this point to be able to claim to Nicholas I that they could not allow their bishops to come to a synod at Rome to deal with the affairs of the Church generally and Lothar's marriage in particular, because Louis II would not grant them safe-conduct; Dümmler 1887b: 114–15.

8 According to AX 866 (sic) (von Simson 1909: 23) Arsenius was received at a general meeting of the Franks; the account given at the beginning of the year in the manuscripts of group 3 says that a meeting between the kings was arranged at Frankfurt, where Louis issued a diploma on June 19 (D LG 118).

9 On these events, which took place in July and August, see AB 865 (Nelson 1991: 123ff.).

10 This account is incomplete. It is clear from AB and from the account in the manuscripts of group 3 that Arsenius returned from west Francia to east Francia and thence to Italy. But it is not certain that the meeting at Cologne mentioned in the group 3 account actually took place in the form described. Charles and Louis met there – cf. AB 865 (Nelson 1991: 128) – but Arsenius's presence is doubtful; Dümmler 1887b: 155.

1 For the improvement in relations between Louis and Carloman see 865 n. 4. In the mid-850s Louis had probably begun to associate his sons in the rule of the east Frankish kingdom: Carloman became margrave in the east, and the young Charles seems to have been given rights in Alemannia; Carloman, Louis and Charles all married into families established in what were to become their future kingdoms. In 865, after Easter, there was a formal division of the kingdom among the three sons. Carloman was to have Bavaria and the marches against the Slavs and Lombards; Louis was to have Franconia, Thuringia and Saxony and the tribute from the peoples along their borders; Charles was to have Alemannia and Rhaetia. While Louis the German lived, his sons were to be assigned certain royal estates in their future kingdoms, and to be allowed to judge minor cases, while appointments to bishoprics, abbeys and counties, control over the fisc and major disputes were reserved to Louis. See BM 1459a; Dümmler 1887b: 119; Borgolte 1977; and below, 872, where Louis explicitly allows his sons to judge cases. Louis, as the second son, may have expected to get more after the difficulties Louis the German had had with Carloman in the

Thuringia and Saxony and drew whoever he could to him to rise against the king.[2] He also involved Counts Werinhar, Uto and Berengar, whom his father had deposed, in his plots and promised that he would give them back their former offices.[3] And he sent Henry, the leader of his army, to Rastiz, asking that he too would agree to support his conspiracy.[4] When this became known, the king left Carloman to guard Bavaria and came swiftly to Francia. He was honourably received by his men, who came streaming from all parts of his kingdom, in Frankfurt,[5] and easily suppressed the conspiracy which had arisen. For the number of supporters he had was so great that the opposing party could without doubt have been tied up, if there had not been fear for his son.[6] Meanwhile Guntbold, one of Carloman's vassals, who had tried to fight against his lord, lost his army and barely escaped alive.[7] The young Louis was reconciled with his father in

previous few years; his attempt at a marriage-alliance with the Adalhards the previous year against his father's will – *AB* 865 (Nelson 1991: 128) – also suggests dissatisfaction. For later disagreements between Louis and his younger sons about the divisions see below, 871, 872, 873.

2 This appears to be the revolt briefly referred to in *AB* 866 (Nelson 1991: 131) among Louis's subjects 'in the Wendish march'.

3 For Werinhar see above, 865 n. 5. Uto and Berengar had been purged in 861 and had gone over to Charles the Bald (see above) but had recently been deprived of office by Charles the Bald. *AB* 865 (Nelson 1991: 129) give incompetence as the reason, but there may have been a connection between the purging of Adalhard and his relatives and Louis the Younger's attempted marriage-alliance with the Adalhards.

4 An alliance with Rastiz is confirmed by *AB* 866 (Nelson 1991: 135). The Henry mentioned here recurs frequently in the annals from now until his death in 886. He was the brother of Poppo (II) of Thuringia (on whom see below, 880, 883(II), 892); through his daughter Hathui, wife of the Liudolfing Otto, he was connected with the Liudolfings. Otto's sister Liutgard was the wife of Louis the Younger (Hlawitschka 1974: 140-65).

5 Louis was still at Regensburg on July 28 (D LG 118) and August 6 (D LG 119); there are then no further diplomata in 866 to confirm his movements. For his agreement with Louis the Younger see *AB* 865 (Nelson 1991: 135). They agreed a truce until October 28, and Louis the German returned to Bavaria to campaign against Rastiz, intending to meet Charles the Bald and Lothar II at Metz on November 3. Hincmar hints at support by Charles the Bald for Louis the Younger (Nelson 1991: 136).

6 *timor filii* may mean either 'fear of' or 'fear for' Louis the Younger. The annal in fact suggests that Louis the Younger had considerable support, as does the subsequent mediation by 'Archbishop Liutbert and other lovers of peace': Louis's party was probably too strong to be overcome directly by force.

7 Gundbold is not otherwise known, though his name occurs in the family of the Count Rihher whom Carloman had deposed (see above, 861 n. 7, and for Rihher, Mitterauer 1963: 124). Possibly the annalist meant Gundachar, who seems also to have been involved in the uprising of 866 (see below, 869 n. 4).

November at Worms through the mediation of Archbishop Liutbert
[of Mainz] and other lovers of peace.[8]

At this time some of Archbishop Liutbert's men were killed at Mainz
in an uprising, and their death was avenged on those responsible with
great severity: some were hanged, others had their fingers and toes cut
off, or were even blinded; many left all their property to escape death
and became exiles.[9]

Ambassadors[10] of the Bulgarians came to the king at Regensburg,
saying that their king and not a few of the people had been converted
to Christianity and asking that the king would not refuse to send them
suitable men to preach the Christian religion.[11]

867

King Louis agreed to the Bulgarians' request and sent Bishop
Ermanrich [of Passau] with priests and deacons to spread the
Catholic faith among that people. But when they came there bishops
sent by the Roman pontiff had already filled the whole of the land with
preaching and baptising; for which reason they returned home with
the permission of the [Bulgar] king.[1]

8 An armistice had been made before November; cf. *AB* 866 (Nelson 1991: 135).

9 Compare the account of an earlier discord at Mainz, above, 848.

10 This paragraph is missing in ms. '2'.

11 For the conversion of Boris-Michael see *AB* 864 (Nelson 1991: 118), and
   compare on this request *AB* 866 (Nelson 1991: 137); Dvornik 1926: 184-95 and
   Vlasto 1970: 155-65 give useful accounts. Louis and Boris had already met in
   864; in the meantime the Christian party in Bulgaria had gained the upper
   hand, and at the same time Michael was less willing than before to rely on the
   Byzantine Church for missionaries, hence his requests to Louis and to Pope
   Nicholas I, on which see *AB* 866 (Nelson 1991: 137-8).

1 Nicholas's legates, Bishops Formosus of Porto and Paul of Populonia, had set
   out in November 866 armed with a lengthy letter from Nicholas to Michael (JE
   2812 = *MGH Epp.* 6: 568-600 no. 99). Ermanrich's mission started consider-
   ably later: materials had to be collected together – compare *AB* 866 (Nelson
   1991: 137) – and priests also. In view of the chronological disorder in the
   annals at this point, Ermanrich's mission need not be put in early 867; any time
   before May 868 (the council of Worms, at which Ermanrich was present;
   Hartmann 1989: 302) would be possible. The choice of Ermanrich shows the
   importance attached to the mission: Ermanrich had been a monk in the Suabian
   monastery of Ellwangen; he was a prominent scholar and author; he had been
   the pupil of the former royal chancellor Bishop Gozbald of Würzburg (on
   whom see above, 855 with n. 7), and was himself probably a member of the
   royal chapel. Certainly he had close links with Louis, to whom he owed his
   promotion to the bishopric of Passau in 866; Dümmler 1887b: 187-92;
   Heuwieser 1939: 143-8; Fleckenstein 1959: 179-80; Löwe 1986. The paragraph
   is missing in ms. '2'.

King Lothar, ignoring the promise about Queen Theotberga which he had made to the apostolic legate,[2] and caring nothing for the oath taken by his magnates, again called Waldrada back from Italy and secretly united himself with her.[3] Whereupon Pope Nicholas, moved by divine zeal, sent letters to kings and bishops through the different provinces of Christianity: Italy, Germany, Neustria and Gaul, in which he excommunicated her, with all those who supported her or communicated with her, from the holy Church until she had made satisfaction through penance.[4] He also sent a letter to the sons of King Louis about the respect due to a father.[5]

Robert,[6] King Charles's count, was killed at the River Loire fighting bravely against the Northmen.[7] He was, so to speak, a second Macchabeus in our times, and if all his battles which he fought with the Bretons and Northmen were fully described they would be on the same level as the deeds of Macchabeus.

There was an earthquake in many places on October 9.

868

Nicholas the Roman pontiff sent two letters to the bishops of Germany: one dealt with the machinations of the Greeks;[1] the other concerned the depositions of Bishops Theotgaud and Gunther, in which he reported that they had committed seven capital offences and said that for this reason they could never for all time be restored to

---

2 See above and *AB* 865 (Nelson 1991: 124–5).

3 At the end of 865; Dümmler 1887b: 138.

4 The annalist seems to have had the text of a letter dated June 13 (866) and addressed to Nicholas's 'brother archbishops and bishops in Italy, Germany, Neustria and Gaul', before him (JE 2808 = *MGH Epp*. 6: 315–16 no. 42); letters to Louis and Charles on this subject, if they existed, have not survived. Nicholas excomunnicated Waldrada on February 2 866.

5 This letter has not survived.

6 This paragraph and the next are missing in ms. '2'.

7 In 866; cf. *AB* 866 (Nelson 1991: 135) for Robert's career and position.

1 All that have survived are letters from Nicholas to Hincmar and the bishops of west Francia (October 23 867; JE 2879 = *MGH Epp*. 6: 600–9 no. 100) and to Charles the Bald and Louis the German (October 24 and October 30 867; JE 2882–3 = *MGH Epp*. 6: 609–10 nos. 101–2); the two kings were asked to summon synods of the bishops in their kingdoms todeal with the problems of the Photian schism and the Bulgarian mission and present a 'united front' of the Latin church to the Greeks.

their old offices.[2]

A synod was held at Worms in May in the presence of King Louis,[3] at which the bishops made a number of canons for the good of the church and issued a suitable responses to the stupidities of the Greeks.[4]

King Lothar set out for Rome[5] and tried very hard to have Waldrada joined to him in marriage with the agreement and support of Pope Nicholas. He found that Nicholas had already died and so went on to Benevento to his brother Louis and asked him to use his influence with Pope Hadrian, who had succeeded Nicholas in the papacy, in support of the union; but his request had no effect.[6]

In the same year there were comets for several nights.[7] Springs and rivers rose greatly because of the unusually heavy rainfall and did not a little damage to buildings and crops in several places. This curse was followed by a great hunger with immense loss of life throughout Germany and Gaul.

869

The Slavs known as the Bohemians made frequent raids across the Bavarian border, setting fire to some *villae* and carrying women off captive. King Louis sent the commanders on the border against them, until he himself should find a suitable time to avenge in arms on the rebels the injuries done to his people. Carloman fought twice with the armies of Rastiz and was victorious, taking not a little plunder, as he

---

2 October 31 867 (JE 2886 = *MGH Epp.* 6: 340-51 no. 53 and JE 2885 = *MGH Epp.* 6: 338-9 no. 52 of October 30 to Louis the German). For Theotgaud and Gunther see above, 863 and 864.

3 DD LG 126-7 are dated there on May 23 and May 25 respectively.

4 May 16 868. The canons were repetitions of conciliar decrees of the Visigothic and Gallic churches, except for a small number which drew on letters from Nicholas I to Charles and Liutbert of Mainz. The 'suitable response' to the Greeks (see n. 1) was probably composed beforehand by one of the participants, who may have drawn on a similar work (now lost) known to have been composed at Hincmar's request by Odo of Beauvais; his text was simply approved by the council; Hartmann 1977: 28-37, 49-76, 125-6; Hartmann 1989: 301-9. For the west Frankish response, see *AB* 867 (Nelson 1991: 141-2).

5 In June 869; *AB* 869 (Nelson 1991: 154).

6 Nicholas I died on November 13 867, so that the annalist is here summarising Lothar's various attempts between 866 and 869 to get his union with Waldrada recognised by the church.

7 Late January 868; Dümmler 1887b: 231 n. 2. This paragraph is missing from ms. '2'.

informed his father by letter.[1] The Sorbs and Siusli[2] joined with the Bohemians and the other peoples of the region and crossed the old[3] Thuringian border: they laid many places waste and killed some who rashly came together to attack them.

Gundachar, Carloman's vassal, who had often been a traitor to King Louis and his sons through perjuries and wicked conspiracies, and had left his own lord and gone over to Rastiz, was killed like Catiline while taking up arms against his fatherland.[4] He is said to have said to those over whom he had been set by Rastiz, as Carloman's *duces* were hurrying up to the battle: 'fight bravely and defend your country, for I shall not be of any use to you in this battle. St Emmeram[5] and the other saints on whose relics I swore to keep faith to King Louis and his sons are holding my spear and sword and press down on my arms and hold me tight as if bound with ropes all over, so that I cannot even raise my hand to my mouth.' As the unhappy man said these words, our men fell on him and killed him, and thus the Lord dealt out a fitting reward for his treachery. When this was reported to the king he ordered all to give thanks together to God for the end of their dead enemy and the bells of all the churches in Regensburg to be rung.

King Lothar broke off the negotiations for which he had come to Rome and planned to return to his own kingdom, but he died at Piacenza in July and many others of his magnates were carried off during the same journey.[6]

1 This has not survived. *AB* 869 (Nelson 1991: 157) give a less favourable picture of Carloman's campaigns in 868 and 869.

2 The Siusli were also a Sorbic tribe; the Sorbs referred to here must therefore have been the Sorbs as a tribe rather than the Sorbic confederation as a whole; Schlesinger 1963: 78.

3 The Latin is *antiquos terminos Thuringiorum*; the sense is uncertain, but perhaps what is meant is that not only the frontier region (the Sorbic march) but also the Thuringian heartland was affected by the attacks.

4 The annalist here shows his familiarity with Sallust's *Catiline Conspiracy*; see below, 875, for a further reference to Sallust. For Gundachar see above, 863 with n. 6, 866 n. 7. It is not known when he lost his marcher command. The passage is generally taken to mean, because of the reference to 'sons' and not just to Carloman, that Gundachar had been involved in Louis the Younger's uprising in 866; cf. e.g. Dümmler 1887a: 155 n. 2; Mitterauer 1963: 176.

5 Patron and legendary founder of the bishopric of Regensburg; as Regensburg was almost a 'capital' for Louis the German, St Emmeram assumed particular importance for the east Frankish kingdom; cf. Schmid 1976: 435-8.

6 Lothar's mission was not as unsuccessful as the annalist makes out; he was restored to communion, and Hadrian expressed willingness to have the affair of his marriage reconsidered by a general synod of the Frankish Church. Gunther of Cologne was also shown some prospect of being restored to his

In August King Louis gathered his troops and divided the army into three parts.[7] The first he sent under his namesake [Louis the Younger] with the Thuringians and Saxons to crush the presumption of the Sorbs. He ordered the Bavarians to assist Carloman, who wished to fight against Zwentibald,the nephew of Rastiz. He himself kept the Franks and Alemans with him to fight against Rastiz. When it was already time to set out he fell ill, and was compelled to leave the leadership of the army to Charles his youngest son and commend the outcome to God.[8] Charles, when he came with the army with which he had been entrusted to Rastiz's huge fortification, quite unlike any built in olden times,[9] with God's help burnt with fire all the walled fortifications of the region, seized and carried off the treasures which had been hidden in the woods or buried in the fields, and killed or put to flight all who came against him. Carloman also laid waste the territory of Zwentibald, Rastiz's nephew, with fire and war. When the whole region had been laid waste the brothers Charles and Carloman came together and congratulated each other on the victories bestowed by heaven. Meanwhile Louis their brother came against the Sorbs, and after he had killed a few forced the rest to turn and run.[10] Many of them were killed, and the Bohemians, whom the Sorbs had brought to fight for pay, were partly killed, partly forced to return to their homes with dishonour, and the remainder surrendered.

While these things were being done King Louis was lying at the city of Regensburg in Bavaria seriously ill, so much so that the doctors despaired of saving his life. Therefore he took all the gold and silver which could be found in his treasuries and distributed it among various monasteries and spent it on the poor. For this he deserved to be cured

bishopric. However, Lothar's death on August 8 (not July as stated above) ended the matter. See *AB* 869 (Nelson 1991: 154–6).

7 Note that here as in 858 Louis's military strength allowed him to put several armies into the field at once.

8 *AB* 869 (Nelson 1991: 162) talk as if the expedition was intended to ratify a peace treaty, not to fight.

9 ...*illam ineffabilem Rastizi munitionem et omnibus antiquissimis dissimilem*, a rather obscure reference. There may be a play on words here: one of the main Moravian cities, possibly the 'capital', was called Staré) Město, which means 'old city', in Latin *urbs antiqua* (see below, 871). The annalist would then be saying that the 'old city' was quite unlike 'older cities'. If this conjecture is correct, it also give the location of Rastiz's stronghold; if not, this is unknown. The annalist seems to be deliberately vague about whether Charles actually took the stronghold or not; the general success of the campaign is confirmed by *AX* 870 (sic) (von Simson 1909: 28) though not by *AB* 869 (Nelson 1991: 162).

10 According to *AB* 869 (Nelson 1991: 163) there were heavy losses on both sides.

by the heavenly Doctor, to whom he commended himself and all his possessions. But King Charles, hearing of his brother Louis's illness, invaded the kingdom of Lothar and disposed of it as he wished; those of that kingdom who would not come to him he deprived of their benefices and hereditary lands. Furthermore, taking the advice of evil men, he had a crown set on his head in the city of Metz by the bishop of that city [Adventius] and ordered that he should be called emperor and *augustus* as one who was to possess two kingdoms.[11]

All King Louis's sons were successful in their campaigns and returned in triumph without loss of their soldiers.[12] The Bohemians asked for and received the handshake[13] from Carloman.

870

King Louis recovered from his illness and in February, on the feast of the Purification of the Virgin Mary [February 2] came to Frankfurt.[1] There he took many leading men of Lothar's kingdom, who had waited for him there a long time, into his lordship and restored the benefices which Charles had taken away. Many also who had at first been with Charles deserted him and came to Louis.[2]

Archbishop Liutbert of Mainz with some of his suffragans came to Cologne, and there ordained the priest Willibert bishop at the order of King Louis and by the election of the whole clergy and people, and

11 For these events see the much fuller account in *AB* 869 (Nelson 1991: 157 ff.). The coronation took place on September 9. The annalist's explanation of the symbolism of the diadem is not confirmed by any other source and indeed is contradicted by the text of the *ordo* given in *AB* (Nelson 1991: 161). The idea that an emperor was a king over kings was, however, a common one in Frankish political thought – the Lorsch Annals for 801 explain the significance of Charles the Great's coronation in 800 thus (*MGH SS* 1: 38), and Widukind of Corvey calls Otto I 'emperor of the Romans, king of the peoples' (III 76; Hirsch and Lohmann 1935: 154). Probably the annalist is here repeating an interpretation of Charles's intentions which was current in east Francia; certainly Charles did not at this point adopt an imperial title; Stengel 1965: 246; Schramm 1968b: 83). See also below, 875 with n. 14 and 876 with n. 4.

12 But see n. 4.

13 *dextras sibi ... dari*: a symbolic gesture for concluding all kinds of agreements (Erler 1971: 1974), it was often used for truces.

1 Where he still was on March 20: D LG 130.

2 Who Louis's Lotharingian supporters were is not known, though they must have included Odilbald of Utrecht, who assisted at Willibert's consecration (see next note and Parisot 1899: 360). Louis felt sufficiently sure of his position after this reception to open negotiations with Charles the Bald under threat of war; *AB* 870 (Nelson 1991: 165).

against Charles's will set him in Gunther's place.[3]

Zwentibald, Rastiz's nephew, took thought for his own interests, and commended himself and the kingdom he held[4] to Carloman. Rastiz was furious at this and laid ambushes in secret for his nephew; he plotted to strangle him at a banquet when he was not suspecting any attack. But by the grace of God he was freed from the peril of death. For before those who were to kill him had entered the house, he was warned by one who knew of the plot, and set out as if to go hawking, and so evaded the ambush laid for him. Rastiz saw that his plot was revealed and followed after his nephew with soldiers to capture him. But by the just judgement of God he was caught in the snare he had set, for he was captured by his nephew, bound and brought to Carloman, who sent him under a guard of soldiers to Bavaria lest he should escape and had him kept in prison until he could be brought to the king's presence. Carloman now entered Rastiz's kingdom without resistance and received the surrender of all its cities and castles. He set the kingdom in order and put his men in charge and then returned home, enriched with the royal treasure.

King Louis celebrated Rogation Days [May 1-3] and Whitsun [May 14] in the *villa* of Bürstadt near Worms. He set out westwards from there in June to a conference at his brother Charles's invitation.[5] But on the way he was resting in a certain gallery[6] when the building collapsed and he fell with it and severely bruised his limbs. He feigned good health, however, at his meeting with Charles, at which they divided up Lothar's kingdom,[7] and then he returned to Aachen, where

3 This took place before Louis's journey to Frankfurt; Willibert wasconsecrated on January 7. Liutbert acted on Louis's orders to prevent Charles the Bald from filling the see of Cologne and thus consolidating his hold on Lotharingia. See *AX* 871 (von Simson 1909: 29); Regino 870 (Kurze 1890: 98); Dümmler 1887b: 290-2; Parisot 1899: 357-62; Weinfurter and Engels 1982: 17; Nelson 1991: 168 n. 13 (who also deals with Charles's successful appointment to Trier, passed over by *AF*).

4 Which part of the Moravian empire constituted Zwentibald's kingdom (*regnum*, which could also be translated as 'province' or 'principality', cf. 883(II) n. 7) is not known. Presumably it was a subkingdom much like those held by Carolingian kings' sons.

5 This conference settled the division of Lotharingia on August 8; for the negotiations leading up to the division see *AB* 870 (Nelson 1991: 166-70).

6 In the royal *villa* of Flamersheim, west of Bonn; *AB* 870 (Nelson 1991: 166); Regino 870 (Kurze 1890: 100-1).

7 For the terms of the treaty of Meersen see *AB* 870 (Nelson 1991: 168-9). They had already agreed to divide Lothar's kingdom in 868 (Nelson 1991: 150 and n. 15), but Charles had tried the previous year to seize the opportunity of taking the whole kingdom.

he lay ill for many days.[8]

At Mainz the sky shone red like blood for many nights, and other portents were seen in the heavens.[9] One night a cloud climbed up from the north and another from the south and east, and they exchanged bolts of lightning continuously. In the end they met overhead and as it were fought a great battle. All who saw this were amazed and afraid and prayed that these monstrous things might be turned to good. The lands around that same city were struck by two earthquakes. Several men gathering in the harvest in the district of Worms were found dead because of the heat of the sun, which was fiercer than usual. Many were also drowned in the Rhine. A certain woman cooked bread for sale on the feast of St Laurence [August 10], while others were going to church. Her neighbours implored her to give the day the honour due to it and go to church, but she did not wish to leave what she had begun and lose her profit. But as she preferred earthly reward to reverence for the saint, she found that the loaves which she put in the oven, made from the same dough from which she had earlier baked fine bread, were suddenly blacker than ink. Bewildered, she hurried outside and showed to all present the sin which she had committed in ignoring so great a feast-day and the loss she had sustained through the spoiling of her bread. There was also a serious cattle pestilence in many parts of Francia, which caused irretrievable loss to many.

At the order of King Louis a synod was held in Cologne on September 26, presided over by the metropolitan bishops of the provinces, Liutbert of Mainz, Bertulf of Trier and Willibert of Cologne, with all the Saxon bishops.[10] When they had discussed many things for the good of the Church they dedicated the church of St Peter, previously unconsecrated.[11] It is said that in the night before the consecration was

8 For two months, according to Regino 870 (Kurze 1890: 100); he issued diplomata there on September 25 and October 17 (DD LG 132-3).

9 Here ms. '1' has a slightly different version: 'and other portents were seen in the heavens in these days. For during three whole nights clouds of various colours climbed up from the north and others from the south and east ....'

10 To deal with the difficulties arising out of the semi-vacancies in Cologne and Trier in the previous seven years. The absence of the archbishop of Salzburg and his suffragans is noticeable; they were holding the synod at which Methodius was condemned at about this time; Dvornik 1970: 152-3; Hartmann 1989: 309-10. The mention of the Saxon bishops is also significant; up till then the bishops of Minden, Münster and Osnabrück and their metropolitan (Cologne) had been in different kingdoms and hence had not met together in synods.

11 Perhaps because newly built; Untermann 1983 suggests that it had been desecrated by Gunther, who had continued to act as archbishop after his deposition in 863.

due to be performed the voices of evil spirits were heard talking to
each other and complaining bitterly that they would have to leave the
homes they had occupied for so long.[12]

While King Louis was staying in the palace at Aachen there came to
him the legates of Louis, emperor of Italy, and of Pope Hadrian, whom
he received and gave leave to depart.[13] Shortly afterwards he left there
and set out around November 1 for Bavaria,[14] where he held a meeting
with his men. He ordered Rastiz to be brought before him bound with
a heavy chain. Rastiz was condemned, by the judgement of the Franks
and Bavarians and Slavs who had come there from various places to
bring gifts to the king,[15] to death; but the king only ordered his eyes
to be put out.[16]

871

Louis and Charles, the sons of King Louis, heard a rumour that King
Louis was planning to take away parts of the kingdoms he had agreed
in his testament that they should have on his death and give them to
their brother Carloman, and took it very badly.[1] They collected a
substantial army, occupied the county of Speyer, and prepared to rebel
against the king. When the king learned of this he set out from Bavaria
and came to Frankfurt on February 1,[2] and tried to reconcile his sons
to him by messengers. But the envoys of both sides failed to come to

12 This sentence is missing in ms. '2'.

13 Louis was still at Aachen on October 17 (D LG 133), but at Frankfurt on
   November 1 (D LG 134). This embassy, consisting of two suburbican bishops
   and a cardinal priest, Wibod, bishop of Parma and Count Bernard (the latter
   two were legates of Louis II), brought letters from Hadrian II about the
   Lotharingian question (in which Hadrian was still supporting the rights of
   Lothar II's brother Louis II) and about the consecration of Willibert of
   Cologne; JE 2930-1 = *MGH Epp.* 6: 730-2 nos. 25-6; *AB* 870 (Nelson 1991:
   170).

14 No diplomata record this visit; he was at Frankfurt on November 1 and again
   on February 15 the following year (DD LG 134, 136).

15 The *dona annua*; see Ganshof 1968: 43; Reuter 1985: 85-6. Note that the Slavs
   took part in the judgement along with the Franks and Bavarians; participation
   by Slav leaders at assemblies was common in the east Frankish–Ottonian
   kingdom.

16 A common form of 'mercy' in cases of high treason where the death penalty
   could have been exacted; the best known example is Louis the Pious's blinding
   of his nephew Bernard of Italy in 818. A blind man was politically dead.

 1 *AB* 871 (Nelson 1991: 170) imply that Queen Emma was behind the revolt.
   Compare also the reasons given for Louis the Younger's revolt in 866.

 2 See 870 n. 14.

a conclusion after long negotiations, except that a meeting place was agreed on[3] and an armistice confirmed by oath. Then the king returned to Bavaria and the sons to the places assigned to them.

Zwentibald, Rastiz's nephew, was accused of breach of fidelity to Carloman and was imprisoned. The Moravian Slavs, thinking that their *dux* was dead, set a certain priest and relative of the *dux*, Sclagamar, over themselves as prince; they threatened to kill him if he did not take up the office of *dux*. Of necessity he agreed, and set out to make war on Engelschalk and William,[4] Carloman's commanders, and drive them from the cities they had occupied. They fought back with equal force and after killing many of his army forced him to flee.

King Louis came to the *villa* of Tribur in May, according to the agreement. There he infuriated his sons by blinding a certain Saxon, so that they refused to come to the meeting with him; for the man who was blinded was the vassal of Count Henry.[5] The king, however, followed his sons to the *villa* of Gernsheim and persuaded them with difficulty to meet him. He was able to some extent to soften them with flattering words and promises of benefices, and then in June he set out for the west and travelled through the places which belonged to him.[6]

Meanwhile Zwentibald, after no one had been able to prove the crimes of which he had been accused, was released by Carloman and returned to his own realm laden with kingly gifts, leading with him an army of Carloman's, with which he was to drive out Sclagamar, for so much he had falsely promised to Carloman, should Carloman allow him to return to his country. But just as humiliation falls on those who are careless and trust too much in themselves, so it befell that army, for Zwentibald left the others to pitch camp and entered the old city of Rastiz.[7] Immediately he denied his fidelity and forgot his oath, in Slavic fashion, and turned his thought and his powers not to driving

---

3 Ms. '1' has 'and deferred until May 1', which could have been derived from the reference in the next paragraph but one.

4 These two were brothers and marcher counts on the Danube (Mitterauer 1963: 178-88); the fate of their children takes up a considerable part of the second continuation (see below, 884(II), 892). Probably they were among the margraves reported by *AB* 871 (Nelson 1991: 175) as killed in the disastrous expedition against Sclagamar later in the year.

5 For the links between Henry and Louis the Younger, see 866 n. 4.

6 Kings normally did this; the fact that it is specifically mentioned here suggests that Louis's control over his kingdom was seriously weakened by the rebellion. Louis was still at Tribur in mid-June (DD LG 137-9).

7 See 869 n. 9.

out Sclagamar but to revenging the injury which Carloman had done him. Then he attacked in great force the Bavarians' camp – they suspected no evil and had were not keeping a sharp watch. He took many alive as prisoners, and killed the rest, except for a few who had prudently left the camp beforehand. All the Bavarians' joy at their many previous victories was turned into grief and weeping.[8] On the news of the slaughter of his army, Carloman was aghast, and forced by necessity he ordered all the hostages in his kingdom to be collected together and returned to Zwentibald; he received scarcely one man from there except for a man called Radbod who returned half-dead.

In August King Louis had a meeting with his brother Charles by the River Meuse,[9] but he was not able to make peace with his sons there either; they refused to come to the meeting because he had put off granting them the benefices he had promised. When a false rumour was heard that Louis, emperor of Italy, had been treacherously killed by Adalgis, *dux* of Benevento,[10] King Louis returned sadly from the palace of Aachen to the eastern parts of his kingdom,[11] and there he met his sons who came to him on the way. After they had received some benefices from him they were reconciled to him with no difficulty.

The king then held a meeting with his men in October in Frankfurt.[12] From there he set out for Bavaria and sent guards of those parts, namely Bishop Arn [of Würzburg] and Count Ruodolt and others with them,[13] to guard his borders against the Bohemians, who were planning an invasion. The enemy had encircled a certain place with a very strong wall and made the entrance to it very narrow, as a trap for the Germans who guarded the frontier, because if any of them should chance to come that way they would be shut in the narrow path unable to turn aside, and could be killed. The Moravian Slavs were celebrating a wedding and bringing back the daughter of a Bohemian *dux*;

8 A biblical reminiscence; cf. e.g. James 4:9.

9 The meeting took place at Maastricht. Louis the Younger and Charles had appealed to Charles the Bald to make peace between them and their father; see *AB* 871 (Nelson 1991: 175).

10 On the falsity of the rumour and its origin in Louis's capture by Adalgis during his Beneventan campaign, see *AB* 871 (Nelson 1991: 176).

11 Louis the German left Lotharingia around the beginning of September; he was at Frankfurt by October 14 (D LG 140).

12 DD LG 140-2 were issued there between October 14 and 20.

13 Found between 822 and 874, he had replaced Ernest as count of the Nordgau in 861 (Mitterauer 1963: 169-75); on Arn see 855 n. 1.

when the leaders already mentioned, that is Arn and the others with him, learnt of this, they immediately followed the army in arms. The enemy, fleeing, came to the wall which has been described, of which they were ignorant. Because of the narrowness of the place they were forced to leave behind their horses and armour and scarcely escaped with their skins. Our men came on behind and found 644 horses, saddled and harnessed, and the same number of shields, which those who fled had thrown away. They collected these without resistance and returned joyfully to their camp.

872

In January around the feast of the Epiphany [January 6] legates with letters and gifts came from Basil, the emperor of the Greeks, with letters and gifts to King Louis at Regensburg.[1] Amongst other gifts they brought him a crystal of marvellous size decorated with gold and precious stones, and quite a large piece of the salvation-bringing Cross. They were received honourably and, after being given an appropriate reply, returned to their own land. The king, however, held a general assembly in mid-Lent [March 9] at the *villa* of Forchheim,[2] where he made peace between his sons who were disputing the division of his kingdom, and laid down clearly which part each was to have to guard after his own death. There also Louis and Charles, his sons, swore an oath in the sight of the whole army[3] that they would be true to him all the days of their life. From there the king returned to Bavaria and celebrated Easter [March 30].

In May he sent the Thuringians and Saxons against the Moravian Slavs; but because they did not have the king with them and would not be at peace with each other,[4] they therefore fled before the enemy and returned in disgrace, having lost many of their number. It is said that some counts fleeing from the expedition were beaten by the women-

---

1 The purpose of this legation is not known; Dümmler 1887b: 337 suggests that it was to establish friendly relations in view of the likelihood of Louis's succeeding to the whole or part of Louis II's kingdom.

2 There are no diplomata at all for 872 to provide a check on the details given in this annal of Louis's itinerary.

3 Hincmar thought that these oaths were insincere; *AB* 872 (Nelson 1991: 178). Note the survival of the idea that an assembly was a *Heerschau*, a mustering of troops.

4 Presumably a reference to aristocratic feuds; compare the entries for 882 and 883 in continuation II below, and the account of the disastrous campaign of 849 above.

folk of the region and clubbed from their horses to the ground. Troops
were sent anew from Francia to Carloman to help him against the
above-mentioned Slavs; others were sent against the Bohemians. With
God's help these put to flight five[5] of their *duces*, by name: Zwentislan,
Witislan, Heriman, Spoitimar, Moyslan, with a great force attempting
to rebel. Some they killed, others they drowned in the River Vltava,[6]
and those who could escape fled into the cities.[7] Then they laid waste
a not inconsiderable part of that province, and returned home
unharmed. Archbishop Liutbert [of Mainz] was the leader in that
expedition. Those who were sent to assist Carloman, however, Bishop
Arn [of Würzburg] and Sigihart, abbot of the monastery of Fulda,[8]
although they fought bravely and pushed the enemy hard, returned
with great difficulty after losing many of their men. But while
Carloman spread fire and slaughter among the Moravians, Zwentibald
sent a large army in secret against the Bavarians who had been left to
guard the ships on the bank of the Danube, and overran them; some he
killed, others he drowned in the river, others again he led away
captive. No one escaped from there except for Embricho, bishop of
Regensburg, with a few men.[9]

The whole summer was ruined by hailstorms and other kinds of
tempest. The hail destroyed the crops in many places, and terrifying
thunder and lightning threatened mortals almost daily with death: it
is said that immense bolts killed men and draught animals in various
places and reduced them to ashes. The cathedral of St Peter at Worms
was also burnt by heavenly fire and the walls nearly destroyed.[10]
Further, there was an earthquake which shook the city of Mainz on
December 3 in the first hour.[11]

5 Ms. '1' also has 'five of their *duces*', but mentions a sixth name, Goriwei. A
   Borivoi plays an important part as an early Christian magnate in Bohemia (cf.
   Havlík 1966: 107; Havlík 1967: 193-5; Dvornik 1970: 166-8 and 206-11), so the
   addition presumably has an authentic basis.

6 Ms. '1' has 'Some they killed, others they wounded; some drowned in the River
   Vltava....'

7 'Cities' = *civitates*, meaning either a unit of Slav government, corresponding
   roughly to a Frankish county, or, as in this case, its physical centre, a
   stronghold fortified by a log and earth rampart.

8 On Arn see 855 n. 1; Sigihard was abbot of Fulda from 869 to 891 (Sandmann
   1978: 187-8).

9 858x864-91.

10 It had been restored recently by Samuel of Worms (d. 856), according to *AX*
   872 (von Simson 1909: 31).

11 These things are perhaps recorded as portents of the event recorded at the
   beginning of 873.

The king, after ordering affairs in the province of the Bavarians,[12] came to Frankfurt in the month of December and celebrated Christmas there.

873

In the month of January he wanted to hold an assembly with his men coming from all parts of the kingdom in the aforementioned place[1] to discuss the state and prosperity of his kingdom. By God's providence his goodness was gloriously demonstrated and the wickedness of some who plotted against his life was laid bare. For when he had entered the court on January 28, a wicked spirit entered into his youngest son Charles and tortured him severely, so that he could scarcely be held down by six of the strongest men, in the presence of the king and of his leading men, that is to say his counts and bishops. And indeed with justice: for he who had wished to deceive the king chosen and ordained by God was himself deceived; he who had treacherously set traps for his father fell himself into the snares of the Devil, so that he might learn from his diabolical torments that there is no counsel against God.[2] But the king and all who were with him were appalled, and wept. When he was led to the church, so that the bishops might pray to God for his recovery, he yammered, sometimes weakly and sometimes at the top of his voice, and threatened with open mouth to bite those who were holding him. The king then turned to his namesake [Louis the Younger] and said: 'Do you not see, my son, whose lordship you accepted, you and your brother, when you thought to carry out wickedness against me? Now you may understand, if you would not before, that as a Word of Truth has it, nothing is hidden which will not be revealed.[3] Confess your sins therefore, and do penance, and pray humbly to God that they may be forgiven you. I also, as far as lies in me, grant you forgiveness.' After the devil's attack was over Charles said aloud in the hearing of many that he had been delivered into the power of the Enemy as many times

---

12 Probably a reference to the replacement of the border counts who had been killed the previous year (cf. above and for the consequences 884(II)); Louis also had a meeting with the Empress Engelberga in May at Trent; *AB* 872 (Nelson 1991: 178).

1 Frankfurt, where he issued diplomata between February 1 and April 9 (DD LG 144–6).

2 Cf. Proverbs 21:30.

3 Matthew 10:28; this quotation is also used in the annal for 858.

as he had plotted against the king.[4]

Charles, the tyrant of Gaul, put aside his paternal feelings, and had his son Carloman, who had been ordained deacon, blinded.[5]

After Lent had passed by and Easter Week was over [April 25] the king left Frankfurt for the *villa* of Bürstadt near Worms, where he had his sons, Louis that is and Charles, judge individual cases; and what they could not resolve themselves they left to their father's judgement.[6] Whence it came about that all of those who came from various parts returned with joy with their grievances lawfully settled. The envoys of Sigifrid,[7] the king of the Danes, also came there, seeking to make peace over the border disputes between themselves and the Saxons[8] and so that merchants of each kingdom might come and go in peace to the other, bringing merchandise to buy and sell; the king promised that for his part these terms would be kept. A certain man from Alemannia, Bertram by name, who had been captured by the Moravian Slavs the previous year, came to the king, having been released by Zwentibald, and expounded the terms of the embassy which had been laid on him by the *dux*, as he had previously promised on oath that he would do.[9]

From there the king came to Mainz about the beginning of May and then sailed down the Rhine and set off for Aachen.[10] There he had a secret meeting with his own men and took Roric, who came to him under the security of hostages, under his lordship.[11]

Then in the month of August, as he held a general assembly at Metz, Halbden, the brother of King Siegfried, also sent his messengers to the

4 On this episode compare *AB* 873 (Nelson 1991: 182), *AX* 873 (von Simson 1909: 31-2) and the illuminating commentary on the accounts of this episode in *AB* and *AF* in Nelson 1988.

5 See *AB* 873 (Nelson 1991: 181) and Nelson 1988 on this.

6 See 866 n. 1.

7 It is not clear when Sigifrid and Halbden succeeded Horic II (on whom see 854 with n. 2; 857 with n. 3), or whether they were related to him; Vogel 1906: 411-12 makes them sons of Ragnar Lodbrok.

8 For earlier clashes between Saxons and Northmen see 845 n. 1.

9 *AB* 873 (Nelson 1991: 184) give further details of the campaigning against and diplomacy with the Moravians and Bohemians in this year.

10 He issued diplomata there between June 10 and 13 (DD LG 147-50).

11 Mentioned also by *AX* 873 (von Simson 1909: 32). Roric had held benefices in Lotharingia from Lothar II (see 857 n. 3); as Lotharingia was now divided, he became the man of both Louis and Charles the Bald; *AB* 870, 872 (Nelson 1991: 169, 180).

king asking the same things which his brother had asked, namely, that the king should send his ambassadors to the River Eider, which separates Danes and Saxons,[12] and that they should meet them there and ratify a perpetual peace on both sides. These same messengers also offered the king a sword with a golden hilt as a gift, and pleaded with him that he should deign to treat their lords, the aforementioned kings, as if they were his sons, while they for their part would venerate him as a father all the days of their life. They also swore on their weapons, according to the custom of that people, that henceforth no one from their lords' kingdom would disturb the king's kingdom, nor inflict damage on anyone in it. The king accepted all these promises gratefully and promised that he would do what was asked. After the messengers had returned to their own country the king went through Alsace to Strasbourg; from there he crossed the Rhine and set out for Bavaria.

In the same year there was a great famine through the whole of Italy and Germany, and many died of hunger.[13] For at the time of the new crops a plague of a new kind and one seen for the first time among the Franks appeared to vex the German people[14] not a little for its sins. For worms like locusts with six feet and flying on four wings came from the east, and covered all the face of the earth like snow, and ate everything green in the fields and meadows. They had a wide mouth and a long stomach and two teeth harder than stone, with which they were able to gnaw through the toughest bark of trees. Their length and thickness was about that of a man's thumb, and they were so numerous that in one hour they devoured a hundred ploughlands of corn near the town of Mainz. When they flew, moreover, they so covered the sky for the space of a mile that the sun's rays scarcely appeared to those on earth; some that were killed in various places were found to have whole grains of corn with the seed and chaff inside them. When some had gone on west others came after them, and for two months their flight presented almost daily a horrible spectacle to those watching. It is said that in Italy in the county of Brescia blood

12 For a similar meeting on the Eider in Charles the Great's time see ARF 811 (Scholz 1972: 93).

13 This is confirmed, as is the account of the plague of locusts which follows, by a number of other east Frankish and Italian annals, e.g. *AX* 873 (von Simson 1909: 33); *AH* 873 (Waitz 1878a: 18); *AC* 873 (Prinz 1982: 106); *AV* 874 (von Simson 1909: 40).

14 *populum Germanicum*, meaning the inhabitants of Louis the German's kingdom. See Eggert 1973: 68-70 and below, 877, 880.

rained from the sky for three days and nights.

In June Rudolf,[15] a certain Northman of royal stock, who had often raided Charles's kingdom with pillage and arson, led a fleet into the kingdom of King Louis, in Albdag's county,[16] and sent messengers ahead with a demand that the inhabitants of the region should pay him tribute. When they replied that they were not bound to pay tribute to anyone except to King Louis and his sons, and that they would not agree to his demands in this matter under any circumstances, he was enraged, and in his pride swore that after all the males had been killed the women and children with all their moveable wealth should be taken off into captivity, not knowing of the revenge which was to pursue him from heaven. He at once invaded their lands and began to make war against them. They, however, invoked the Lord, who had so often preserved them from their enemies, and opposed their evil enemy in arms; battle was joined and Rudolf himself fell first, and with him eight hundred men.[17] But the rest, since they could not reach their ships, took refuge in a certain building. The Frisians laid siege to this and took counsel with each other as to what should be done with them. Different people had said different things, when a Northman who had become a Christian and had long lived among these Frisians and was the leader of their attack, addressed the others as follows: 'O my good fellow-soldiers, it is enough for us to have fought thus far, for it is not due to our strength but to God's that we few have prevailed against so many enemies. You know also that we are absolutely exhausted and many of us are seriously wounded; those who lie here within are in desperation. If we begin to fight against them, we shall not defeat them without bloodshed; if they turn out to be stronger – for the outcome of battle is uncertain – then perhaps they will overcome us and depart in safety, still able to do us harm. It seems more sensible to me, therefore, that we should take hostages from them and allow some of them to leave unwounded for the ships. We will meanwhile retain the hostages until they send us all the treasure which they have in the ships, and they will first take an oath that they will never return to King Louis's kingdom.' The others agreed to this plan, and after taking hostages allowed some to leave for the boats. These sent back a really immense treasure and received their hostages back, after first,

15 On him see *AB* 864, 872, 873 (Nelson 1991: 112, 180, 184), where the battle here described is briefly mentioned; see also *AX* 873 (von Simson 1909: 32).

16 The Ostergau in Frisia, around Dokkum (Vogel 1906: 244).

17 Five hundred, according to *AB* 873 (Nelson 1991: 184) and *AX* 875 (von Simson 1909: 32-3).

as I have said, taking an oath that they would never again return to King Louis's kingdom. Then they departed with great shame and loss, and without their *dux*, to their own country.

In November Archbishop Agathon, the ambassador of Basil the emperor of the Greeks, came to King Louis at Regensburg with letters and gifts, for the purpose of renewing the former friendship between the two. The king received him with honour and allowed him to depart.[18]

Count Thachulf, *dux* of the Sorbian march, died in August.[19]

874

The winter was very hard and longer than usual;[1] there were also great falls of snow from November 1 to the vernal equinox [March 21] without intermission, and these caused great difficulty to men wanting to go to the woods to collect fuel. Hence it came about that not only animals but also many men died of cold. The Rhine and the Main were frozen by the intense cold and for a long time would bear the weight of those who set foot on them.

The Sorbs and the Siusli[2] and their neighbours rebelled on the death of Thachulf. Archbishop Liutbert [of Mainz] and Ratolf, Thachulf's successor,[3] crossed the River Saale in January and by pillaging and burning crushed their insolence without battle and reduced them to their former servility.

In the same year Louis the Younger held a secret meeting with certain of his father's counsellors at Sts Marcellinus and Peter [Seligenstadt], which brought his father from Bavaria to Francia. For he came around February 1[4] to Frankfurt and took counsel with his faithful men about the peace and state of his kingdom. In Lent [February 25], when he had left off dealing with secular affairs and was spending his time in

18 See above, 872 with n.1, to which the 'former friendship' presumably also refers.

19 On him see 849 with n. 2; 858 with n. 8. He died on August 1 873; Schmid *et al.* 1978b: 385-6.

1 *AB* 874 (Nelson 1991: 185) also notes the exceptionally severe winter.

2 See above, 869 n. 2.

3 Ratolf's family connections and previous history are unknown; by 880 atthe latest he had been replaced by Poppo; see below.

4 In fact rather later; he was still at Augsburg on February 2 (D LG 151), and issued a diploma at Frankfurt on February 26 (D LG 153). Note that Louis's problems with his sons were still not settled.

prayer,[5] he saw in a dream one night his father, the Emperor Louis, in
dire straits, who addressed him in Latin speech in the following way:
'I implore you by our Lord Jesus Christ and by the Triune Majesty
that you will save me from these torments in which I am held, so that
I can at last come to eternal life.' Horrified by this vision he therefore
sent letters[6] to all the monasteries of his kingdom, asking urgently
that they might intervene with the Lord through their prayers for a
soul placed in torment. From this it may be understood that although
the said emperor had done many praiseworthy things pleasing to God,
nevertheless he allowed many things against God's law in his
kingdom. For if – to mention nothing else – he had strongly opposed
the heresy of the Nicolaitans[7] and taken care to observe the warnings
of the Archangel Gabriel which Abbot Einhard wrote down in twelve
chapters and offered to him that he might read them and carry them
out,[8] perhaps he would not have suffered such punishments. But since
God, as it is written,[9] does not let any sin go unpunished, and since
according to the Apostle not only those who do evil deeds but also
those who consent to them are worthy of death [Rom. 1:32], so he has
deservedly been condemned to suffer penalties, since he would not
correct the errors of those who had been entrusted to him while he
could, even after he had been warned.

In Easter Week[10] King Louis came to the monastery of Fulda to pray
and returning from there held a general assembly in the *villa* of
Tribur.[11] From there he set off for Italy across the Norican Alps[12] and
held a meeting with his nephew Louis [II] and John [VIII] the

5 See Kottje 1975 on Louis's practice of spending Lent in prayer.

6 These have not survived, though Flodoard, *Historia Remensis Ecclesiae* III 20
   (*MGH SS* 13: 513) mentions that Hincmar received one and replied to it at
   length.

7 A reference to married clerics.

8 These are referred to by Einhard in the *Translatio SS Marcellini et Petri* III, 15
   (*MGH SS* 15: 252-3); they were conveyed to one of the monks at Einhard's
   monastery of Seligenstadt in a dream, written down, and sent to the emperor,
   but have unfortunately not survived.

9 Not in the Bible, though the thought is common enough.

10 This should mean the week following Easter (April 11–18), but as it was Louis
    the German's custom to visit monasteries during Lent to pray (see the
    annalist's remark at the beginning of the year), perhaps the annalist meant the
    week before Easter (Holy Week).

11 Not precisely datable.

12 Meaning presumably the Brenner Pass.

Roman pontiff not far from the town of Verona.[13] From there he returned and spoke with Carloman and Louis his sons in the *villa* of Forchheim[14] and there he received the ambassadors of Zwentibald who sought peace and promised fidelity. The head of the embassy was John, a priest of Venice, who even confirmed whatever he said with an oath so that the king might have all doubt removed and believe what he said, namely that Zwentibald would remain faithful to the king all the days of his life and would pay the tribute ordained by the king annually, if he were only allowed to live peacefully and rule quietly.[15] The king also heard the messengers of the Bohemians and gave them leave to depart, and after this he took himself to Bavaria. In July he came from Bavaria to Frankfurt[16] and from there he went on after a short time to the *villa* of Biberich whence he took ship and came to the palace of Aachen. He stayed there quite a long time; at length he had a meeting in December with his brother Charles at St Lambert [Liège][17] and returned to Francia. He came to Mainz on December 20 and from there he went to Frankfurt and celebrated Christmas there.[18]

In this year, through the hunger and pestilence which raged through the whole of Gaul and Germany, nearly a third of the population was destroyed.[19] Also Queen Emma suffered a stroke and lost the use of her voice.

13 Nothing is known for certain about the date or purpose of the meeting, but it was presumably held in connection with the succession to Italy and the imperial title on Louis II's death. The talks Louis had on his return from Italy with Carloman and Louis probably also concerned the Italian succession question (Arnaldi 1990: 59-67).

14 Date unknown.

15 Zwentibald had already offered peace terms the previous year, according to *AB* 873 (Nelson 1991: 186); this time they seem to have been accepted, though the annalist does not say so directly, as there are no further references to troubles with Moravia for a number of years. Althoff 1988: 14-15 argues that Zwentibald had been primarily concerned in 871-74 to restore his 'honour' after his mistreatment in 871 than to secure 'independence'.

16 There are no diplomata for the second half of the year to give details of the itinerary.

17 Cf. *AB* 874 (Nelson 1991: 137), where the meeting is said to have taken place at Herstal on the Meuse. Louis's long stay in Aachen was due to Charles's illness and delay in agreeing to meet him. Here again it is probable that the Italian succession question was discussed.

18 *AB* 874 (Nelson 1991: 187) has Louis at Aachen for Christmas and going on to Frankfurt afterwards; it is not known which is correct.

19 There is a reference to serious crop failures in *AB* 874 (Nelson 1991: 186).

875

King Louis wintered in Frankfurt[1] and after Easter [March 27] set
out for Bavaria to see the queen.[2] From there he came back and around
June 1[3] he came to Tribur and held a general assembly there. There
there was a really serious dispute which arose between Franks and
Saxons, and if the young Louis had not quickly intervened with his
men they would have slaughtered each other with their already drawn
swords.[4]

A comet appeared in the first hour of the night of June 6 in the north,
shining more brightly than is usual and with a spread-out tail,
foretelling by its appearance the remarkable and indeed tragic event
which quickly followed, although for our sins it may be feared that it
signified still more serious matters. For a certain *villa* in the Niddagau
called Eschborn, which has no rivers or streams near it, was almost
completely destroyed by a flash flood, and eighty-eight people of both
sexes were killed. For when the people of the place had gone to sleep
on July 3, not suspecting anything, so much rain fell in a moment from
the sky that it uprooted all the trees and vines it touched in the *villa*,
overthrew the foundations of buildings, and hurled the draught
animals and beasts with everything which was in the houses to
destruction. The church of the *villa* with its altar was also so
completely destroyed that those who now look at the spot can see no
sign that there was once a building there. There was a further
lamentable sight: as women reached out their hands to their children
and husbands to their wives to try to help them, they were seized by
the force of the waters and drowned along with those whom they had
wished to help. Even corpses long buried were swept from their graves
by the force of the waters, along with the coffins which they lay in, and
were found within the bounds of another *villa*.

1 Where he issued diplomata on February 26 and April 3 (DD LG 157-60).
2 He was at Regensburg on May 18 (D LG 161); this diploma grants the Mary
  chapel at Regensburg to the monastery of Berg 'for the salvation [*salute*, which
  could mean 'health'] of our lord grandfather and father and of our beloved wife
  Hemma and our beloved offspring', which may be a reference to Emma's illness
  but is more likely to refer to her eternal salvation.
3 'Around' must here mean 'before', since *AB* 875 (Nelson 1991: 187) say that the
  meeting took place in May and that unfinished business was postponed to
  another meeting summoned to Tribur for August (see below). Louis was at
  Frankfurt on June 14 (D LG 162).
4 Note that Louis the Younger is here already in effect in charge of the kingdom
  allotted to him.

In August King Louis had a meeting with his faithful men and his sons in the *villa* of Tribur.[5] Meanwhile Louis, emperor of Italy [died][6] and his body was taken to Milan and buried in the basilica of St Ambrose.[7] When Charles, the tyrant of Gaul, learnt of this,[8] he immediately invaded the kingdom of Italy and dragged together with his crooked hand all the treasure he could find. King Louis was enraged at this, and sent Carloman with an army through Bavaria to Italy. He himself joined with his namesake [Louis the Younger] and invaded Charles's kingdom with a great army in order to compel him to come out of Italy. But the army which followed the king turned to plunder and seized or destroyed everything it found.[9] Charles, when he heard of Carloman's arrival in Italy, tried at first to defend himself at the mouths of the Alpine passes, but he was unsuccessful, for Carloman had already taken up positions with his men in places which were difficult to reach. Charles, however, fearing that the business would have to be settled with iron – for he is as fearful as a hare[10] – turned to his customary trickery. He offered gold, silver, and a great number of precious stones to Carloman if he would be reconciled with him and leave his father's allegiance. He swore that he would quickly depart from Italy and would leave the disposing of the kingdom to the judgement of his brother Louis, if Carloman would go away.[11]

5 A continuation of the earlier assembly (see n. 1); Louis issued diplomata there on August 11 (DD LG 163 and 164).

6 August 12 875. The manuscripts have a gap in the text; ms. '2' has 'died' added in another hand, and mss. '3c', '3d' and '3e' (folios are missing in '3' itself at this point) have 'date and place to be inquired' which probably stood as a marginal note in their common ancestor.

7 Not without a dispute between the bishop of Brescia and the archbishop of Milan over where his body was to be buried; Andreas of Bergamo, c. 18 (Waitz 1878b: 229).

8 It is probable that Louis the German and Louis II had reached an agreement that Carloman should succeed Louis II; the evidence is summarised by Dümmler 1887b: 388. Carloman himself claimed to have been designated as successor by Louis II (D Carloman 4). According to *AB* 875 (Nelson 1991: 188) and Andreas of Bergamo, c. 19 (Waitz 1878b: 229-30) Louis first sent an expedition under his youngest son Charles; Carloman's army was a substantial one, and included Berengar, margrave of Friuli and other Italian magnates (Dümmler 1887b: 389 n. 1).

9 Compare *AB* 875 (Nelson 1991: 188). Louis issued diplomata from Metz in late November (DD LG 166-9).

10 The use of the present tense makes it likely that this entry was written before Charles's death in 877.

11 *AB* 875 (Nelson 1991: 188) and the Italian chronicler Andreas of Bergamo, c. 19 (Waitz 1878b: 230) agree that Charles the Bald and Carloman came to an agreement, but Hincmar suggests that this was simply for Carloman to withdraw in the face of superior force, while Andreas implies a truce.

Carloman believed his promises and left, and he broke all that he had
promised and set off for Rome as fast as he could. Like Jugurtha[12] he
bribed the whole senate[13] and people of Rome and allied with them, so
that even Pope John gave way to his wishes and, placing a crown on
his head, ordered him to be called Emperor and Augustus.[14] How he
carved up that kingdom with his followers,[15] how he returned with the
treasures he bore to his own kingdom, and what slaughterings and
burnings he did on the way, I have not wished to relate, since I have
no certain report. For it is better to be silent than to speak lies.

876

King Louis was moved by mercy and yielded to the prayers of many
that Gaul should not be ruined because of Charles's stupidity, and
returned to his kingdom in January.[1] He came to Mainz after Epiphany
[January 6] and from there to Frankfurt, where he held an assembly
with his men in the following month; he did the same thing in
mid-Lent [March 25].

Queen Emma died in the city of Regensburg in Bavaria and was buried
in the church of St Emmeram the Martyr.[2]

12 A reference to Sallust's *Jugurthine War*. The two sentences at the end of this
   annal also reflect the influence of Sallust, in the way they hint at wickedness
   without describing it fully and thus leave the reader to imagine the worst
   (Smalley 1970: 172), though they also echo the Rule of St Benedict 1, 12: 'about
   whom it is better to be silent than to talk'.

13 There is no evidence for the continued existence of a senate in Rome at this
   time, and the terms 'senate' and 'senators' seem to be used as a literary
   reminiscence simply to mean 'leading members of the Roman nobility'
   (Toubert 1973: 965-6).

14 Charles was crowned on December 25 875, the day having been postponed so
   that it would fall on the anniversary of Charles the Great's imperial coronation
   in 800. The annalist is mistaken (or misleading) in implying that John VIII was
   forced to crown Charles; he was only too willing to do so. The gifts made to
   the pope and the Romans are mentioned in several sources – see *AB* 875-76
   (Nelson 1991: 189) and for the others Dümmler 1887b: 398 n. 1 – but only *AF*
   and Regino 874 and 877 (Kurze 1890: 110, 113) imply bribery.

15 A somewhat unfavourable view; for Charles's support in Italy see *AB* 875-76
   (Nelson 1991: 189 and Arnaldi 1990: 9-28).

 1 For the negotiations which led to Louis's retreat see *AB* 875 (Nelson 1991:
   188-9). There are virtually no diplomata from 876 to give details of Louis's
   itinerary.

 2 January 31 876. Emma was the sister of Judith, Louis the Pious's second wife.
   She had suffered a stroke in 874. Schmid 1976 argues that Emma was not in
   fact buried in St Emmeram, but this is convincingly refuted by Fuchs 1992.

The Frisians known as Westerners[3] fought with the Northmen and were victorious and took away all the treasures which the Northmen had collected together in plundering various places and divided them up among themselves.

King Charles returned from Italy to Gaul and is said to have adopted new and unaccustomed modes of dress: for he used to go to church on Sundays and feast-days dressed in a dalmatic down to his ankles and with a sword-belt girdled over it, his head wrapped in a silk veil with a diadem on top. For, despising all the customs of the Frankish kings, he held the glories of the Greeks to be the best, and so that he might show his overweeningness more fully he put aside the name of king and ordered that he should be called Emperor and Augustus of all kings on this side of the sea.[4] He also threatened that he would do many incredible things to King Louis and his kingdom; among other boasting claims he is said to have boasted that he would collect so large an army from different places that the River Rhine would be drunk dry by their horses and he himself would cross the dry bed of the river to lay waste the whole of Louis's kingdom. His threats were easily silenced, for Louis collected his army and he was filled with fear and sent ambassadors to beg for peace. When legates from both sides had been exchanged often and had sought to make peace between them,[5] Louis fell seriously ill, and grew worse daily. He died on August 28 in the palace at Frankfurt. His namesake [Louis the Younger] bore his corpse away and buried it honourably in the monastery of St Nazarius, which is called Lorsch.[6] But Charles, when he learned of Louis's death, was led by greed to invade his kingdom, thinking, as it was rumoured, that he could not only tyrannically obtain the part of Lothar's kingdom which Louis held and which he had left to his sons to guard but also add all the cities of Louis's kingdom on the west bank of the Rhine, that is, Mainz, Worms and Speyer, to his kingdom and

---

3 The inhabitants of the Westergau on the Frisian coast.

4 Schramm 1968b: 132-4 describes this as a tendentious account of Charles's Byzantinising in his last years, for which see *AB* 876 (Nelson 1991: 190, 194); for a similarly unfriendly view by the annalist of Charles's aspirations see above, 869.

5 On these negotiations see also *AB* 876 (Nelson 1991: 195).

6 Wehlt 1970: 34-5 argues that Louis the German's burial in Lorsch was intended and points to the numerous donations Louis made to the monastery; Fried 1984: 13, sees these as insignificant and suggests that Louis the Younger was concerned to secure a burial place for a legitimate Carolingian within his own kingdom in face of the threat from Charles the Bald. Note that Emma had been buried in Regensburg (above, n. 2).

so oppress his brother's sons with his power that none would dare to resist or contradict him.[7] He therefore made first for the palace of Aachen and set out from there with all his army and held court in Cologne.[8] He also sent ambassadors beforehand to Louis's leading men to urge them to desert their own lord and come to him, promising many benefices and gifts to those who came, and threatening those who did otherwise with the loss of their worldly goods or with liquidation. Louis, who had succeeded his father as heir in those parts,[9] came against him with a few men and pitched camp on the northern bank of the Rhine and awaited the arrival of his army. Meanwhile he sent messengers to Charles saying: 'Why have you raised war against me? for the Old People were absolutely forbidden to make war even on the nations around them unless these had first refused peace.[10] Go back in peace, I pray, to your kingdom and be content with your own glory and do not tyrannously invade the kingdom left to us by our father in hereditary right and in consequence violate the laws of kinship, which naturally hold between us, by this kind of machination. Remember also your oaths, which you took to my father not just once or twice;[11] consider also the danger to the Christian people if you persist in this obstinacy without turning back. It may be that you trust in the size of the army which you have raised from various parts, and so it delights you to make war. But why do you not think of the fact that God can liberate both from small and from great things? [I Macc. 3:18] Restrain your mind from this kind of desire, for you do not know in the least what the outcome of what you are planning will be.' But when Charles, goaded by avarice, would not reasonably agree to a meeting in spite of this and other similar arguments, Louis left his camp one night with his men, crossed the Rhine, and took up position in the castle of Andernach. Almost all his army scattered to different places

7 The significant part of this sentence is Charles's intention to seize the territories of Mainz, Worms and Speyer; they were assigned to the east Frankish kingdom after special negotiations before the treaty of Verdun (Regino 842 [Kurze 1890: 75]) and contained a substantial quantity of fiscal lands. Their addition to Charles's kingdom would indeed have enabled Charles to 'oppress his brother's sons with his power'.

8 See *AB* 876 (Nelson 1991: 195-6), for Charles's journey through Lotharingia. Charles was in Aachen by September 15 (Prinz 1977: 544-5), so that he must have been informed of Louis's condition before his death and had time to make preparations.

9 See 866 n. 1 and 876 with n. 18 for the division of the east Frankish kingdom.

10 Cf. Deuteronomy 20:10-21.

11 For example in 842 (Strasbourg), 849 (cf. *AB* 849 [Nelson 1991: 67], which implies a public promise if not a formal oath), 860 (Koblenz) and 865 (Tusey).

to collect fodder for the horses, but he again sent messengers to
Charles to make peace between them. Charles pretended peace but
planned treachery in his heart and promised falsely that he would send
ambassadors to Louis and agree to peace for the common good.[12] For
in the same night he hurried out with all his army, intending to kill the
others and capture and blind Louis, so that afterwards he could take
over his kingdom without resistance. But Willibert, bishop of the city
of Cologne, discovered Charles's treacherous plans and, while others
shuddered, boldly went to meet him, begging him urgently that he
would not do such cruel and barbarous things to a nephew who sought
peace. When he could not turn him from his evil will, he sent a certain
priest of his called Hartwig by a shorter route to warn Louis of the
ambushes laid for him and the arrival of Charles himself. Immediately
he [Louis] put on his mail-coat and putting all his trust in God boldly
went against Charles with the few who were with him (for he could not
call together his scattered men). He ordered all on his side to wear
white garments so that they could recognise their own fellows. The
Saxons, who were placed in the front line against the enemy, began the
battle at first, but were terrified by the great number of their opponents and soon turned to flight for a while. But the eastern Franks on
both wings fought bravely, killed Charles's standard-bearers and put
the rest to flight. Louis pursued them and dealt out considerable
slaughter. He also took alive many of Charles's leading men, whom in
his humanity he ordered to be spared unharmed.[13] Charles ran away in
cowardly fashion, and, leaving behind the treasure he had with him,
escaped almost naked with the few men he had with him. Those who
were with Louis turned back to despoil the dead, and no one can relate
how much booty they took in gold, silver, clothes, arms, armour,
horses and different kinds of apparatus. Without doubt God fought
against Charles in these battles, for, as the prisoners who were led
away reported, when Louis and those who were with him appeared,
such fear filled all Charles's army that they thought themselves
defeated before battle had begun, and, what is still more remarkable,
though they scored and gashed the flanks of the horses on which they
sat with their spurs, these remained standing as if tied to posts. They
fought also with their arms, but wounded few, for the edges of their

12 This account of Charles's duplicity is confirmed by *AB* 876: 196.

13 For names see *AB* 876 (Nelson 1991: 197); the captured included Bishop Ottulf
    of Troyes and Gauzlin, abbot of St-Denis and Charles's chancellor, as well as
    a number of lay nobles.

weapons were as if blunted and hardly damaged anyone.[14] This happened on October 8 against the new Sennacherib,[15] so that he who in his self-confidence would not remember God may now, defeated and shamed, realise that victory in war lies not in the greatness of armies but that strength comes from heaven, and may also at last set some bounds to his greed and pride.[16] Louis came to the palace of Aachen after Charles's flight and after he had dealt as he wished with his affairs there returned in triumph to Frankfurt.[17]

In the following month Carloman and Louis and Charles, the sons of King Louis, met in the county of Ries and divided their father's kingdom among themselves and promised each other to keep faith and confirmed this with an oath, whose text, written in the German tongue, can be found in many places.[18]

877

King Louis held a general assembly at Frankfurt in January,[1] and sent the men of Charles's kingdom whom he held captive back to Gaul.

The Slavs called Linones and the Siusli their neighbours planned to rebel and refused to pay the usual tribute.[2] King Louis sent certain of his faithful men there around mid-Lent [March 17], and they suppressed the rebellion without fighting; they took some hostages and not a few gifts and reduced these peoples to their former state of servility.

Charles, the tyrant[3] of Gaul, set out for Italy in the summer and took

14 For other accounts of the battle at Andernach see *AV* (von Simson 1909: 41); *AB* (Nelson 1991: 196-8); and Regino (Kurze 1890: 112).

15 Cf. 2 Kings 19.

16 Like the passage noted above (875 n. 10), this appears to have been written during Charles's lifetime.

17 He was there by November 11 (D LY 1).

18 These oaths have not survived. The division is reported by Regino 876 (Kurze 1890: 112); it correspondend to those made in the lifetime of Louis the German, except that the lion's share of Lotharingia went to Louis the Younger, with Charles the Fat only getting 'a few cities'. *AB* 876 (Nelson 1991: 198) give a different account of the diplomacy between the three brothers. See 866 n. 1, and below, 877 with n. 10 for the subsequent division of 'east Frankish' Lotharingia.

1 He issued diplomata there on January 4 and 26 (D LY 2-4).

2 See 858 with n. 7 and 869 with n. 2 for these tribes.

3 Here, as in the references to Charles as tyrant above under 873 and 875, meaning 'unjust ruler', though it is probably also an attack on Charles's 'imperial' pretensions (cf. 869 with n. 11 and 876 with n. 4). For the normal Carolingian meaning of the term see 879 with n. 10.

up residence in Pavia, from where he made great efforts to prevent Carloman, who was on his way, from entering the province.[4] But Carloman came into Italy with a great army of Bavarians and various Slav peoples, and prepared to fight against Charles.[5] When Charles learnt this, he took to flight immediately, as was his wont; for all the days of his life, whenever it was necessary to resist his opponents, he either fled openly or else secretly deserted his own soldiers.[6] On this same flight he caught dysentery and perished in great misery.[7] When his bodyguards wanted to take the corpse back to the vault he had prepared for himself at St-Denis, they were forced to bury it at a certain monastery in Burgundy,[8] because of the terrible stench of the putrid corpse by which the army was greatly afflicted. Carloman received the leading men of Italy, who came to him, and after ordering the region as he wished returned to Bavaria.[9]

King Louis divided his portion of Lothar's kingdom equally with his brothers Carloman and Charles.[10] Louis, the son of King Charles, afraid because of the injuries his father had done the king [Louis the Younger], sent ambassadors to him and sought to exculpate himself of everything which his father had done against Louis; the king heard

---

4 Carloman arrived in Italy in mid-September; for his claims to the kingdom see above, 874 with n. 13 and 875 with n. 8, and for Charles the Bald's expedition to Italy in 877 see *AB* 877 (Nelson 1991: 200-2) and Regino 877 (Kurze 1890: 112-13).

5 Carloman issued diplomata in Italy between October 16 and November 22 (DD Carloman 4-10).

6 Evidently obituary rather than comment; for examples of Charles's leaving his men see above 858. *AB* 877 (Nelson 1991: 202) depict Carloman as the one who fled.

7 On October 6; *AB* 877 (Nelson 1991: 202).

8 Nantua, west of Geneva.

9 The brief period during which he issued diplomata there (see n. 5) suggests that he did not make a serious attempt to rule until after Charles the Bald's retreat. He was back across the Alps by early December, before he had been able to gain recognition from John VIII; D Carloman 10 is dated November 20 from Verona, D Carloman 11 is dated December 3 from Ötting. His hurried return was forced on him by serious illness, from which he was never really to recover; see *AB* 877 (Nelson 1991: 203), and below, 879.

10 The main purpose of this 'spontaneous' share-out of Lotharingia seems to have been to establish a claim to part of Italy on the basis of the agreement of Ries (cf. 876 with n. 18), hence Carloman's immediate rejection of it (cf. 878 with n. 1). For Louis the Younger's interest in Italy see 878 and 879, and the statement he made at Fouron; *AB* 878 (Nelson 1991: 213. Charles appears to have received Alsace and the northern Burgundian *pagi*, Louis the remainder; Parisot 1899: 422-7.

them and allowed them to depart.[11] After this he set out for the palace of Aachen and there he celebrated Christmas.

In this year Italian fever and an eye-sickness troubled the German people,[12] especially those living around the Rhine; and a terrible malady followed Carloman's army on its return from Italy, so that many coughed up their lives.

878

In January the king came from Aachen to Frankfurt and there held an assembly with his men in the following month. Carloman gave back to Louis the part of Lothar's kingdom which he had received from his brothers the previous year to keep.[1] King Louis remained from Lent [February 5] until May in the royal *villa* called Salz,[2] and from there went to Frankfurt, where he held a general assembly.[3] He sent envoys to his brother Charles and divided with him the part of Lothar's kingdom which he had accepted from Carloman.

Lambert,[4] son of Wido, and Adalbert,[5] son of Boniface, entered Rome with a large army, and, after placing John, the Roman pontiff, under guard, forced the leading men of the Romans to affirm their allegiance to Carloman with an oath.[6] After they had gone, the same pope came to the church of St Peter's and took all the treasures which he found there to the Lateran and covered up the altar with sackcloth and closed all the doors of the church. No service was celebrated there for many days, and – shame to tell – entrance was denied to all those who had come there to pray, and everything there was in utter confusion. The

11 Louis the Stammerer had been crowned at Compiègne on December 8 877; see *AB* 877 (Nelson 1991: 204).

12 See 873 n. 14.

1 Cf. 877 n. 10.

2 He issued a diploma there on April 10 (D LY 8).

3 He issued a diploma at Frankfurt on May 26 (D LY 9).

4 Margrave of Spoleto, *c.* 860-*c.* 879. The older brother of Wido II of Spoleto, the later emperor (see 882(I) n. 5), his sister Rotilde was married to Adalbert; Hofmeister 1907: 353, 362-5; Hlawitschka 1983: 66-77..

5 Margrave of Tuscany, 834-86, and brother-in-law of Lambert of Spoleto (see n. 4); Hofmeister 1907: 333, 336-7, 345-7.

6 Lambert and Adalbert may have been acting on Carloman's behalf, as they were probably among the leading men who had acknowledged him at Pavia the previous year. But their action was also a continuation of earlier attacks on the papal state by the two margraves. See *MGH Epp.* 7: 68-71 nos. 73-4, 99-100 nos. 83-4 and Dümmler 1888: 73 for details.

said pope then took ship across the Tyrrhenian sea to Charles's kingdom and remained there almost a year.[7] In the end he called to him Count Boso, who had poisoned his own wife and taken the daughter of Louis the emperor of Italy by force, and returned with great plans to Italy and plotted with him to take away the kingdom of Italy from Carloman's power and give it to him to protect.[8]

King Louis came to Aachen in the month of October[9] and held a meeting not far from there with his namesake, the son of King Charles.[10]

There was an eclipse of the moon on the ides of the same month [October 15], in the last hour of the night. The sun also was so dimmed for about half an hour after the ninth hour of October 29, that stars appeared in the sky and all thought that night was threatening. There was a terrible cattle plague in Germany, especially around the Rhine, and this was followed by many deaths. There is a certain *villa* in the county of Worms, not far from the palace of Ingelheim, called *Walahesheim,*[11] where a remarkable thing happened. The dead animals were dragged daily from their stalls to the fields, where the village dogs, as is their wont, tore up and devoured them. One day almost all the dogs gathered together in one place and went off, so that none of them could be found afterwards either alive or dead.

879

King Louis celebrated Christmas in Forchheim, and from there he set off into Bavaria to see Carloman, who was seriously ill, having lost the

---

7 See *AB* 878 (Nelson 1991: 207–12) for this journey, which lasted more like six months (March to November 878).

8 On Boso see *AB* 876, 878, 879 (Nelson 1991: 189–90, 212, 219); Bautier 1973; Bouchard 1988. It is normally held, not least on the strength of this passage, that John VIII intended to crown Boso as emperor, but it is more likely that the Fulda annalist misunderstood what was really happening: John VIII intended to crown Louis the Stammerer as emperor – Boso had simply been sent back with him as a stop-gap to give him some support against Lambert and Adalbert (Fried 1976). The lady referred to is Ermengard; the marriage took place in 876, i.e. after the death of Louis II.

9 Before that he had been in Alsace (D LY 10, issued from Modern near Colmar on September 13).

10 At Fouron; see *AB* 878 (Nelson 1991: 207–13) for the treaty agreed there.

11 Exact location unknown; possibly Heidesheim on the Rhine between Mainz and Bingen.

ability to speak after a stroke.[1] There he received the leading men of the region who came to him, so that after Carloman's death they would not take any other as king over them nor allow any other to rule.[2] From there he moved on and celebrated Easter [April 12] in Frankfurt.

Louis, son of King Charles, died on April 11 in the palace at Compiègne, and was buried there. When the king learnt this he set off for Gaul with a large army and came as far as Verdun.[3] But the army which followed him, when it could not buy the necessary victuals from the citizens at the just price, took to looting, and plundered almost the whole city. The king sent some of his faithful men beyond the Meuse to the leading men of that region and returned to Francia[4] and came first to Mainz and from there to Frankfurt. There he received Count Erambert from Bavaria and some others who came to him, whom Arnulf had deprived of their public offices and expelled from the kingdom because of a dispute between them and his father Carloman.[5] On their behalf the king set off for Bavaria and restored peace to some extent between the disputants and gave them back their former offices.[6] This caused offence to some, as if the king had failed to keep

1 Perhaps following the attack on him in the previous year; see n. 5. But cf. 877 with n. 9 for the circumstances under which he left Italy; the phrase used here by the annalist echoes precisely what is said of his mother Emma in 874. Carloman was evidently still regarded as ruler in Italy, as most of his diplomata for 878 and 879 were issued for Italian, not Bavarian recipients (DD Carloman 12, 13, 16, 17, 22-8).

2 This was directed both against Louis's younger brother Charles, who got Italy (see n. 9) and against Carloman's illegitimate son Arnulf, prefect of Carinthia.

3 He issued a diploma at Metz on May 10 (D LY 12).

4 Date uncertain; see *AB* 879/80 (Nelson 1991: 216-20 with notes) and Werner 1979 for the background to Louis the Younger's expedition to west Francia, which was backed by Gauzlin and opposed by Hugh 'the Abbot'. In the end the west Franks agreed on a division between Louis the Stammerer's sons Louis and Carloman to keep Louis the Younger out.

5 *AS* 878 (*MGH SS* 30: 742) record that 'King Carloman was besieged at Ergolding by Count Erambert and his partners; Erambert was received by Louis in Francia.' Erambert was count of the Isargau, and so attacked Carloman on home ground (Ergolding is on the Isar, downstream from Landshut). The attack may have been the result of a private feud, or have had a more 'political' character and been intended to prevent Arnulf's succeeding to Carloman's kingdom – from the account above it is clear that he was already ruling *de facto* during his father's illness. See Bresslau 1923: 49-50; and for Erambert's fate below, 898.

6 Louis was in Regensburg on November 22 (D LY 13).

his oath. Those who know about the oath judge otherwise;[7] for Carloman, who was the oldest by birth, bound himself by oath first among the brothers and promised that he would keep all the terms of the oath; and then Louis swore on the same terms, on the understanding, however, that if Carloman kept the vows he had made intact he also would observe his promises. But when Carloman held his oath to be void in the division of the kingdom of the Lombards,[8] without doubt he released Louis from the terms of his oath; and hence Louis cannot be held guilty of the crime of perjury. Carloman, however, finally called Louis to him, and, since he could not speak, commended himself and his wife and son and the whole kingdom to him in writing.[9] The king placed bishoprics and abbacies and counties at his service, and after ordering the region as he wished returned to Francia.

Meanwhile Hugh, Lothar's son by Waldrada, was playing the tyrant in Gaul.[10] Against him the king sent certain of his faithful men to drive him out. When they arrived they besieged some of his men in a certain castle near Verdun, and after taking the castle they killed some, sent others into exile, and others they scalped and flayed and drove out from there in disgrace; then they destroyed the castle.

7 On the oath and the division see 876 with n. 10. For a similar piece of casuistry about royal motivation see the account of Louis the German's dilemma when confronted with the 'request' by west Frankish notables in 858.

8 See 877 n. 10.

9 Louis issued a diploma for Salzburg in Regensburg on November 22 (D LY 13). Carloman's testament has not survived; the mention of Carloman's wife and son (Arnulf) implies a degree of reconciliation between Louis and Arnulf, and in fact Arnulf kept his *honores* under Louis the Younger – noted by Regino 880 (Kurze 1890: 117) – and Charles the Fat. At about the same time as the transfer of Bavaria, Carloman surrendered his claims to the kingdom of Italy to his younger brother Charles: *Erchanberti continuatio* (*MGH SS* 2: 329) and see for the precise chronology BM 1505a and Dümmler 1888: 97-112. His last diploma for an Italian recipient was issued on August 11 (D Carloman 28); Charles's first was issued on November 15 (D C III 12).

10 For Hugh see Hincmar's account of the synod of Troyes – *AB* 878 (Nelson 1991: 211) – and further *AB* 867, 879, 880, 881, 882 (Nelson 1991: 139 and n. 7, 219, 221, 225). He had previously held benefices in Alsace from Louis the German. 'Playing the tyrant' does not refer to the nature of Hugh's rule but to its legitimacy (see 877 n. 3); in the eyes of the authors of *AF* and *AB* Hugh was not a legitimate king and they used appropriate terms for him and his following, which was in fact substantial; Parisot 1899: 444; Tellenbach 1979: 286-8.

880

The winter was hard and longer than usual: the Rhine and Main were frozen in the great cold and could be crossed on foot for a long time.

King Louis celebrated Christmas in Frankfurt; afterwards he left for Gaul, received the sons of Louis, who came to him, and took the whole of Lothar's kingdom into his power.[1] From there he turned his army to driving out the Northmen who had long been settled on the River Scheldt.[2] There was a battle in which more than five thousand of them were killed; the king's son Hugh also fell in that battle.[3]

There was an unhappy battle in Saxony against the Northmen, for the Northmen were victorious and killed two bishops: Thiotrih [of Minden] and Marcwart [of Hildesheim] and twelve counts: Brun, dux and the queen's brother, Wigmann, Bardo, a second and third Bardo, Thiotheri, Gerrich, Liutolf, Folcwart, Avan, Thiotric, Liuthar, with all who followed them. Besides this they killed eighteen royal vassals with their men: Adera, Alfwini, Addasta, Aida, another Aida, Dudo, Bodo, Wal, Haulf, Hildiwart, Ruodtag, Hitti, another Wal, Rather, Adalwin, Werinhart, Thiotrih, Ailwart, not to mention a great number whom they led off into captivity.[4]

The king returned from Gaul to Francia and celebrated Easter [April 3] at Frankfurt.[5] The Slavs called Daleminzi,[6] the Bohemians, and the

1 A reference to the treaty of Ribemont of February 880, by which Louis the Younger acquired the western half of Lotharingia; Parisot 1899: 437. For its practical implications (the west Frankish rulers evidently retained possession of parts of Lotharingia) see *AB* 882 (Nelson 1991: 223 with n. 2). For Louis's dealings with west Francia in 879/80 see above, 879 with n. 4. No diplomata survive to reveal his itinerary in this period.

2 In fact only since the previous year; they had come there from England; D'Haenens 1969: 45-9.

3 The battle took place at Thimeon, north of the Sambre. Hugh was an illegitimate son of Louis the Younger, whose only legitimate son had died after an accident the previous year; Dümmler 1888: 166-7.

4 The battle, whose precise location is unknown, took place on February 2. In spite of the very heavy losses, there do not seem to have been any serious consequences. The queen referred to is the Liudolfing Liutgard (see 866 n. 4); the other counts and royal vassals (*satellites regios*) cannot be identified with certainty, though from their names it is likely that Wigmann was an ancestor of the later Billung dukes of Saxony, and that Bardo, Liutolf and possibly Liuthar were related to the Liudolfings. See in general Harthausen 1966: 34-43. Lists of names of the kind found above are likely to be derived from arrangements made to preserve the memory of those killed by having their names recorded in *libri memoriales*.

5 D LY 14 was issued there already on March 23.

6 See 856 n. 4.

Sorbs and the other tribes in the neighbourhood, when they heard of the slaughter of the Saxons by the Northmen, came together and threatened to invade the lands of the Thuringians, and attacked the Slavs around the Saale faithful to the Thuringians with plunder and burning. Count Poppo,[7] *dux* of the Sorbian march, came against them with the Thuringians, and with God's help so defeated them that not one out of a great multitude remained.

Carloman, brother of Louis and Charles, died on March 22.[8]

Louis held an assembly with his men in mid-August at Worms and sent some of his faithful men to meet the envoys of his nephews at Gondreville,[9] and others against Hugh, who was playing the tyrant in Gaul.[10] But Henry and Adalhard[11] and the rest who were with them began a battle with Theobald,[12] the leader of Hugh's army, who had the bulk of his forces with him; and many died of their wounds on both sides. In this battle Henry won a bloody victory. When those who returned from Gondreville and those who returned from the battle joined together, they all set out with Louis's sons to fight against Boso in Gaul and, capturing the town of Mâcon, received the surrender of Bernard, who had ruled there. But Boso fled over the Rhone and took refuge in Vienne.[13]

The Northmen plundered and burnt in Gaul and among the many places and monasteries which were laid waste was Birten, where a great number of the Frisians lived, which they burnt. Turning away

7 Brother of Margrave Henry. In the group 3 manuscripts this sentence runs: 'Count Poppo came against them and defeated them with God's help'; ms. '2' omits 'with the Thuringians'.

8 This date, confirmed by other sources including perhaps Regino 880 (Kurze 1890: 116), who has the impossible 'VII. Non. Aprilis' instead of 'XI Kal. Aprilis' is probably correct, but another tradition has September 22 as the date of Carloman's death (see Dümmler 1888: 138; Bresslau 1923: 51; BM 1547c). He had in any case not effectively ruled for some time; see 879 with n. 9.

9 This meeting had been arranged earlier in the year; according to *AB* 880 (Nelson 1991: 221) Louis was unable to go himself because of illness.

10 See 879 n. 10.

11 For Henry see 866 with n. 4. Adalhard was count of Metz and lay abbot of Echternach from 878 to 890 (Parisot 1899: 399).

12 Son of Hubert, lay abbot of St-Maurice d'Agaune and brother of Lothar II's rejected wife Theutberga. Surprisingly enough, he was married to Bertha, Hugh's sister and the daughter of Lothar II's mistress Waldrada. This may imply a closing of ranks by 'native Lotharingians' against 'outsiders'; see Parisot 1899: 444–6 and Nelson 1991: 221 n. 6.

13 For Boso see above, 878 with n. 8; on Bernard's identity see *AB* 880 (Nelson 1991: 221 and n. 9).

from there they put a strong rampart and wall around Nimwegen and made themselves winter quarters in the king's palace. Louis came against them with a strong army, and returned without having accomplished much, because of the harshness of the winter and the strength of the fortifications.

In this year there was a harvest failure and a general shortage of everything in the counties of Worms and Nidda and in many places in Louis's kingdom, which affected the German people[14] not a little.

881

The winter was very long and bad for animals of all kinds. For the earth was still frozen in spring and denied the animals their accustomed fodder, and for the most part they died of hunger and the great cold, especially because of the shortage of the previous year.

The king set out for Gaul after Easter [April 23] and took Hugh, Lothar's son by Waldrada, who came to him, into his lordship, and gave him monasteries and counties in benefice so that he would keep faith with him. But he took the advice of wicked men and betrayed his allegiance and rebelled against the king; for which the king's army pursued him and forced him to flee into Burgundy.[1]

The king had a fitting meeting with his nephew Louis in Gondreville;[2] leaving there he spent the whole summer in Bavaria.[3] His nephew fought with the Northmen and triumphed nobly; for he is said to have killed nine thousand of their horsemen.[4] But they renewed their army and increased the number of horsemen and pillaged many places in the lands of our king: Cambrai, Utrecht, the county of Hesbaye and the whole of Ripuaria, especially the monasteries of Prüm, Cornelimünster, Stavelot, Malmedy and the palace of Aachen, where they used the king's chapel as a stable for their horses. Besides this they burnt Cologne and Bonn with their churches and buildings. Those who could escape, whether canons or nuns, fled to Mainz, bringing

14 *Germanicus populus*; see 873 n. 14.

1 See above, 879 and 880 for Hugh and his following.

2 Nothing more is known about this meeting.

3 Not confirmable; Louis was at Frankfurt on June 5 and September 22 (DD LY 19, 20) and at Regensburg on October 14 (D LY 21).

4 At Saucourt on August 3, the occasion for the *Ludwigslied* (see Fouracre 1985). Other accounts are given by *AV* 881 (von Simson 1909: 50), *AB* 881 (Nelson 1991: 222), with an unfavourable account and Regino 883 (Kurze 1890: 120); see Fouracre 1985 and Yeandle 1989 for commentary and background.

their church treasures and the relics of the saints with them. The king was seriously ill in Frankfurt, and as he could not go himself he sent his army against the Northmen.

There was a great earthquake just before cockcrow on December 30 at Mainz; the buildings were shaken and pots, as the potters claimed, were crashed together and broken.

882

A comet appeared on January 18 in the first hour of the night with an exceptionally long tail, which prefigured by its appearance the disaster which quickly followed. For Louis's illness grew worse and on January 20 he died.[1] His body was taken up and buried next to his father in the monastery of St Nazarius, which is called Lorsch.[2] Hearing this the army which had been sent against the Northmen broke off the attack and returned without finishing the business. The Northmen followed the tracks of the departing army and burnt with fire all that they had previously left intact, as far as the castle of Koblenz, where the Moselle enters the Rhine. The restoration of the city walls of Mainz was begun and a ditch was built around the walls outside the city.[3] The Northmen left their fortification and attacked the city of Trier, driving out or killing its inhabitants and burning it down completely on April 5. Wala, bishop of Metz, came against them rashly with a small army and was killed.[4]

[continuation in ms. 2]

The Emperor Charles, hearing of his brother's death, came from Italy to Bavaria and received his brother's leading men, who came to him, into his lordship.[5] From there he came to Worms and took counsel with his men who came from all sides as to how he might drive out the

1 He was still well enough to be credited with issuing diplomas on January 17 and 18 (DD LY 23 and 24).

2 On Lorsch as a burial-place see 876 n. 6.

3 The text of ms. '1' breaks off at this point.

4 The battle took place near Remich on the Moselle on April 10; Dümmler 1888: 162, and compare *AB* 882 (Nelson 1991: 224), with Hincmar's characteristically acid implication that the defeat served Wala right for breaking canon law by bearing arms, something which was common practice in the east Frankish kingdom, as *AF* shows; see in general Prinz 1971.

5 Charles did not hurry back from Italy: he was still in Pavia on April 17 (D C III 56) and the assembly at Worms was not held until the second half of May (DD C III 57, 58).

Northmen from his kingdom. A time was agreed among them and made known, and there came from various provinces innumerable men, an army to be feared by any enemy, if it had had a suitable leader and one it agreed on. There were Franks, Bavarians, Alemans, Thuringians and Saxons;[6] and they set out with one accord against the Northmen, wanting to fight them. When they got there, they laid siege to the Northmen's fortification, which is called Asselt.[7]

When the fortress was about to fall, and those within were struck with fear and despaired of escaping death, one of the emperor's counsellors, a false bishop called Liutward,[8] without the knowledge of the other counsellors who had been accustomed to assist the emperor's father, got together with the most treacherous Count Wigbert[9] and went to the emperor and persuaded him not to attack the enemy, having been bribed to do so, and presented the enemy *dux* Godafrid to the emperor. Like Ahab[10] the emperor received him as if he were a friend and made peace with him; and hostages were exchanged. The Northmen took this as a good sign, and so that it might not be doubted that they would observe the peace, they hoisted a shield on high after their fashion and threw open the doors of their fortress. Our men, knowing nothing of their treacherousness, went into the fortress, some to trade, some to look around the fortifications. The Northmen reverted to their usual treacherousness by hauling down the shield of peace and closing

6 *AF* 882(II) and Regino 882 (Kurze 1890: 119) mention Lombards as well, a sign that Charles could draw on troops from other kingdoms, as also in 884(II) when the Bavarians were sent off to Italy.

7 The manuscripts have *Ascloha*, where Charles issued a diploma (D C III 59) on July 20. The place is often identified with Elsloo on the Meuse, north of Maastricht. Asselt (near Swalmen, upstream from Venloo) seems more likely however, as Elsloo is far more than 14 miles from the Rhine (cf. 882 [II]). D'Haenens 1969: 312-15 reviews the evidence for both possibilities.

8 Bishop of Vercelli (880-900), Charles's archchancellor from 878 and archchaplain from 883 at the latest until his fall in 887 (see below). 'Counsellor' as a title implies a certain formal position, though more so south than north of the Alps; Keller 1967. The reference to the 'other counsellors' is to the replacement of Liutbert of Mainz, archchancellor under Louis the German and Louis the Younger, by Liutward. The annalist seems to have been closely connected with Liutbert of Mainz, which explains the hostility in his account to Liutward and to Charles III so long as Liutward was chancellor; Fleckenstein 1959: 186, 190-1; Keller 1966: 336-41; introduction, 8-9.

9 An associate of Hugh of Lotharingia; see Regino 883 (Kurze 1890: 120-1) and Keller 1966: 345 n. 33.

10 See 3 Kings 20—22 and the commentary by Hrabanus Maurus, *PL* 109: 214-20. Ahab was deceived by false prophets and had made peace with Benedad against God's declared will.

the gates: all our men inside were either killed or bound in chains and kept for later ransoming. But the emperor ignored the shame inflicted on his army, raised the aforementioned Godafrid from the baptismal font, and made the man who before had been the greatest enemy and traitor to his kingdom into a co-ruler over it. For the counties and benefices which the Northman Roric, a faithful man of the Frankish kings, had held in Kennemerland,[11] he gave to that same enemy and to his men to live in. What was still more of a crime, he did not blush to pay tribute to a man from whom he ought to have taken hostages and exacted tribute, doing this on the advice of evil men and against the custom of his ancestors the kings of the Franks. He took away the churches' treasures, which had been hidden for fear of the enemy, and to his own shame and that of all the army which followed him, gave to those same enemies 2,412[12] pounds of purest gold and silver. Moreover, he ordered that anyone in his army who should, moved by divine zeal in defence of Holy Church, kill a Northman who was trying to break into the camp, should either be strangled or blinded. The army was greatly saddened at this, and regretted that such a prince had come to rule over them, one who favoured the enemy and had snatched victory over the enemy away from them; and they returned to their homes greatly shamed. The Northmen, however, sent ships back to their country, loaded with treasure and captives two hundred in number;[13] they themselves remained in a safe place, waiting until there should again be a suitable opportunity for plundering.[14]

The emperor left there and came to Mainz, and from there to the *villa* of Tribur, where he stayed for many days. He held an assembly at Worms,[15] and issued decrees of little use. The Northmen burned the port called in the Frisian tongue Deventer, where St Liafwin lies, with

11 So also *AV* 882 (von Simson 1909: 51). For Roric see above, 850 with n. 2, 857 with n. 3. Kennemerland is the strip of Dutch coast running up from Harlem; the territory controlled by Godafrid was probably greater than this, as in 885 he is found with other counts under him, according to Regino 885 (Kurze 1890: 123).

12 The difference in quantity between the two versions is not explicable. According to *AB* 882 (Nelson 1991: 224–5) these payments were made to Sigifrid and Wurm, not to Godafrid; note that Hincmar also stresses the use of church treasures for paying the 'Danegeld'.

13 Or 'two hundred ships ... loaded with treasure and a number of captives'.

14 See 882 (II); there may also be a reference here to the raids on west Francia, for which see *AB* 882 (Nelson 1991: 225).

15 On November 1, according to *AB* 882 (Nelson 1991: 225); DD C III 61-4 are dated from Worms between November 4 and 13. This is a rare reference to an east Frankish ruler's having issued capitularies; cf. 852 n. 10.

great loss of life.

John the Roman pontiff died. In his place Marinus, who was already a bishop, succeeded, contrary to canon law.[16] A very wealthy man called Gregory, whom the Romans used to call a 'superista', was killed by his colleague in the forecourt of St Peter's, and the floor of the church was drenched with his blood as he was dragged over it.[17]

883

The emperor set out for Italy and consulted with his faithful men at the town of Verona[1] about the state of his kingdom.

Counts Poppo and Egino, *duces* of the Thuringians, clashed with each other and not a few men were killed. In the battle Poppo was defeated and scarcely escaped with a few men, the rest being killed.[2]

Godafrid the Northman, who had been baptised the previous year, made an alliance with Hugh, Lothar's son, and took his sister to wife. Hugh became bolder as a result of this, and planned to bring his father's kingdom under his own rule.[3]

The emperor remained in Italy the whole summer,[4] and alienated the leading men of the region. For he dismissed Wido[5] and some others

16 John VIII died on December 15 882; see 883(II), for a more detailed account of his death with notes. Marinus had been bishop of Caere (though he may have resigned; cf. Zimmermann 1968: 51-2) and had been a close adviser of Popes Nicholas I, Hadrian II and John VIII; Dümmler 1888: 214-15. Canon law forbade the translation of a bishop from one diocese to another, and the pope was the bishop of Rome.

17 There is almost certainly a connection between this and the death of John VIII, but what is unclear. Gregory may perhaps be identified with the *nomenclator* Gregory who was one of John VIII's main opponents in Rome; *AB* 878 (Nelson 1991: 208). However, the *superista* was a military office and the *nomenclator* was in charge of the charitable works in Rome; Noble 1984: 226-7, 248-9. Arnaldi 1990: 21 makes the two separate but related individuals.

1 Set out' does not mean immediately after the beginning of the year; Charles travelled through Alsace via Ulm to Regensburg (cf DD C III 66-75), where he was on April 5. He reached Verona by May 7 (D C III 77).

2 See 882(II) with n. 10, 883(II) with n. 8.

3 Hugh's sister was called Gisela. Regino 882 (Kurze 1890: 120) says that this marriage was part of the peace settlement between the Franks and Vikings the previous year.

4 His last diploma was issued in Italy on October 23 (D C III 93).

5 Wido II, margrave of Spoleto and Camerino, and later king of Italy and emperor. He had succeded Wido III, the son of Lambert (see 878 n. 4). See Hofmeister 1907: 365-9, Hlawitschka 1983, and below, 883(II), 884 (I & II)

and gave the benefices which they and their fathers and their grandfathers and their great-grandfathers had held to persons of much lower standing.[6] They took this very badly and with one accord planned to rebel against him, claiming back much more than they had previously held.

A mountain slipped from its place in Italy and fell into the Adige, blocking its flow. Those who lived in Verona and in places near to the same river had to do without it until it had, so to speak, made tunnels through the mountain and could return to its former bed.

The Northmen came up the Rhine and burned many places lately rebuilt, taking not a little plunder. Archbishop Liutbert of Mainz came against them with a few men; but he killed not a few of them and took back the plunder. Cologne was rebuilt apart from its churches and monasteries and its walls were provided with gates, bars and locks.

884

The Northmen tried to invade the Saxons. Count Henry and Bishop Arn [of Würzburg] came against them with a strong force of the eastern Franks, and when battle was joined many fell on both sides.[1] But in the end with God's help the Christians had the victory. It is said that Northmen of a beauty and size of body never before seen among the Frankish people were killed in this battle.

The emperor had a meeting with his men about the time of the Purification of the Blessed Mary [February 2] in the place in Alsace which is called Colmar,[2] and from there he sent bishops, abbots and counts against the Northmen to guard the frontiers of his kingdom.[3] The Northmen fought not just once or twice with Henry, and were defeated, and wherever they wished to go to plunder, they were put to

885 (II); Wido's dismissal was not an arbitrary action on Charles's part but was almost certainly connected with Wido's attacks on papal lands. See Dümmler 1888: 217–18.

6 In view of the annalist's account of the fall of Liutward of Vercelli (below, 887(I) with n. 3) this might be a reference to Liutward's party. For a similar insistence on the heritability of benefices at about this time see *AB* 882 (Nelson 1991: 225).

1 See 885(II) with n. 9.

2 DD C III 94–5 were issued there on February 14 and 15; by the 19th he was in Sélestat (D C III 96).

3 Regino 884 (Kurze 1890: 122) says that they had been allowed to pass up the Rhine by Godafrid; he also confirms the success of Henry's defence.

flight and killed, God giving them what they deserved. Then, as the
Christians came together as one, seeking to attack their stronghold,
they were struck with fear and fled at night; Henry followed them to
the crossing of the Rhine, and finding them in a certain place slew one
hundred and two of them without loss to his own men.

The emperor had a meeting at Worms in the middle of May[4] and from
there he sent guardians of his frontiers against the Northmen.
Lothar'sdaughter, who had been sent to the emperor by Godafrid, to
whom she had been given in marriage, also came there. The emperor
kept her with him for a time and did not allow her to return to her
husband.[5]

The emperor had a meeting with Zwentibald on the Bavarian–Slav
border.[6] From there he set off for Italy and there he was reconciled to
Wido and the others whom he had offended the previous year.[7]

The Northmen fought with the Frisians in a place called Norden and
were defeated and many of them were killed. There is a letter about
this battle, which Rimbert, bishop of the same place, sent to Archbishop Liutbert of Mainz, which runs as follows: ....[8]

Charles [Carloman], the young king of Gaul, is said to have been
killed by a boar while hunting; in fact he was unintentionally wounded
by one of his vassals while hunting, and died.[9] As a result of this the
Northmen, who for a long time had wearied his land with plundering
and burning, became bolder, and demanded 12,000 pounds of gold and

---

4 DD C III 100-1 were issued there on May 22 and 23; 103 on June 11.

5 See 883(I) n. 3; according to Regino 885 (Kurze 1890: 124) Gisela was still with
  Godafrid when he was killed the following year.

6 See 884(II) for the background to this. Charles was at Regensburg in mid-
  September (D C III 107-8).

7 Wido of Spoleto; see above, 883 with n. 5. Charles was in Friuli by November
  16 (D C III 110) and at Pavia by Christmas (884(II)).

8 The letter is not in the manuscript, nor has it survived elsewhere. Rimbert
  (865-88) was (arch)bishop of Bremen, not of Norden; he was the pupil and
  biographer of Ansgar (Weinfurter and Engels 1984: 16-17).

9 On December 12. AV 884 (von Simson 1909: 55) also has this story, naming the
  vassal as Bertold, while Regino 884 (Kurze 1890: 121-2) offers both 'wounded
  by a boar', and, 'as some say', the story above, with the gloss that the king
  himself concealed the truth so that his follower should not be put to death as
  an innocent man. Both here and in what follows the annalist suppresses all
  mention of the fact that Charles III of east Francia was invited by the west
  Frankish nobility to succeed the dead Carloman as king, and accepted in June
  885; cf. AV 884 (von Simson 1909: 56), Regino 884 (Kurze 1890: 122) and
  Dümmler 1888: 234.

silver from the region as tribute, and even after that did not keep the faith which they had promised, for they killed their hostages and did not cease at all from plundering.[10]

885

The same Northmen invaded the Hesbaye and occupied the regions around it and, gathering crops of various kind together, made plans to over-winter there and live there, as if there were none to resist them. They set aside for their service those men and women whom they could find. Archbishop Liutbert [of Mainz] and Count Henry and some others came upon them unexpectedly and, having killed many of them, forced the rest to take refuge in a certain small fortification and took away from them the supplies which they had gathered together. Besieged for a long time, and wearied by hunger, they did not dare to risk open battle and fled one night.[1]

Godafrid the Northman, who had become a Christian and promised on oath to keep faith with the emperor and the Christian people, broke his faith, gathered not a small army from his people, and prepared to come up the River Rhine and put many places under his dominion. He had begun to do this around the middle of May, but God was against it and he was unable to carry out his plan. For he was invited to a meeting by Henry and other faithful men of the emperor and accused of treason; and, when he had infuriated them by abuse and scornful words, he was killed, along with all who were with him. God gave him the due reward for his treachery.[2]

10 The demands of the Viking Great Army for a tribute of 12,000 pounds had been made early in the year and a truce arranged until October, in which time the money was to be collected; *AV* 884 (von Simson 1909: 55). The tribute-payment thus preceded Carloman's death. According to Regino 884 (Kurze 1890: 122), the Northmen claimed on hearing of Carloman's death that their treaty had been with him and 'whoever it might be who succeeded him in the kingdom he would have to pay the same sum and quantity of money if he wished to hold rule in peace and quiet', which might explain the account in *AF*.

1 On these campaigns, in which forces from west Francia also took part, see *AV* 885 (von Simson 1909: 56-7) and Regino 884 (Kurze 1890: 122).

2 Regino 885 (Kurze 1890: 123-4) gives a much fuller account of this, confirmed in a short notice by *AV* (von Simson 1909: 57). Regino says that Godafrid made demands through his followers Gerulf and Gardulf of Charles III for fiscal lands at Koblenz, Andernach, Sinzig and other places, so that he could have adequate supplies of wine – Regino's gloss is that if this were granted he would be able to spy out the land and if not he would have a good excuse for breaking the agreement of 882. Henry went together with Archbishop Willibert of Cologne to meet Godafrid on an island at *Herespich* where the Rhine and the

But the Northmen whom he had summoned did not know what had
been done and set off for Saxony to plunder. A few Saxons came
against them, but, fearing to offer resistance to so large an army, fled;
and the Northmen, although they were already a long way from their
ships, followed the fleeing men as if to take them prisoner. Meanwhile
the Frisians who are called the 'Destarbenzon',[3] as if sent by God, came
along in tiny ships, as is their custom, and began to attack the
Northmen from the rear. When they saw this, the Saxons, who had at
first fled, returned and made a fierce counter-attack, and so battle was
joined from both sides against the Northmen. At length the Christians
made such a slaughter of them that very few were left of the whole
multitude. After this had been done, the same Frisians attacked their
ships, and there they found such treasure in gold, silver and other
kinds of moveable goods that all from the smallest to the greatest were
made rich.

It was alleged to the emperor that Hugh, the son of King Lothar,
whose sister the aforementioned Godafrid had taken to wife, had taken
part in the conspiracy which Godafrid had organised against the
emperor's kingdom. For this reason he was summoned to the emperor
and convicted of the crime; he was blinded, together with his uncle,
and shut away in the monastery of St Boniface at Fulda, and so there
was an end to his tyranny.[4] The others who were with him were stripped
of their horses, arms, and clothing, and scarcely escaped naked.[5]

The emperor held an assembly with his men at Frankfurt[6] and sent
envoys to Rome to invite Pope Hadrian to Francia. For he wished, as
the rumour went, to depose certain bishops unreasonably and set up
Bernard, his son by a concubine, as heir to the kingdom after him, and

Waal meet; Willibert persuaded Gisela to leave the island and talk of peace, and
in the meantime Godafrid and his following were provoked in the course of a
discussion of the losses incurred by Eberhard, a Frisian count, and killed.

3 The inhabitants of Testerbant.

4 See above, 879 with n. 10, 883 with n. 3, 884 with n. 5, for Hugh's attempts to
establish himself in Lotharingia and his alliance with Godafrid and for the
terms 'tyrant', 'tyranny'. Hugh's uncle appears here only (Parisot 1899: 477).
Regino 885 (Kurze 1890: 125) adds that Hugh was taken first to St Gallen,
then 'recalled to his country', and finally sent to Prüm. AV 885 (von Simson
1909: 57) ascribe the action to the Babenberger Henry. Tellenbach 1979 and
Parisot 1899: 442-77 give good commentaries on Hugh's late career.

5 I.e. they were a landless armed following; cf. Reuter 1985: 83-4. Regino 883
(Kurze 1890: 120-1) mentions a number of Hugh's more high-ranking
followers, who were evidently not affected by his fate.

6 He issued diplomata there between September 6 and September 23 (DD C III
130-2).

because he doubted that he could do this himself, he wanted to have it done by the Roman pontiff, as if by apostolic authority.[7] By the judgement of God his deceitful plans were frustrated; for the Roman pontiff had set out from Rome and crossed the River Po when he ended this life and was buried in the monastery of Nonantula.[8] When the emperor heard of this, he was greatly saddened, because he had not been able to accomplish what he had wished in this matter. After a few days, therefore, he came to Mainz, and from there to Worms; from there, after he had had a meeting with the bishops and counts of Gaul,[9] he set out for Bavaria, where he celebrated Christmas.

When the Romans heard of the death of their pontiff, they set up Stephen in his place. The emperor was furious at the fact that they had presumed to ordain anybody without consulting him, and sent Liutward [of Vercelli] and some bishops of the Roman see[10] to depose him. But they were unable to do this. For the said pontiff sent by ambassadors to the emperor the names of more than thirty bishops, and of all the cardinal priests and deacons and persons of lesser rank, and also letters from the leading laymen of the region, who had all unanimously elected him and subscribed his ordination.[11]

7 From this point on, Charles's reign was increasingly dominated by the succession question; presumably he no longer expected to have legitimate heirs by his wife Richgardis (see below, 887(I) n. 5). The deposition of the bishops and the acceptance of Bernard as heir were evidently connected; the episcopal opposition was probably led by Liutbert of Mainz. Bernard was seen by Notker the Stammerer as a successor – *Gesta Karoli* II, 14–15 (Haefele 1959: 74, 78) – and Charles may have revived these plans in early 887, since a letter from Stephen V (JL 3428 = *MGH Epp.* 7: 340, no. 14) shows that he had asked the pope to attend an assembly a fortnight after Easter. See Hlawitschka 1978: 23–4 and for a general discussion of the succession and Charles's reign Reuter 1991: 117–20.

8 The date of Hadrian's death is not known precisely; his predecessor Marinus was pope for one year and between three and five months, and he himself was pope for one year and four months. This puts his death in August or September of 885, which conforms with the account above but adds no extra precision to it.

9 He was at Worms on October 1 (D C III 133) and at Regensburg on January 7 (D C III 134). This passage is the only hint in this text that Charles had become king in west Francia, though his diplomata (DD C III 116-26) show him as having spent May and June there.

10 I. e. suburbican bishops, bishops whose bishoprics lay in the province of Rome.

11 Charles thought that the pope should first have sworn fidelity to him, as laid down by the *Constitutio Romana* of 824; *MGH Capit.* 1: 322-3 no.161, and cf. Noble 1984: 310-23. In fact Stephen had acted in agreement with the imperial legate in Rome, according to *Liber Pontificalis*, c. 112 (Duchesne 1892: 191-2), and it was presumably for this reason rather than because of the notice of election that Charles had to back down.

886

In the month of February an army of the eastern Franks was sent into Gaul against the Northmen, who were near Paris. On the journey they suffered not inconsiderable losses to their horses through floods and sudden cold. However, when they had arrived there, the Northmen, who were well stocked with all things in their fortifications, did not want to fight with them, nor did they dare to. So the whole of Lent [February 9] and the time up to Rogation Day [May 1] was wasted in empty effort, except that Henry, finding some outside the fortifications, killed them. They took many horses and oxen from there and returned to their homes.[1] Meanwhile Hugh and Gauzlin, abbots and the leading generals of Gaul, in whom lay all the hope of the Gauls against the Northmen, died.[2] At this the Northmen became bolder, and came out from their fortifications, and took possession of the whole region, and were able to hunt and sport with no one to prevent them.

The best quarter of the city of Mainz, where the Frisians lived, burnt down in March after mid-Lent [February 27]. And in May, June and July there was such rainfall day and night without stopping that no one of the present age was able to say that he had seen such abundance of water. As a result rivers swelled in many places and did great damage to all kinds of crops. For the Rhine burst its banks and swept away all the corn, flax, and hay at places close to it from where it rises to the place where it enters the sea. The Po is said to have behaved in a similar fashion in Italy.

In the month of July the emperor had a meeting with his men in the town of Metz and from there set off against the Northmen.[3] While he was staying there Count Henry was abandoned by his men, sur-

---

1 This first unsuccessful relief expedition by the eastern Franks is also mentioned by Regino 887 (Kurze 1890: 125), *AV* 886 (von Simson 1909: 59) and Abbo, *De Bello Parisiaco* II, verses 3-34 (Waquet 1942: 66-9). *AV* say that Henry's help was requested by Bishop Gauzlin of Paris after the loss of a tower built against the besiegers with those inside it.

2 Hugh, lay abbot of Auxerre, died on May 12; Gauzlin, bishop of Paris, on April 16. On them see Werner 1979, Nelson 1991, *passim* and Abbo, *De bello Parisiaco* II, verses 70-6 (Waquet 1942: 70-3).

3 He issued a diploma at Metz on July 30 (D C III 137), another at Attigny on August 16 (D C III 138), and reached Paris in slow stages by October 24 at the latest (D C III 142).

rounded by the enemy, and killed.[4] Meanwhile Sigifrid came with a
great host of Northmen to bring help to the others who were already
in residence, and caused great fear among the Christians. At this the
emperor, terrified, gave leave to some to go plundering through
Burgundy, and promised much money to others if they would leave his
kingdom by a time agreed between them.[4] He, however, hurried
swiftly away from there and took himself off into Alsace, where he lay
ill for many days.[5]

887

The winter was hard and longer than usual; there was an unusually
severe plague among cattle and sheep in Francia, so that almost none
of these kinds of animal was left alive.

The emperor held a meeting with his men in Waiblingen.[1] In earlier
times, that is from when he was set up as king in Alemannia, he had
exalted one of his men of low birth called Liutward above all who were
in his kingdom, so that he surpassed in both rank and dignity that
Haman who is mentioned in the book of Esther.[2] For Haman was
second after King Ahasuerus; but Liutward was greater than the
emperor and was honoured and feared by all more than the emperor.
For he carried off the daughters of the most noble men in Alemannia
and Italy without opposition, and gave them to his relatives in
marriage. He went so far in his stupidity, indeed in his madness, that
he invaded the nunnery in Brescia and had certain of his friends carry

---

4 Henry, who had been sent on ahead, was killed on August 28; his horse fell into
   a kind of tank trap built by the Northmen and he was cut off from his followers
   and killed; *AV* 886 (von Simson 1909: 61-2); Regino 886 (Kurze 1890: 125-6);
   Dümmler 1888: 269 n. 2 gives the date of death and further references.

5 *AV* 886 (von Simson 1909: 62) mention winter as a further reason for the
   armistice, though they regard the peace settlement as disgraceful. The
   diversion of the Northmen to Burgundy, according to Regino 887: 127, was
   because 'the inhabitants of those regions refused to obey him', a reference
   perhaps to a Burgundian refusal to join Charles's army, perhaps to Boso. Abbo,
   De bello Parisiaco II, verses 330-46 (Waquet 1942: 90-3) says that Charles
   offered 700 pounds of silver to the Northmen to be gone by March.

6 He was still at Paris on November 6 (D C III 149); by November 12 he was
   already on his way (D C III 150 was issued at *Iovilla nova*, perhaps Janville near
   Compiègne); in January he is found at Schlettstadt (DD C III 152, 153, 155)
   and in February at Rottweil (DD C III 156-7).

1 He issued a diploma there on May 7 (D C III 158).

2 Cf. Esther 3, and, for the annalist's attitude to Liutward, above, 882(I).

off by force the daughter of Count Unruoch,[3] a relative of the emperor, and gave her to his relative in marriage. But the nuns of that same place turned to prayer, and beseeched God that he would revenge the shame brought upon that holy place; and their prayers were heard on the spot. For the man, who was about to consummate his marriage with the girl in the usual way, died that same night, by the hand of God, and the girl remained a virgin. This was revealed to one of the nuns called ...[4] in that nunnery and she told the story to the others. However, after the aforementioned Liutward had been doing this kind of thing in the emperor's kingdom for many years, puffed up with vanity and blinded by greed, he at length sought to pervert the Catholic faith and diminish our Redeemer, saying that he was one in the unity of substance, not of person, whereas Holy Church believes and confesses Him to have had one person in two substances. Whoever denies this immediately blasphemes Him who came to seek and to save that which is lost. For if He were not truly God, He would not have brought salvation; if He were not truly man, He would not have offered an example.[5] But the same King of Kings in this year turned the emperor's mind against the blasphemer; having had discussions with his men in a place called Kirchen[6] he deposed him from his office of archchaplain, took many benefices away from him, and expelled him from the palace with ignominy as a heretic and a man hated by all. But Liutward took himself to Arnulf in Bavaria and began to plot with him how he might deprive the emperor of his kingdom; and this was done.[7]

3 On the rivalry between Liutward and Berengar, see 886(II) with n. 8. Unruoch I, Berengar's brother, had died in 874 (Hlawitschka 1960: 276-7); he was a descendant of Louis the Pious through Gisela and Eberhard of Friuli, and hence Charles III's relative.

4 The name is missing in the manuscript.

5 A further charge brought against Liutward was that of adultery with Queen Richgardis, according to Regino 888 (Kurze 1890: 127); she cleared herself by claiming that she was still a virgin after more than ten years of marriage, and retired to the monastery she had founded at Andlau in Alsace; Dümmler 1888: 284 n. 2.

6 May–June 887. On May 30 887 Liutward was still acting as archchancellor (D C III 159); by June 16 he had been replaced by Liutbert of Mainz (DD C III 160-1). It is almost certainly not a coincidence that Charles had a meeting with Boso's son, Louis (the Blind) at this time: see 887(II) with n. 6.

7 Liutward's role in the fall of Charles is mentioned here only. He was sufficiently close to Arnulf to have taken part in a prominent position in the synod of Mainz in May 888 (Hartmann 1989: 361), but seems after that to have retired to Italy, where he was killed by the Hungarians in June 900;Regino 901 (Kurze 1890: 148) and Dümmler 1888: 509 n. 1. A diploma of Charles's (D C III 170) which can be dated either to December (Keller 1966: 362-7) or more probably to September 887 restores lands to a relative of Liutward's and

For as the same emperor was staying in the *villa* of Tribur, waiting for the arrival of his men from all sides, Arnulf came on him with a strong army of Bavarians and Slavs, and was a great trouble to him.[8] For all the leading men of the Franks who had conspired against the emperor came to him, and he received them into his allegiance. Those who refused to come he deprived of their benefices, and he left nothing to the emperor except the vilest of persons to serve him. The emperor sent to him by Archbishop Liutbert [of Mainz] the wood of the Holy Cross on which he had formerly sworn loyalty to him, so that he might be reminded of his oaths and not behave so cruelly and barbarously to him. He is said to have shed tears at the sight; however, having ordered the kingdom as he wished, he returned to Bavaria.[9] The emperor, however, together with the few who were with him, went back to Alemannia.[10]

suggests that there was at least a partial reconciliation before Charles's deposition.

8 For these events see also 887(II). Further accounts of significance are in Regino 887 (Kurze 1890: 127-8): 'After these events the emperor began to sicken in body and mind. In November around the feast of St Martin [November 11] he came to Tribur and summoned a general assembly. When the leading men of the kingdom saw that his powers not only of body but also of mind were deserting him they of their own accord summoned Arnulf, son of Carloman to the kingdom, and after conspiring suddenly deserted the emperor and went over to Arnulf in a body, so that within the space of three days hardly anyone remained who would even fulfil the duty of humanity to him. He received food and drink by the kindness of (Arch)bishop Liutbert' [after which Charles commended his son Bernard to Arnulf and received from him a few estates in Alemannia to live on]; in *AV* 887 (von Simson 1909: 64): 'The eastern Franks, seeing that the emperor's strength was inadequate to rule the empire, ejected him from the kingdom and set his nephew, Arnulf son of Carloman, on the throne'; and in *AH* 887 (Waitz 1878b: 19): 'Charles came to Tribur, and as he held a general assembly after the feast of St Martin, there was a conspiracy against him, and the eastern Franks left him and elected Arnulf as king, and Charles submitted to Arnulf.' See also the account in *ASC* 888 cited 888(II) n. 2. These passages have received much attention from German historians, since the deposition of Charles III and elevation of Arnulf can be seen as marking at least an important stage in the emergence of a German kingdom. What is quite clear is that it was the eastern Franks who acted; what is not clear is how far they saw themselves acting for the whole of the Frankish empire, and whether the leading men of east Francia or Arnulf himself played the more important role. These are questions which probably cannot be answered without pressing the sources too far. For recent discussions see Keller 1966; Hlawitschka 1968: 31-64; Hlawitschka 1969; Schlesinger 1969; Hlawitschka 1978; Reuter 1991: 119-20.

9 Arnulf was in Forchheim on December 11 and in Regensburg by January 1 (DD A 2, 5).

10 Where his support was and where, according to Regino 887: 128 and the Bavarian continuator 887(II), Arnulf had granted him estates.

The Northmen, hearing of the dissensions among the Franks and the casting-down of their emperor, laid waste places which they had previously hardly touched. They are said to have come as far as the town of Rheims, but God for the merits of St Remigius surrounded the monastery outside the city and the city itself with a dense fog for the space of three days, so that they could not find or even see either the monastery or the city. So, amazed, and ashamed as well, they departed.[11]

[882: continuation in the manuscripts of group 3]

The Northmen seized everything that they could and – what was worse and more horrible to see – burnt some places and churches and ruined others and returned to their fortress which was surrounded by a wall and situated on the banks of the Meuse in a place called Asselt,[1] fourteen miles from the Rhine.

When Charles heard of the death of his elder brother, he made his way from Italy through Bavaria to Francia, and held a general assembly at Worms in the month of May, receiving the leading men from his brother's kingdom.[2] After this he gathered troops from the whole of his kingdom. He took the Lombards, Alemans and Franks with him and moved up the western bank of the Rhine against the Northmen; the Bavarians proceeded up the eastern bank as far as Andernach, where they crossed over. There the army divided: the Bavarians, under their prince, Arnulf,[3] and the Franks under Henry[4] were sent with a strong force in advance of the king and the army so that they might find an unprepared and unsuspecting army outside their fortifications and capture them in ambushes, following the thought in the poet's famous verse:[5]

What do I care whether I win by force or tricks?

11 Vogel 1906: 342-7 gives details of these attacks, which affected the eastern part of Neustria and northern Burgundy.

1 For the location see 882(I) with n. 7.

2 For the chronology see 882(I) n. 5.

3 Note that Arnulf appears here commanding all the Bavarians; he had actually preserved his position under Louis the Younger, cf. 879 n. 9 and Regino 880 (Kurze 1890: 117): 'The king also conceded Carinthia to Arnulf, which his father had already allowed him; here there is a most well-fortified castle called Mosapurc because the place is surrounded by an impenetrable marsh and thus makes access to it most difficult for those who wish to enter it.'

4 See 866 n. 4.

5 The author here cited has not been identified.

And so it would have turned out, if some of our men from among the Franks, bribed as it was said, had not been traitors and prevented it.[6] However, having killed a few men, they returned to the king. On their return the king straightaway set out with all his army and occupied the Northmen's territory and besieged their fortifications with their kings inside, that is Sigifrid and Godafrid and the princes Wurm and Hals. He had the camps of the army set up in a circle around the city and so held it besieged for twelve days. Then one day a thing remarkable for both besiegers and besieged occurred. For on July 21 in the afternoon a sudden darkness covered the whole of the sun, and with thunder and lightning there was such a hailstorm that no mortal could claim to have seen anything like it before. The hailstones were not, as they usually are, smooth and equal in size, but jagged and unequal and with rough edges, so that they offered to all who beheld them an unusual and extraordinary spectacle. It is remarkable and incredible to relate that they could scarcely or not at all be spanned with one's thumb and middle finger. The horses were so startled that they uprooted their tethering-posts and tore their bridles and ran around wildly and in fright both inside and outside the camps. A great part of the city which they were besieging also collapsed under the storm, so that a column in formation could have ridden in if the wall which surrounded it had not held them back. Because the siege had gone on for so many days in the summer, the great army began to fall ill and be nauseated by the putrefaction of the many corpses. Those who were trapped inside were no less oppressed. There were negotiations between the two sides, and it was agreed that we should give hostages, and that Sigifrid,[7] who was stronger, should come outside the fortifications for a distance of six miles to the king. First he swore on oath that from that hour onwards as long as the Emperor Charles should live he would never again come into his kingdom to plunder it as a enemy.[8] Then he accepted Christianity, and the emperor himself stood godfather at his baptism. They spent two days there together in joy, and then our hostages were sent back from the fortification, and he contrariwise returned home with great gifts. These were the gifts: in gold and silver 2,080 pounds or a little more[9] (we reckon a pound as being twenty *solidi*). Once the affair had been settled in this way the

---

6 Compare the much more explicit accusations in 882(I).

7 Presumably a slip of the pen for Godafrid.

8 Note the parallel with the agreement of 872 above.

9 See 882(I) with n. 12.

king departed and in the castle of Koblenz he graciously allowed his army leave to go home.

Civil war broke out between the Saxons and the Thuringians at the instigation of Count Poppo, the brother of Henry, and Count Egino.[10] After a great slaughter, Poppo and the Thuringians were defeated.

When the Bavarians had returned home, a great and terrible plague broke out in the whole of Bavaria, so that often two bodies were buried in one grave. The king, however, remained in Germany,[11] and held an assembly at Worms before Christmas.[12] Here he received all kinds of embassies from the Moravians and other peoples,[13] and after hearing them and settling affairs returned to Alemannia. Henry, however, was sent against the Northmen.[14] He settled matters as well as he could, and returned.

883

Caesar celebrated Christmas in Alemannia.[1] From there he gradually made his way towards Bavaria and spent Easter [March 31] with ceremony in the city of Regensburg.[2] There he held a meeting, and having heard a number of things from Italy, returned to that country.[3] For at Rome, the bishop of the apostolic see, John by name, was first poisoned by his relative and then, as he was thought by this man and other companions in his crime to be likely to live longer than would suit their desires — for they wanted both his treasure and to seize the ruling of the bishopric — was struck with a hammer until his skull was bashed in, and died. But the perpetrator of this evil deed, terrified by the raging crowd around him, was seen to die on the spot, though he

10 For Poppo see 880 n. 6. Egino was a count in eastern Franconia who died in 886 (Schmid *et al.* 1978b: 382); nothing is known about the causes of the feud.

11 *Germania*, here probably meaning Franconia.

12 November 1, according to *AB* 882: 225; Charles issued diplomata there from November 4 to 13 (DD C III 62-4).

13 Including the west Franks, who wanted to do a deal over the implementation of the 880 treaties on Lotharingia; see *AB* 882 (Nelson 1991: 225).

14 Who had raided Deventer; see 882(I).

 1 His power-base, though whereabouts in Alemannia is not known; he was at Colmar on January 9 (D C III 66).

 2 He was at Colmar on January 9, Mindersdorf near Zollern in mid-February, Ulm on February 25 and Regensburg from March 23 to April 5 (DD C III 66-75).

 3 He was in Verona on May 7 (D C III 76). Note 'returned'; Italy was an important source of power for Charles.

was not wounded or harmed by anyone. In John's place it was agreed
unanimously by acclamation of the whole Roman people that Marinus
should be ordained, who at that time was held in the city of Rome to
be an archdeacon.[4] The emperor set out to meet the pope and receive
him with the honour due to him at a place called Nonantula.[5] There
among other things Wido,[6] count of the Tuscans, was accused of
treason, which he avoided by taking flight. But that flight immediately
shook the whole of Italy with fear; for he straightaway made a firm
alliance with a strong band of pagans from the people of the Moors.
Berengar, a relative of the emperor's, was sent to deprive Wido of his
kingdom.[7] This he did in part, and would have completed, if illness and
weakness amongst his army had not forced him to return. And indeed
the human race throughout Italy was affected by the spread of the
sickness, to such an extent that the disease even penetrated to the
court and among the king's bodyguard and to the king himself.

A feud, followed by cruel fighting, again broke out between Poppo and
Egino. Poppo, as he had been before, was the loser.[8] Henry, that is
Poppo's brother, as soon as he learnt that a strong army of the
Northmen was coming, crushed them with his men, so that it is said
that not one escaped.[9] But he himself was also wounded.

4 See 882(I) with n. 16. The Latin is ambiguous – it could either mean that Marinus
   was thought to be an archdeacon (and hence not to be a bishop, so that there
   would be no canonical objection to his becoming pope) or that he held the office
   of archdeacon. It is extremely improbable that the Romans did not know that
   Marinus was a bishop, if he in fact was one, even if the annalist was uncertain.

5 Late in May; he issued a diploma there on May 24 (D C III 78).

6 Wido II, margrave of Spoleto and later king of Italy and emperor; why he is
   here called count of the Tuscans is unclear. On him see 883(I) with n. 5.

7 Margrave of Friuli, c. 874-88; king and subsequently emperor of Italy. His
   mother Gisela was a daughter of Louis the Pious, hence he and Charles the Fat
   were cousins (Werner 1967: table). Kingdom (*regnum*) means here, as often in
   Carolingian narrative sources, a region with its own historically developed
   political consciousness, such as Aquitaine, Bavaria or as in this case Spoleto; it
   does not imply that Wido was a king. See Werner 1981: 175-222; Goetz 1987:
   171-90.

8 See 882(II) with n. 10.

9 The raids referred to here and in 884 (I) are difficult to sort out, particularly
   as the manuscript reading of 883(II) is uncertain: ms. '3' has *Prumiam*, i.e.
   'when he heard that a strong army of the Northmen was coming to Prüm',
   while '3c' and '3e' have *primum*, as translated above. If Prüm were accepted,
   then Henry's battle would seem to fit in with the campaigning in the Rhine
   valley, in which Liutbert also took part. It seems more probable, however, that
   primum should be read, not least because Regino has no mention of such a raid.
   If so, the account here probably refers to the same events as are described at
   the beginning of 884(I) Cf. Hellmann 1908: 56 n. 4.

884

After the king had returned to Alemannia a general assembly was held in the *villa* called Colmar. There it was decreed that the Bavarians should leave for Italy to fight against Wido.[1]

Pannonia suffered great losses; how this came about we shall now proceed to explain. Two brothers, William and Engelschalk, had been given the frontier of the kingdom of the Bavarians by the king, that is Louis the Elder, to hold against the Moravians, and they are said to have fought hard in defence of the fatherland.[2] At length, when they had ended their lives, still in action, their office was not given to their sons, but rather to Arbo, by the concession of the lord king, succeeded to the county. The sons of the said men, and their relatives, took this badly, and said that one of two things would happen: either Count Arbo, if he did not give up their ancestors' county, or they themselves should die at the edge of the sword. Arbo was frightened at the news of this, and entered into a friendship with Zwentibald, *dux* of the Moravian people, and when the agreement had been completed he did not shrink from giving his son[3] as a hostage. The said sons won over to their side some of the leading men of the Bavarian people and gathered together their relatives and troops came to them from all sides, so that they had a strong army. They expelled with dishonour the count installed by the king, and usurped the county for their own use.[4] This was done after the death of Louis and of his children Carloman and Louis, whose successor, their younger brother, holds the kingdom. He gave Arbo the county back as he had held it before, but as the consequence of this was that Pannonia suffered great loss, we have inserted four small verses on how it happened into our text for the delectation of the reader, as follows:

Jesus says that no kingdom can remain firm
When divided in itself; and no discord can be stable
From this come betrayal and fear to you, most beautiful land,
From this comes trouble for Pannonia, once happy.

For in the same year as those sons robbed the aforementioned count,

1 February 2; see 884(I). On Wido's revolt see 883(I), 883(II), and below 884(II).

2 On them see above, 871.

3 Presumably the Isanrich who is found in 898 in close contact with the *duces* of Moravia; see below.

4 Presumably in 882, since later on the annalist talks of the feud having lasted two and a half years.

that is Arbo, of the honours which had been bestowed on him by the king, Zwentibald, *dux* of the Moravians, a man with a mind full of trickery and cunning, remembering how much his people had suffered from the ancestors of those sons when they were in charge of the Bavarian march, and also the friendship and the oath which he had sworn to Arbo, set out to avenge this injury, and succeeded in doing so. For on the north side of the Danube they captured Werinhar, the middle of the three sons of Engelschalk, and Count Wezzilo who was their relative, and cut off their right hands, their tongues, and – horrible to relate – their genitals, so that not a trace of them could be seen.[5] Some of their men returned without either their right or their left hand. The army destroyed everything with fire at the *dux's* orders; moreover, they sent scouts across the Danube and everywhere that they could find the lands or the property of the said sons they burnt them forthwith. The trouble resulting from the actions of the aforementioned children lasted for about a year. When they realised that they could not expect anything good from the king, because of the crimes which they had committed against Arbo, they withdrew, and decided to become the men of Arnulf, the son of King Carloman, who then held Pannonia.[6] When the *dux* Zwentibald heard this, he sent messengers to him and said to him: 'You are supporting my enemies; if you do not dismiss them you cannot continue in peace with me.' And on another occasion he accused him as follows: 'Your men have conspired treacherously with the Bulgarians against my life and also against my kingdom', for the Bulgarians had in the previous year devastated his kingdom,[7] 'I demand that you swear an oath to me that this is not true'; to which Arnulf replied that he would never do either of these things. On this the *dux* collected troops from all the Slav lands in a short time and invaded Pannonia with a large army, killing cruelly and inhumanly like a wolf, and destroying and consuming with fire and sword a great part of it, so that not unjustly this verse was composed on the disaster:

This is at once the complaint of the land and its miserable death.

And when all this had been done as a result of the actions of the sons

5 For a (highly conjectural) genealogical table of the family see Mitterauer 1963: 187.

6 Note the indication of tension between Charles III and Arnulf, with Charles, Arbo and Zwentibald opposed to Arnulf and the Wilhemines.

7 For 'kingdom' see above, 883(II) n. 7; for earlier co-operation between Franks and Bulgars against the Moravians see 863 n. 4. .

already mentioned within the space of a year the *dux* returned unharmed with his army to his own lands. But in the same year that we set down these things[8] the *dux* again gathered a multitude and brought a hostile army into Pannonia, so that if anything remained from the year before he could now swallow it up completely in his wolf's mouth. For he brought such a multitude on that expedition that in one place his army was seen to pass from the rising to the setting of the sun. He remained with an army of this size in Arnulf's kingdom[9] for twelve days, plundering; then, just as he wished, returned safely, and afterwards also sent some of his army across the Danube. Hearing this the sons of William and Engelschalk who were oldest, namely Megingoz and Pabo, took some of the Pannonians with them and went rashly against them. But it was not profitable to have begun the battle, for the Moravians had the victory. Megingoz and Pabo, seeking flight, were drowned in the River Raab; but Count Berchtold's brother,[10] with many others, were captured by the Slavs. Let those who scorn the truth now pay attention, judge and compare; and those whom the original plan and actions pleased, let them also be pleased at the evils which followed. They despised the peace, which in being preserved preserved Pannonia, but which being broken led to Pannonia's being laid waste from the Raab eastwards within the space of two and a half years. Male and female slaves with their children were killed, many of the leading men were captured, killed, or – what is more disgraceful – had their hand or tongue or genitals cut off and were sent back. Without doubt this all happened either through the mercy or through the anger of God. But we say that God's anger is a just punishment which without doubt, as we are convinced, only falls when it is justified.

The emperor set out through Bavaria to the east, and coming to the River Tullnbach, had a meeting at *Mons Comianus*.[11] To this there came among others the *dux* Zwentibald with his nobles and became by joining of hands, as is the custom, the emperor's vassal.[12] He swore

8 The annal is evidently roughly contemporary.

9 As n. 7.

10 Berchtold is probably the count of the palace in Alemannia under Charles III and Arnulf (Dümmler 1888: 183, 294, 486; Borgolte 1986: 79-80; Mitterauer 1963: 182-3 speculates on other possible identifications), though it is not clear why his brother should have been involved in this feud.

11 The Kaumberg near Tulln at the northern edge of the Wienerwald; cf. BM nos. 307a and 1646b.

12 He was already allied with Arbo and Charles III; see the account of the Pannonian feud in the previous paragraph.

fidelity to him with an oath that as long as Charles should live he would never come into his kingdom with a hostile army. Then the *dux* Brazlavo came, who at that time held the kingdom between the Drava and the Sava, and was accepted as a vassal;[13] and the king proceeded through Carinthia into Italy, and he celebrated Christmas in prosperity at Pavia.

885

On the day after Epiphany [January 7] a general assembly was held and Wido, *dux* of the Spoletans, who had previously defected from the emperor by flight, cleared himself by oath of the charge of high treason and was restored to the king's fidelity.[1] After the death of King Carloman, who at that time ruled Gaul, Caesar went to that kingdom and having received the leading men and disposed affairs there as he wished, returned to Francia to meet the pope at the assembly which had been arranged at Worms.[2] But while the pope was in the middle of his journey he was struck down by a sudden illness and died.[3]

King Godafrid was accused of plotting with the Northmen against the kingdom of the Franks, and was killed by his accusers themselves.[4]

Hugh, the son of King Lothar, acted unwisely in the emperor's kingdom, and was blinded.[5]

Peace was confirmed in the east between Arnulf and Zwentibald by oaths in the presence of the Bavarian nobles.[6]

---

13 *sui miliciae subditus.* On Brazlavo, who ruled between the Drava and Sava, that is in much the same area as the Slav princeling Liudewit whose rebellion is recorded in *ARF* for 819-23 (Scholz 1972: 104-13 *passim*), see Wolfram 1987: 355-7. He appears several times in the 890s as an ally of Arnulf; see below, 892 and 896.

1 See above, 883(I and II), 884(II).

2 Carloman of west Francia died on December 12 884; Charles III is found there in May and June 885 (DD C III 116-26). See also 884-85(I) for Charles III's succession in west Francia and for the planned meeting with the pope at Worms.

3 See above, 885(I) with n. 7.

4 See 885(I) with n. 2; the 'kingdom of the Franks' here probably means the whole area over which Charles ruled (cf. 'the emperor's kingdom' in the next paragraph, and Eggert 1973: 104-5).

5 See 885(I) with n. 4.

6 Note here, as in the previous year, Arnulf's semi-independent position in Pannonia.

886

The emperor celebrated Christmas at Regensburg.[1] From there he set out for Italy at the invitation of the pope [Stephen V], and sent Bishop Liutward to Rome.[2] There many matters were arranged as he wished: among other things, the supreme pontiff decreed at the king's request that bishops whose dioceses had been quite obviously devastated by the fire of the heathen might be granted other vacant sees.[3]

On Palm Sunday there was a regrettable riot involving the king's bodyguards and the citizens of the town of Pavia. For many of the former were killed and many of the citizens of the town were wounded, and for fear of the emperor, who was nearby at the time celebrating Easter [March 27] at Corte Olona, took flight and ended their life on the road.[4]

After Easter the emperor held a general assembly at Pavia and went through Burgundy to Gaul against the Northmen who were then at Paris.[5] Henry, the margrave of the Franks, who held Neustria at that time, was killed there,[6] and the king returned to his own lands, having accomplished little.[7]

A feud broke out between Berengar, the king's relative, who held Friuli, and Bishop Liutward [of Vercelli].[8] For this reason Berengar moved to plunder the town of Vercelli and coming there he carried off as much of the bishop's property as he wished, and returned.

In the autumn there was unusual and unexpected flooding. For in the

---

1 He was there between January 6 and 10 (DD C III 133-5); there are no Italian diplomata to record his visit there.

2 See 885(I) with n. 11 for the background to this.

3 This would have amounted to a translation, and was thus contrary to canon law (see 882(I) n. 16); for the specific problem see the case of Frothar of Bordeaux/Bourges dealt with at the council of Ponthion in 876, though Frothar's translation was in the end accepted; AB 876 (Nelson 1991: 194). Arnulf's attempt to make Wiching bishop of Passau in 899 (see below) is another example.

4 Such clashes between imperial armies and Italian cities were common in Ottonian and later times; this is probably the earliest recorded example.

5 For the siege see 886(I).

6 August 28; see 886(I) with n. 4.

7 See 886(I) and notes for the chronology of this.

8 The two were reconciled shortly before Liutward's fall the following year. This feud may be what lies behind the extraordinary story in 887(I) about Liutward and the nunnery in Brescia.

east the rivers burst their banks and surrounded *villae* unexpectedly and are said to have suddenly swept them away with their inhabitants, men, women and children, so that they could be seen levelled to the ground. In the Alpine regions, moreover, there were such severe floods and landslides that the windings and traces of the roads on the sides of the mountains were rendered completely invisible.

887

The emperor was afflicted by a severe illness in Alsace.[1] Afterwards he recovered somewhat and set out for Alemannia, and coming to the *curtis* of Bodman he had blood let to relieve pain in his head.[2] After Easter [April 16] had passed an assembly was held at Waiblingen;[3] there among other things Berengar returned to Caesar's fidelity and compounded for the injury which he had done to Liutward in the previous year with great gifts.[4]

Boso died, leaving a small son by the daughter of Louis, king of Italy.[5] The emperor came to meet him at the *villa* of Kirchen on the Rhine, and received him with honour to be his man, as if he were his adopted son.[6]

The Alemans conspired treacherously against Bishop Liutward, who at that time was the chief counsellor in the king's palace, and forced him to withdraw from the king's presence, stripped of all his honours.[7]

1 See 886(I) n. 6.

2 *pro dolore capitis incisionem accepit.* This is generally taken to mean that Charles was trepanned, but this seems improbable, since although Charles was evidently ill in the second half of the year and died in early 888, he was still well enough to transact business up until June, which is scarcely compatible with his having undergone a serious head operation. See Oesterle 1979, who also discusses briefly the nature of the illness which afflicted several of the Carolingians of the east Frankish line (Emma, Carloman, Charles III, Arnulf) – perhaps epilepsy, but the evidence is too vague for a certain diagnosis.

3 Around May 7 (D C III 158); see 887(I) n. 1.

4 See 886(II) with n. 8; note that there is here as yet no sign of Liutward's imminent fall from power.

5 Boso died on January 11; the daughter was Ermengard (above, 878 n. 8).

6 *honorifice ad hominem sibi quasi adoptivum filium eum iniunxit.* It is generally assumed that Louis was indeed adopted by Charles at this point, possibly with the intention of making him Charles's successor in the empire: Ewig 1962; Hlawitschka 1978: 21 n. 7 and 26-31, who points to a parallel in Flodoard, *Historia Remensis Ecclesiae*, III, 24 (*MGH SS* 13: 537). It is however unclear whether adoption in this sense was known to the Franks, and it could equally be that Charles was simply making his peace with the son of a man whom he and the other Carolingians had never accepted as a legitimate ruler.

7 See 887(I) for a discussion of this.

And soon Caesar was struck by a most serious illness. From that day the Franks and, after their usual fashion, the Saxons and the Thuringians, together with some of the leading men of the Bavarians and the Alemans, entered into an evil conspiracy and began to think of defecting from the emperor's fidelity; and indeed they did this. So, when the Emperor Charles came to Frankfurt, these men invited Arnulf, the son of King Carloman, and chose him for their lord, and without delay decided that he should be made king.[8] Charles began to make war against King Arnulf, but had no success; for the Alemans, on whom the king chiefly relied for the conduct of the affairs of his kingdom,[9] were struck with fear, and all straightaway defected from him, so that even his servants left him and hurried to join up with King Arnulf. Charles, recognising that he was deserted by his men on all sides, did not know what could be done for his cause, but at length sent gifts to the king asking that in his mercy he would grant him a few places in Alemannia for his use until the end of his life; and the king agreed to do this.[10] However, he did not enjoy them for long; for he lived in piety in the places which had been granted to him by the king for a few days, and then after Christmas, on January 13, ended his life happily. And, wonderfully, until the time when he was buried with honour in the church of the Reichenau, the heavens were seen open by many beholders, so that it could be clearly shown that he who had been spurned by men and stripped of earthly honour had been deemed worthy by God to be held as a servant of His heavenly country in happiness.[11]

8 For a discussion of this see 887(I) with n. 8.

9 Alemannia was Charles's power-base, even after he had acquired the rest of the Frankish kingdoms; both Liutward of Vercelli and Liutbert of Mainz were Alemans, as were Charles's wife Richgardis and several of his most important aristocratic followers. Note that it was the Alemans who conspired against Liutward of Vercelli, according to the annalist. See 866 n. 1 on the divisions of Louis the German's kingdoms.

10 For a parallel see Louis the Younger's behaviour to Carloman, above, 879.

11 Charles's rapid death evidently gave rise to rumours and legends: *AV* 887 (von Simson 1909: 64) say 'after losing rule he is said to have been strangled by his men'; Regino 888 (Kurze 1890: 128-9) gives a highly moral account of Charles's edifying end.

888

King Arnulf received at Regensburg the leading men of the Bavarians, the eastern Franks, the Saxons, the Thuringians, the Alemans and a great part of the Slavs, and celebrated Christmas and Easter [April 7] there with honour. While he long delayed there,[1] many kinglets sprang up in Europe, that is to say the kingdom of his uncle Charles.[2] For Berengar, the son of Eberhard, made himself king in Italy;[3] Rudolf,

1 In fact Arnulf did not stay at Regensburg the whole winter; the evidence of his diplomata shows that he left Regensburg in mid-February and visited his own power-base in Pannonia in Lent (DD A 15-22). See Bowlus 1987 for speculation on the reasons for this.

2 This famous passage should be read in conjunction with two other accounts. The first is Regino 888 (Kurze 1890: 129): 'After his [Charles III's] death the kingdoms which had obeyed his authority, as if lacking a lawful heir, dissolved into separate parts and, without waiting for their natural lord, each chose a king from its own bowels. This was the origin of great wars; not that the Franks lacked princes who by nobility, courage, and wisdom were capable of ruling kingdoms, but rather because the equality of descent, authority and power increased the discord among them: none so outshone the others that the rest deigned to submit to his rule.' The second is *ASC* for 887 (Whitelock 1979: 199): 'And the same year Charles, king of the Franks, died; and six weeks before he died his brother's son Arnulf had deprived him of the kingdom. The kingdom was then divided into five, and five kings were consecrated to it. It was done, however, with Arnulf's consent and they said that they would hold it under him, for not one of them was born to it in the male line but him alone. Arnulf then lived in the land east of the Rhine, and Rudolf succeeded to the middle kingdom and Odo to the western portion; and Berengar and Guido to Lombardy and the lands on that side of the Alps; and they held it with much discord and fought two general engagements, and ravaged the land again and again, and each repeatedly drove out the other.' Note that *AF* ascribe the 'dissolution' to Arnulf's delay, while for Regino – who writes from a Lotharingian standpoint – it would seem that the deposition of Charles III was valid only in east Francia, and not until Charles III's death was a new ruler required (though 'without waiting for their natural lord' presumably refers to Arnulf). The Anglo-Saxon annal offers a contemporary but *ex post facto* view; in view of the Italian reference it cannot have been composed before 889, by which time it may have looked from abroad as if Arnulf had intended his hegemonial position from the start. For most of the kings about to be mentioned it is uncertain whether their claim was made before Charles's death (January 13 888, but one must also allow time for the news to have reached other parts of the Frankish empire); at least for some of them it seems to have been a reaction to the deposition of Charles and elevation of Arnulf.

3 For Berengar see above, 883(II) n. 7. The regnal years in Berengar's diplomata suggest that his reign began between December 26 and January 2, i.e. before the death of Charles III, though this is not absolutely certain; Dümmler 1888: 313 n. 1, Schiaparelli 1902: 83-4; Hirsch 1910: 175-7. His rival in Italy was to be the Wido mentioned above; see below with n. 5. Liudprand, *Antapodosis* I, 14 (Becker 1915: 16-17), says that Berengar and Wido had made a pact that Berengar should have Italy and Wido should have Francia.

the son of Conrad, decreed that he would hold upper Burgundy in kingly fashion;[4] and then Louis, the son of Boso, and Wido, the son of Lambert, claimed to hold Belgian Gaul and Provence as kings;[5] Odo, the son of Robert, usurped the lands as far as the Loire or the province of Aquitaine for his own use;[6] and from there Ramnulf decreed that he should be held as king.[7] Hearing these things, the king set out for Francia, and after holding a general assembly at Frankfurt, prepared to come to Worms.[8] Odo, when he learnt this, adopted the sensible plan of saying that he would prefer to hold his kingdom in peace by the grace of the king than to rebel in pride contrary to his fidelity, and coming there humbly to the king he was received with grace.[9] When things had been successfully arranged according to the wishes of both sides, each returned to his own lands. The king set out for Alsace against Rudolf.[10] From there he sent an army of the Alemans against

4 The Welf Rudolf had, like his father Conrad, previously been *dux* in the region around the Jura; the kingdom he set up is the only one for which there were no Carolingian precedents, but it is probable that he intended to claim Lotharingia. See Parisot 1899: 261-4; Hlawitschka 1968: 70, 79

5 The kingdoms are given in reverse order: Louis claimed Provence (see above, 887(II) with n. 6), though he did not have himself crowned until he had come to terms with Arnulf (see below, 890 with n. 5). Wido, supported by his relative, Archbishop Fulco of Rheims, first tried to claim west Francia, and then Lotharingia, where he was crowned as king in Langres by Bishop Geilo. Neither of these attempts met with any great success, and he had returned to Italy by the summer; see below, n. 12. On Wido's previous career see 883(I) with n. 5; on his actions in 888 see *AV* 888 (von Simson 1909: 64-5); Dümmler 1888: 314f.; Hlawitschka 1968: 73-4.

6 He was anointed king by Archbishop Walter of Sens on February 29, but was not at first recognised in Aquitaine, or Brittany, and faced a strong internal opposition led by Archbishop Fulco of Rheims. See the references given in n. 5 above.

7 Ramnulf certainly did not recognise Odo's authority as king in west Francia; but *AF* are the only source which ascribes kingly status to him. *AV* 889 (von Simson 1909: 67) show him as guardian of the young Carolingian Charles the Simple and as acknowledging Odo in 889; on the titles he used see Brunner 1973: 228-9.

8 Arnulf is found at Frankfurt from June 8 to July 3 (DD A 26-34); the meeting at Worms presumably took place in August (diplomata are dated from Tribur and Gernsheim in that month: DD A 35-7). At least some of the leading men of west Francia, including Fulco of Rheims, wanted to offer Arnulf himself the crown, but he refused: cf. *AV* 888 (von Simson 1909: 65); and Flodoard, *Historia Remensis Ecclesiae* IV, 5 (*MGH SS* 13: 563). Hlawitschka 1968: 73-7 is a good recent discussion.

9 Arnulf seems to have reconciled Odo with his opponents; Odo was crowned with a crown supplied by Arnulf at Rheims on November 13. See the references in n. 8 above and Dümmler 1888: 322.

10 In September, judging by the dates of DD A 37-8.

him, and he himself returned to Bavaria through Francia. But Rudolf
negotiated with the leading men of the Alemans and came of his own
free will to the king at the town of Regensburg.[11] After many things
had been agreed on between them, he returned to his own lands as he
had come, in peace and with the king's permission. The king also
decided to go to Italy with an army, but Berengar, who shortly before
had fought a bloody battle with the tyrant Wido, was concerned to
prevent this, lest the Italian kingdom should suffer damage by the
entry of so great an army, and so sent his leading men ahead of him
and himself came to the king at the town of Trent.[12] For this reason
he was received graciously by the king, and none of the kingdom
which he had acquired was taken from him, except for the *curtes* of
Navus and Sagus.[13] Then without delay the army was given leave to
depart for home. But the king, taking a few men with him, went into
Friuli, and celebrated Christmas at the *curtis* of Karnburg.[14] More
horses died in that journey than any mortal can remember.

11 Arnulf issued a diploma at Regensburg on October 9 (D A 38). Rudolf's negotiations with the Alemans are a hint at the weakness of Arnulf's position in
Alemannia, Charles III's homeland; see below, 890 with n. 6 and 891 with n. 5.
The outcome of the negotiations between Rudolf and Arnulf is uncertain;
according to the Anglo-Saxon Chronicle (see 888(II) n. 1) Rudolf was recognised as king by Arnulf, but though this fits the passage here, it does not square
with the persistent later hostility of Arnulf and his son Zwentibold to Rudolf.
Cf. Regino 888 (Kurze 1890: 130): 'All the days of their life Arnulf and his son
Zwentibold persecuted Rudolf, but were unable to harm him because, as was
said above, the inaccessible regions [of Rudolf's kingdom], where in many
places only goats could go, repelled the concerted attacks of the armies sent
against him.' A plausible interpretation is that Rudolf at first claimed the whole
of Lotharingia, thus arousing Arnulf's enmity, and then at the meeting with
Arnulf agreed to confine himself to upper Burgundy and to recognise Arnulf's
overlordship; so Hlawitschka 1968: 68-70, 78-83.

12 The meeting must have taken place between early November and Christmas
(cf. DD A 40, 42). Wido had returned to Italy in the summer and gathered a
substantial army from his home base of Spoleto but also from Lombardy.
Sometime in the autumn he and Berengar fought a battle near Brescia;
Berengar's forces won, but both sides were so weakened that a truce was made
until January 6 889; Dümmler 1888: 324-5. See 890 with n. 2 and 893 with n.
7 for the further development of Italian affairs, and Wickham 1981: 170-2 and
Delogu 1968 for a commentary.

13 *excipiuntur curtes navum et sagum*. It is not entirely certain that *navum/ navus* and
sagum/ sagus are place-names rather than otherwise unknown terms for royal
rights or taxes, but it is likely – however, the places have not been satisfactorily
identified; Dümmler 1888: 325 n. 1.

14 He issued a diploma there on December 26 (D A 42).

889

Liutbert, the noble archbishop of the city of Mainz, departed from this life.[1] It would be a long story to relate how upright his manner of living was; however, it may be possible to give some brief idea in these few verses:

> He was very generous, patient, humble and benign,
> And remained an example to all in his goodness;
> There where the Danube flows and the twin-horned Rhine runs,
> He was more learned than those learned in letters.

A terrible time began in this year. For an attack of whooping-cough from Italy troubled many; there were more floods than usual; civil wars disturbed the regions all around; and plague here and there and unexpected famine were exceptionally bad. The harvest was destroyed by hailstorms and men suffered the lack of crops in misery. But above all else there was a detestable portent in the lands of the Thuringians. For water fell from the heavens not, as usual, in raindrops, but all together like a waterfall, and in three *villae* the houses were carried away in a moment by the shock and three hundred human corpses were collected after they had been swept on to the fields by the force of the waters.

At the end of May the king held a general assembly in the *villa* which is called Forchheim.[2] There there was a discussion about the state of the kingdom, and it was agreed that the leading men of the Franks should confirm by oath, like the Bavarians, that they would not withdraw from the rulership and government of his sons, that is of Zwentibald and Ratold, who had been born to him by concubines. This some of the Franks refused to do for a time, but at length they satisfied the king's will and did not refuse to give their right hands on it,[3] but with the reservation that this should only hold good if he did not have an heir by his lawful wife.[4] There came there also ambassadors from

1 February 17 889; note the use of the entry for the priest Probus under 859 as a model for what follows.

2 DD A 47-51 are dated from Forchheim between June 5 and June 20.

3 See 869 n. 13.

4 The opposition may have been as much to the idea of dividing the kingdom as to the succession of 'illegimate' sons; see Schlesinger 1963: 268, Hlawitschka 1968: 209-11, Schlesinger 1969, Hlawitschka 1969 for a discussion. The opposition was presumably led by the 'Conradines', who could expect to (and later did) profit from the succession of a legitimate son born to Arnulf's Conradine wife Uota.

the nations all around, that is to say from the Northmen in the north and from the Slavs, asking for peace, whom the king heard and gave leave to depart without delay. Then it was agreed that an army should go against the Abodrites; but before that it pleased the king to hold an assembly at the royal *curtis* of Frankfurt with the Franks.[5] Then, as had already been arranged, he went against the Abodrites with a great army, but little was accomplished there, however, and the king gave the army leave to depart and returned to Frankfurt in great haste.[6] From there he travelled slowly through Alemannia and celebrated Christmas in state in Bavaria at the town of Regensburg.[7]

890

In mid-Lent [March 22] the king set out for Pannonia and held a general assembly with the *dux* Zwentibald in the place which is called *Omuntesperch*[1] in the common tongue. There among other things the said *dux*, at the request of the pope, asked the king urgently that he should visit the church of St Peter in the town of Rome, and should deign to rescue the Italian kingdom from the evildoing of Christians and the threats of the pagans, and hold it for his own use to control it.[2]

5 In early July; cf. DD A 53-6.

6 He is found in Frankfurt again from mid-October: DD A 62-9; D A 60 is dated from Einbeck on August 20 and D A 61 from Wölfis in Thuringia (near Ohrdruf) on October 10, which dates the campaign to September. On the background see Friedmann 1986: 166-9, who suggests that this campaign was a reprisal for the hostilities in 886 in which Wulfhar bishop of Minden was killed.

7 DD A 70-2 show him at Wiesloch in Baden, Ulm and Augsburg in late November and early December; after that there are no diplomata until early January.

1 *Omuntesperch* has not been identified. Arnulf was at Regensburg on March 16 (uncertain) and again on April 14 and at his own centre *Mosapurc* on March 21 (DD A 74-6). See Bowlus 1987 on this journey. Regino 890 (Kurze 1890: 134) says that Arnulf conceded overlordship over the Bohemians to Zwentibald at this meeting, and their friendship was confirmed by Zwentibald's acting as godfather to Arnulf's illegitimate son of the same name (the use of the name makes the story very plausible, but the baptism must have taken place before 890).

2 Wido had defeated Berengar in the battle of the Trebbia in early 889, and was sole ruler in Italy (Dümmler 1888: 365-6), Berengar being confined to his own base of Friuli. Although he had been supported by Pope Stephen V, who had adopted him before the death of Charles III and thus perhaps designated him as future ruler, he now seemed a threat to the papacy (cf. above, 878 with n. 5 for relations between John VIII and the margraves of Spoleto). Stephen's embassy was a last attempt to avoid having to accept Wido as emperor, and he had already had to crown Wido on February 21 891 (Dümmler 1888: 368).

But the king, because of many problems which had arisen within his own kingdom, had to refuse what was asked, although unwillingly.[3] After Easter [April 12], in the month of May, he held a meeting with his men in the *villa* which is called Forchheim.[4] There the daughter of Louis [II], king of Italy, the widow of the tyrant Boso, came to him with great gifts and was received with honour and sent back to her own lands.[5] The king, after settling affairs there as he wished, came to the Reichenau and Constance in Alemannia to pray.[7] Returning from there he celebrated Christmas in the city of Regensburg.

Salomon, the bishop of Constance, a man of most commendable life, died. He was succeeded by his namesake, the younger Salomon, who was the third of that name to hold the episcopal see.[7]

Zwentibald's role as an intermediary shows the connections between the Moravian rulers and the papacy, which were independent of the Frankish Church; see the letters of Stephen V to Zwentibald and the Moravians, JL 3407-8 (= *MGH Epp.* 7: 354 no. 1 and 352 no. 33).

3 problems' refers probably to Bernard's uprising in Alemannia; see below, n. 13.

4 D A 78 is dated there on June 1.

5 Arnulf and Louis may have been rivals for the succession to Charles III (see above, 887(II) with n. 6). At first there seems to have been some coolness between Arnulf and the Bosonids; Arnulf's rule was not recognised in Provence, and diplomata were dated by formulae like 'in the first year following the death of Boso/Charles'. A diploma of Arnulf for the Empress Engelberga, Louis's grandmother, is dated from Forchheim on June 12 889 (D A 49), and presumably marks the beginning of a reconciliation; following the present meeting between Arnulf and Ermengard, Louis, the son of Boso and Ermengard, was crowned king of Provence in Valence with Arnulf's approval (and that of Stephen V!) in the autumn of 890; *MGH Capit.* 2: 367-8 no. 289. Arnulf's support for Louis was presumably directed against Rudolf of Burgundy. Dümmler 1888: 332-3; Poupardin 1901: 15-20; Hlawitschka 1968: 84-108. For 'tyrant' see above, 879 n. 10.

6 He was at Ulm on June 26 (D A 79). Prayer was not the only reason for his journey; in 890 there was a rebellion in Alemannia by Charles III's illegitimate son Bernard, which can be reconstructed largely from charter evidence for the confiscations which followed. Bernard was supported by Count Ulrich of the Linz- and Argengau and Abbot Bernard of St Gallen; the revolt was checked by Arnulf's supporters, the ex-chaplains Salomon (later abbot of St Gallen and bishop of Constance) and Hatto (abbot of the Reichenau; on these two see Fleckenstein 1959: 199-200), but continuing Aleman opposition to Arnulf is clear from the account of the following year, and it was not until Bernard was killed by Count Rudolf of Raetia in 891 or 892 that Alemannia quietened down. See Dümmler 1888: 341ff.; Borgolte 1986: 226-7, 263.

7 Salomon II died on December 23 889; Salomon III succeeded him in 890 and also to the abbey of St Gallen. Both were members of an 'episcopal dynasty' which provided three bishops of Constance (Salomon I 835x847-71, Salomon II 875-89, Salomon III 890-919) as well as bishops of Freising (Waldo, 884-906) and Chur (Waldo, ?913-49). Dümmler 1857: 110 has worked out the genealogy.

891

The king sent his ambassadors to the Moravians to renew peace.[1]

Embricho, bishop of Regensburg,

a man who was patient, sober, humble and faithful,[2]

died happily in old age. But the city [of Regensburg] itself was by divine judgement suddenly set on fire and burnt down on August 10 with all its buildings and even its churches except for the church of St Emmeram the Martyr and the church of St Cassian in the middle of the town, which were protected by God from the fire.[3]

Then the Northmen invaded the lands of the western Franks, and an army was sent from Francia to repel them. There Sunderolt, the archbishop of Mainz, attacked them rashly and was killed, and in his place Hatto, abbot of the Reichenau, a man of subtle mind, was made archbishop.[4] Therefore King Arnulf set out with the Franks, after gathering to him a useless Aleman army, to avenge this on the Northmen. But the Alemans pretended to be sick and left the king and returned home.[5] But he continued successfully with the Franks to the west.[6] The Northmen, having laid waste a great part of Lothar's kingdom,[7] pitched their camp, untroubled, by the River Dyle in the place which is called Louvain, and after their fashion surrounded it with a fortified ditch.[8] The king and his army then arrived

---

1 See 890 n. 1; Schwarzmeier 1972 edits a letter written by Margrave Arbo to Arnulf about the state of affairs on the Moravian border which refers to these ambassadors.

2 A hexameter verse in the original Latin.

3 Embricho died on July 14. The destruction of Regensburg by fire is recorded in other annals but was not so complete that Arnulf was no longer able to stay there. It remained the place he visited most frequently, though he did build a new palace, presumably to replace the older one. See Schmid 1976: 51, 53-8, 189-91.

4 Sunderolt was killed on June 25 (Dümmler 1888: 348 n. 1); the precise date of Hatto's succession is unknown.

5 An indication of the continuing hostility to Arnulf in Alemannia; cf. above, 890 n. 6. This is presumably the unsuccessful expedition recorded by *AV* 891 (von Simson 1909: 69-70).

6 Arnulf was still in Bavaria at the end of July (D A 91); he issued a diploma at Maastricht on October 1 (D A 92).

7 I.e. Lotharingia.

8 On Viking practice see above 882(I and II) and in general Foote and Wilson 1980: 267.

unexpectedly at that place. They quickly crossed the river and thought of joining battle without delay. The king indeed hesitated to risk so large an army, because with a marsh on one side and the bank of the river on the other there was not room for cavalry to attack. He looked the position over, he thought about it, and took advice as to what plan was needed, for the Franks are not used to fighting while advancing step by step.[9] He considered the matter anxiously, and at length the hero called the leaders of the Franks to him and addressed them in a relaxed manner as follows:

Men, while you have honoured God, and have always protected the fatherland under God's grace, you have been invincible. Take courage, when you think of revenging the blood of your pious relatives shed by an enemy raging in a most pagan fashion, when you behold the overthrow even in your fatherland of holy churches dedicated to the honour of saints and of your Creator, and when you see the deaths of God's ministers of the highest rank. Now, soldiers, act! you have the authors of these crimes before your eyes, and when I get down from my horse and signal with my hand, follow me! Let us attack our enemies in God's name, avenging not our shame but that of Him who can do all things.

Stirred up by this speech, all, young and old, with equal will and boldness, prepared to give battle on foot. First they begged the king that he would see to it with cavalry that they should have nothing to fear from attacks by the enemy in the rear. The shouts of the Christians rose to heaven, and the pagans after their fashion shouted no less; terrible battle-standards moved through the camps. Swords were drawn on both sides, and the armies clashed like iron on stone. The Danes were there, the most powerful people among the Northmen, who had never been heard to have been captured or conquered in any fortification. There was a fierce battle, but after a short time, with the aid of God's grace, the victory fell to the Christians. The Northmen sought safety in flight and found that the river, which before they had thought of as a wall to their rear, was now their death. For with the Christians bringing death from the other side

9 *pedetemptim*; on this passage, which has been cited since the time of Waitz and Brunner as a key text showing the importance for the Franks of fighting on horseback, see Bachrach 1970: 51-3. His interpretation – that it was only the difficulty of advancing slowly through the marshes on foot, not fighting on foot as such that worried the warriors and was worth noting in this annal – should be considered in the light of Regino's account of the battle (Kurze 1890: 137-8): 'The king ... ordered the army to dismount and to fight with the enemy on foot.'

they were forced to throw themselves into the river, and, grasping at each other in heaps by hand, neck and limbs, they sank in hundreds and thousands, so that their corpses blocked the river bed and it seemed to run dry. In that battle two of their kings were killed, that is Sigifrid and Godafrid,[10] and sixteen royal standards were carried off and were sent to Bavaria as a witness. In the same place, on the … kalends of …,[11] the king ordered litanies to be celebrated, and he went in procession there with his army singing praises to God, who had given such a victory to his men, with only one man found to have been killed on the Christian side, and so many thousands perishing onthe other side.

892

The king returned in triumph from Francia to Alemannia, and celebrated Christmas in state at the royal *curtis* of Ulm. From there he set out to the east,[1] hoping to meet the *dux* Zwentibald; but the latter in his usual fashion refused to come to the king and betrayed his fidelity and all the things which he had promised before.[2] The king was enraged at this, and held a meeting in *Hengistfeld* with the *dux* Brazlavo,[3] and tried to arrange there among other things a time and place to invade the lands of the Moravians; for it was agreed that three armies should invade that kingdom.[4] And so the king, taking with him Franks, Bavarians and Alemans, came to Moravia in the month of July,[5] and there spent four weeks with a great army – the Hungarians

---

10 There seems to be a confusion here with the names of the two Viking kings given in the accounts of the siege of Asselt in 882; see above, 882(I) and (II). Sigifrid was killed in 887 according to *AV* (von Simson 1909: 63, and see Dümmler 1888: 334) and the Godafrid of 882 had been killed in 885 (see above, 885(I) with n. 4). If the names are correct they presumably refer to close relatives of the kings of 882.

11 There are gaps in ms '3' at this point, presumably so that the date could be filled in: cf. 875 n. 6. For the litanies after a victory see above, 869 and McCormick 1986: 354-5.

1 He was still near Ulm on January 21 (D A 96); his diplomata then show him at Ötting on February 15 and at Salzburg on April 3 (DD A 97-8).

2 See above, 890 with n. 1, 891 with n. 1.

3 On him see above, 884(II) with n. 13. *Hengistfeld* is probably south of Wildon in Styria; cf. Chroust 1890: 587-91.

4 Note the extent of east Frankish military power, and compare above, 858, 869, 871, 882(I and II).

5 He was still at Ranshofen near Salzburg on July 2 (D A 103).

also came to him there with an army[6] – going about laying waste the whole of the land with fire.

He also sent his men with gifts from there in the month of September to the Bulgarians and their king, Lodomir, to renew the former peace[7] and to ask that they should not sell salt to the Moravians. The ambassadors, not being able to travel by land because of the ambushes laid by the *dux* Zwentibald, went from the kingdom[8] of Brazlavo by the River Odra as far as Kulpa, and then by ship along the River Sava into Bulgaria. There they were received with honour by the king, and returned with gifts by the same route by which they had come, arriving back in the month of May.

Poppo, the *dux* of the Thuringians, was deprived of his offices.[9]

893

Before Lent [February 21] the king went through the whole province of the western Franks visiting monasteries and bishoprics for the sake of prayer.[1]

Engelschalk, a man of youthful boldness, who had been in exile among the Moravians for a time after carrying off the king's daughter by a concubine, returned not long after into the king's grace, and was made

---

6 The Hungarians appear here for the first time in *AF*. Regino 889 (Kurze 1890: 131-3) gives a much more bloody account from the perspective of two decades later, from which most later accounts including the Hungarian chronicles are derived; Silagi 1988. For their later career see below, and Fasoli 1945; De Vajay 1968; Bartha 1975.

7 See 884(II) n. 6.

8 *regnum*: see above, 883(II) n. 7.

9 On him see above, 883(II) and 884(II). Regino 892 (Kurze 1890: 140) reports that it was on Poppo's advice that Bishop Arn of Würzburg had led an attack against the Slavs earlier in the year and been killed. The deposition may have been a punishment for this, but in view of the fact that two members of the 'Conradine' family, Conrad and Rudolf, succeeded Poppo and Arn respectively, and that the Conradines and Babenberger were shortly afterwards found in a state of feud (cf. Regino 897 [Kurze 1890: 145]), it also seems possible that Arnulf was changing his support from one family to the other. See Geldner 1971: 15-20. He was restored to most of his lands in 899 (D A 174).

1 The 'western Franks' here are the Lotharingians. Regino 893 (Kurze 1890: 141) also mentions Arnulf's tour and says that the bishops brought him 'huge gifts'. He was at Frankfurt on January 6 (D A 110), issued diplomata for Toul (D A 112) and Trier (D A 113) in early February, and was back at Ingelheim by February 11 (D A 114; falsified but probably retaining the date of a genuine diploma).

margrave in the east.[2] There he acted over-boldly against the leading men of Bavaria in the affairs which were committed to his charge, and by their judgement he was blinded at the town of Regensburg as he carelessly made to enter the king's palace, without being brought before the king.[3] Following this William, his uncle's son, who sent messengers to the *dux* Zwentibald, was convicted of high treason, and beheaded. His brother, who was hiding in exile among the Moravians, was killed by a treacherous plot of the *dux*'s, along with many others.[4] The king therefore broke off his journey and again invaded the kingdom of the *dux* Zwentibald with an army, and after laying waste a great part of the land returned with great difficulty, because of the ambushes that were laid, to Bavaria to the queen at the *curtis* of Ötting.[5] A son was born to him by her not long afterwards, whom Hatto, archbishop of Mainz, and Adalbero, bishop of Augsburg, anointed with the holy spring of baptism and named Louis, after his grandfather.[6]

Legates of Pope Formosus came to the king in Bavaria with letters, accompanied by the leading men of the Italian kingdom, begging urgently that he should come and take into his own hands from those of evil Christians the affairs of St Peter and of the Italian kingdom; at

---

2 For Engelschalk see above, 871 with n. 4, 884(II); he is found intervening in DD A 64 and 109, which confirms the reconciliation after Arnulf's rise to kingship. The daughter of Arnulf mentioned here may have been the Ellinrat recorded as still alive in 914; cf. Werner 1967: 460 and table.

3 The vagueness of the annalist here is unfortunate; among the leading men will certainly have been Arbo, the old opponent of Arnulf and the Wilhemines (see above, 884(II)), who had retained the eastern march after Arnulf's accession and for whom Engelschalk's appointment represented a loss of power. See Dümmler 1888: 360-1; Mitterauer 1963: 181. The fact that Engelschalk could be blinded under Arnulf's nose is very revealing about east Frankish power structures in the 890s.

4 *AA* 893 (Lendi 1971: 184): 'William killed; Engelschalk blinded; Rupert was killed', so the brother was presumably called Rupert. Why Zwentibald killed him rather than supporting him is unclear. Arnulf was at Regensburg in May and June (DD A 115-17).

5 The expedition probably took place in July/August; Arnulf is found in Regensburg on June 23 (D A 117), in *Eberesburc* on August 21 (D A 118) and in Regensburg again on September 2 (D A 119). *Eberesburc* according to Kehr 1940: 173 is Mautern near Krems in Austria (not Ebersberg south-east of Freising in Bavaria). In either case Arnulf must then have been returning from the campaign; BM 1890a puts the campaign between August 21 and September 2, but this seems too short a time.

6 The later King Louis the Child (900-11).

that time the tyrant Wido was principally attempting to do this.[7] The king received them with honour at the city of Regensburg, and allowed them to depart with gifts after agreeing to what had been requested.

The winter was fierce and longer than usual, so that in the month of March in some places a foot of snow fell on five consecutive days. As a result of this there was a great shortage of wine throughout Bavaria; and sheep and bees were lost.[8]

894

There was a great thunderclap on January 28.

The king soon set out on his journey and stayed for Christmas at the royal *curtis* of Aibling.[1] From there he entered Italy with an army of the Alemans. The first town which he found was resisting him was Bergamo under Wido's count, Ambrosius.[2] Enraged at this the king ordered the camps of the army to be moved forward to the walls of the town while he rode around the hills above. The day was already drawing towards evening, and the two sides had begun to fight so fiercely that both besiegers and besieged had to keep watch for the remaining part of the night. As dawn came the king heard mass and then ranged his army around to storm the town. He himself remained at the top of the hill with his battle-standard to give assistance to those attacking the wall. Great courage was given to both sides, both besiegers and besieged; both stood unshaken in their formations like the wall between them. For on the first assault there was such a noise of stones thrown at the shields that it seemed to sound like thunder to the men guarding the king's camp, which was over a mile away. The king's bodyguard fought with great effort before him and at length

7 The letters have not survived; the leading men will have included Berengar, and conceivably some of those mentioned in the account of Arnulf's Italian expedition in 894. On Wido see above, 888 with n. 5 and n. 12, 890 n. 2; for the term 'tyrant' see the note on Hugh of Lotharingia, 879 n. 10. Formosus had succeeded Stephen V in September 891, and had crowned Wido's son Lambert emperor on April 30 892 (Dümmler 1888: 372). Tensions may have increased following a visit by Wido to Rome in 892; Schiaparelli 1905: 63.

8 This sentence is a marginal note in ms. '3'.

1 Near Rosenheim, hence already *en route* for the Alps. Arnulf had already sent his son Zwentibald with an Aleman army into Italy in the autumn of 893; Dümmler 1888: 373 and n. 4.

2 D A 121 was issued at Bergamo on February 1. Ambrosius is not otherwise known; Hlawitschka 1960: 123-4.

they reached the wall. They held their shields above them like a roof
and tried to dig through the walls built in antiquity. Meanwhile the
unfortunate townsmen emptied containers full of stones on them in
vain, and after throwing all their lances, finally tried to tip the
ramparts down on them. But those below, with all their strength and
at God's will caused the wall to collapse to the ground. There was a
great shout from the people outside, and within there was fear and
flight. The army broke into the town on all sides like a whirlwind.
Count Ambrosius, the instigator of resistance to the king, sought to
take refuge in a certain turret, but in vain; for he was captured and, by
the enraged judgement of the army, immediately hung from a gallows.
His wife and sons were handed over to the king with a great treasure.
Moreover, the bishop of the same town, Adalbert by name, was
captured there and given to Bishop Hatto [of Mainz] to guard. At the
news of this such a terror spread through the whole of Italy that the
great towns, that is Milan and Pavia, came of their own free will to the
king and surrendered themselves.[3] So also the leading margraves of
the Italian kingdom, that is Adalbert and his brother Boniface,[4]
Hildebrand and Gerard,[5] presented themselves to the king. But, as
they demanded in their presumption excessive benefices, they were all
made prisoner and given into the hands of the princes for safe-keeping.
But the king did not keep this up for long; for, moved by mercy, he
allowed their release and asked that they should swear fidelity to him
by an oath. Two of them, Adalbert and Boniface, betrayed their
fidelity, and defected from the king by flight. The king came as far as
Piacenza,[6] and then, because the army was exhausted by the length of
the journey, returned and celebrated Easter [March 31] near the
castle of Ivrea.[7] A count of Wido's called Ansgar, with vassals of King
Rudolf of Burgundy who had been sent to make sure that the king did

3 On the siege of Bergamo see Jarnut 1974, who points out that Bergamo was of
    great strategic significance for east–west communications in Lombardy, and
    also that the speed with which the city was taken made further resistance seem
    pointless and dangerous; cf. Regino 894 (Kurze 1890: 142). Bergamo had
    traditionally favoured the east Frankish claimants to Italy, hence the descrip-
    tion of Ambrosius as 'instigator of resistance' and his fate.

4 Adalbert II of Tuscany (884x889-915); see Hofmeister 1907: 348, 388-92, and
    346-7, 388 on his brother Boniface, of whom little is known.

5 Hildebrand was a Tuscan count (Hofmeister 1907: 337-43); Gerard seems to be
    unknown. None of the magnates mentioned here (except Adalbert, who in some
    sources is referred to as *dux*) were margraves in the sense that they 'ruled' over
    a wider area with counts subject to them.

6 Where he issued diplomata on February 17 and March 11 (DD A 122-3).

7 DD A 124-5 are dated from there on April 16 and 17 respectively.

not return that way,[8] defended this castle as well as the passes, which were strongly fortified with a stone castle on top. The king, when he saw that the road was defended and could not be stormed without danger to his men, climbed the Alps with great effort with the help of guides. Because of the size of his army they lost the way, and they came to steep cliffs. At length they came on the third day only with great danger to themselves to the valley of Aosta, and in remarkable fashion; the horses had to jump from the tops of the cliffs, as if from a wall, over the stones to land below, pausing for breath as it were on the shelves of the cliff. The king, having sent his army before him, forced King Rudolf to flee;[9] he himself returned through upper Burgundy to Alemannia, where the queen came to meet him at the *curtis* of Kirchen.[10]

A general assembly was held at Worms,[11] and there among other things the boy Charles, a youth of childish disposition, the son of Louis the son of King Charles [the Bald] of western Francia and the king's relative, came to him; the king received him with love and allowed him to depart.[12]

The Alemans were sent in force under Zwentibald, the king's son by a concubine, against King Rudolf. He defended himself by the protection of the Alps, and the Alemans returned home after they had laid waste a great part of his lands.[13]

8 Rudolf was evidently expecting the later attacks on him; see n. 9 and 13. Ansgar, one of Wido's most prominent supporters, was margrave of Ivrea; Hlawitschka 1960: 128-9.

9 But was unable to do Rudolf any serious damage; Regino 894 (Kurze 1890: 142) reports that Rudolf 'climbed up the mountains and hid himself in the safest places'. See below, n. 13.

10 Presumably in May; see n. 11.

11 Arnulf issued diplomata there between June 5 and 13: DD A 126-8.

12 Charles the Simple had been crowned king in west Francia in opposition to Odo on January 28 893; neither side had been able to subdue the other and an armistice was arranged in September 893 to last until Easter 894. The text above is not very informative; Regino 893 (Kurze 1890: 141) and *AV* 894 (von Simson 1909: 74) say more definitely that Arnulf recognised Charles as king. Why, is not entirely clear; the explanation offered by Hlawitschka, that Arnulf was creating a 'Carolingian' alliance (Charles, Louis of Provence, Berengar and himself) against the non-Carolingians Wido and Rudolf, seems forced. See Dümmler 1888: 383-8; Hlawitschka 1968: 115-32.

13 According to Regino 894 (Kurze 1890: 142), Arnulf had granted to Louis of Provence, who came to him together with Ermengard at Lorsch after the assembly at Worms, 'certain cities with their surrounding counties, which Rudolf held'; the expedition was presumably intended to make the grant effective, but Regino reports that Louis was unable to dispossess Rudolf. See Hlawitschka 1968: 125-6.

Wido, the tyrant of the Italian kingdom, was attacked by a fever and died; his son Lambert tried to seize the kingdom in a similar fashion after him.[14]

Zwentibald, the *dux* of the Moravians and the source of all treachery, who had disturbed all the lands around him with tricks and cunning and circled around thirsting for human blood, made an unhappy end, exhorting his men at the last that they should not be lovers of peace but rather continue in enmity with their neighbours.[15]

The Avars, who are called Hungarians,[16] penetrated across the Danube at this time, and did many terrible things. They killed men and old women outright, and carried off the young women alone with them like cattle to satisfy their lusts, and reduced the whole of Pannonia to a desert.

In the autumn peace was made between the Bavarians and the Moravians.[17]

Anastasius, an ambassador of Leo, emperor of the Greeks, came with gifts to the king at the town of Regensburg. The king heard him and gave him leave to depart on the same day.[18]

895

There was a great famine throughout the whole of Bavaria, so that in many places people died of hunger.

Engildeo, the margrave of Bavaria, was deprived of his offices. In his place Liutpold, the king's relative, was appointed.[1] Hildegard, the

---

14 Wido died in December 894 (Dümmler 1888: 381 n. 3); for Lambert see above, 893 n. 7.

15 The succession was disputed between Zwentibald II and Moimir II; see below, 898.

16 On the Hungarians, who were not the same as the Avars, see 892 with n. 6.

17 Following the hostilities which had broken out again in 892-93; see above.

18 Arnulf was at Regensburg in August and again in January, so he probably spent the whole autumn there (DD A 129-31). The purpose of the embassy, which is known only from the reference here, was perhaps to make common cause against the growing threat from the Hungarians; Arnulf does not seem to have paid it much attention.

1 'Relative' = *nepos*, which cannot be translated here as 'nephew'. Liutpold, the ancestor of the tenth-century *duces* of Bavaria, was perhaps related to Arnulf through the latter's mother Liutswind; Tellenbach 1939: 54; Reindel 1953: 3-4. This probably happened in May; cf. n. 2.

daughter of Louis [the Younger], king of the Franks, was accused of acting contrary to her fidelity to the king, and as a result was deprived of her benefices and shut away in Bavaria on an island in the marsh of Chiemsee.[2]

Twenty-six bishops came together in Francia from the whole of Lotharingia, Saxony, Alemannia and Bavaria, and held a great synod at the *curtis* [royal estate] of Tribur, which was presided over by the metropolitans Hatto, archbishop of the town of Mainz, Herimann, archbishop of the town of Cologne, and Ratbod, archbishop of Trier. They considered many things useful to the Christian religion, and they set down their decisions in written canons so that they could be retained in memory for their successors.[3]

A royal assembly was also held at Worms.[4] There Odo, king of Gaul, came to the king's fidelity with gifts; he was honourably received by him and after a few days returned to his own lands as he had come, with friendly leave to depart.[5]

Zwentibald, the king's son, received the royal crown from his father, and was made king in Burgundy and the whole of Lothar's kingdom after he had received the leading men of those parts.[6]

2 'Benefices' has here been used to translate the *publicis honoribus* of the original, since it is unlikely that Hildegard held offices. Hildegard had most of her lands restored later, according to Regino 894: 142. There may have been a connection between the two disgraces, since Engildeo and Hildegard are mentioned in a diploma of Arnulf's as having unlawfully dispossessed a Megingoz, vassal of Bishop Erkenbald of Eichstätt, of land which was restored to him 'by the judgement of the Franks, Bavarians, Saxons and Alemans' (D A 132, May 5 895). See Dümmler 1888: 393-4; Reindel 1953:2-4.

3 The synod met in May 895 (Arnulf issued diplomata there on May 5 and May 14: DD A 133-4), and was, apart from the council of Mainz of 847, legislatively the most important ecclesiastical asembly held in the east Frankish kingdom. Its canons (*MGH Capit.* 2: 196-247 no. 252) dealt among other things with marriage law, sacrilege and penance. The older view that it was a display of ecclesiastical support for Arnulf against the lay magnates is untenable. See Lehn 1987; Hartmann 1989: 367-71.

4 Arnulf issued a diploma there on May 25 (D A 135).

5 According to *AV* 895 (von Simson 1909: 75-6), Arnulf, concerned at the civil war in west Francia, had summoned both Odo and Charles to appear before him. Odo came; Charles did not. These annals also report Zwentibald's coronation 'in the presence of King Odo'; Odo's recognition of Zwentibald was perhaps the price of Arnulf's support. See Dümmler 1888: 407-8; Hlawitschka 1968: 133-7.

6 Note that Zwentibald was made king in Lotharingia *and* Burgundy; for the rivalry between Arnulf/Zwentibald and Rudolf see above, 888 with n. 11, and 894. Regino 894 (Kurze 1890: 142), reports that Arnulf had already tried to have Zwentibald crowned at the assembly at Worms the previous year, but

At the same time there were great earthquakes in many places among the western Franks.

Ambassadors of the Abodrites came to the royal *curtis* of Salz bringing gifts with them, hoping to make peace with the king. When the king heard them, he immediately agreed to their requests and allowed them to depart.[7]

The Avars [Hungarians] invaded the lands of the Bulgars and were driven off by them, and a great part of their army was killed.[8]

In the middle of July a general assembly was held at the town of Regensburg.[9] There came there from Sclavania all the *duces* of the Bohemians, whom the *dux* Zwentibald had long kept by force from the alliance and control of the Bavarian people.[10] The leading ones were Spitignevo and Witizla, and they came to the king and were honourably received by him, and, as is the custom, surrendered themselves to the king's power by joining hands, and were reconciled.

The king was again asked urgently by Pope Formosus through letters and messengers to come to Rome.[11] The king, when he had decided with the advice of his bishops to give satisfaction to these demands,

that the leading men of Lotharingia had not agreed; under 892 (Kurze 1890: 140) he notes that Zwentibald had received some of the benefices of the Lotharingian count Megingaud. Evidently the plan realised here was of long standing. Zwentibald's kingdom seems to have been a genuinely independent one: he controlled all royal rights in Lotharingia, and Arnulf ceased to issue diplomata for Lotharingian recipients. Zwentibald even felt able to offer support to Charles the Simple shortly after becoming king! See Hlawitschka 1968: 132, 136-9, 158-9.

7 The meeting is not precisely datable, but presumably took place in June. See above, 892, for Arnulf's dealings with the Abodrites. Friedmann 1986: 166-9 suggests that the Abodrites sought peace because of Danish pressure and because the decline in Moravian power left them without alternative allies.

8 This is probably the attack described in more detail in the annal for 896.

9 D A 136 is dated at Regensburg on July 16.

10 Bohemian *duces* had submitted to Louis the German in 845 and in subsequent years the Bohemians are generally found under Bavarian influence, but see 890 with n. 1 for Zwentibald and the Bohemians and for the earlier history of Franco-Bohemian relations above, 845 with n. 3, 856, 869, 871, 874; for Bohemian–Moravian relations see also below, 897.

11 See above, 893 with n. 7, for the earlier request. Formosus presumably wished to be freed from Lambert's control, though at the same time he was writing to Archbishop Fulco of Rheims to tell him of his friendship for Lambert (Flodoard, *Historia Remensis Ecclesiae* IV 3 and 5 (*MGH SS* 13: 561, 566). By the time of the siege Lambert's mother Angeltrude was actually in Rome, where she had been left by Lambert to lead the resistance; cf. Regino 896 (Kurze 1890: 144).

sent an army in the month of October from Francia and Alemannia into Italy.[12] They came to beyond the Po, and there the army was divided: he allowed the Alemans to go by Bologna to the town of Florence, while he and the Franks came across the northern part of the Apennines to the *curtis* which is called Turris, and from there to the city of Luni. There he celebrated Christmas.

896

Now the whole army was held up on the cliffs of the mountain-tops by violent storms and exceptional rainfall and flooding. It wandered round and about and came through with difficulty. As a result of this there was a great sickness among the horses, more than usual because of the difficulty of the march, so much so indeed that almost the whole army had to transport its baggage in unaccustomed fashion on oxen saddled like horses. Besides this, there was an evil rumour which disturbed the king and the army, to the effect that Berengar, the king's relative,[1] had defected from his fidelity and for this reason had already returned to Italy,[2] while Adalbert, that is the margrave of Tuscany,[3] had been brought to agree in meetings with Berengar that he would not in any way return to his fidelity to the king. After hearing these and similar rumours the king in great anxiety and the whole army with great worry and want finally arrived at the city of Rome.[4] On top of all these things there was a new problem for the army, for as they were arriving, Angeltrude, Wido's widow, had all the doors around the wall shut and barred, so that entrance to the church of St Peter was denied to all alike. The king took this badly, and by common counsel met with the whole army at the church of St Pancras.[5] After celebrating mass the king asked the army what it was best to do. All came together, promised their fidelity with tears and did public confession before the priests. Then it was agreed by common acclamation that there would be one day of fasting and then the city would be

12 He was at Pavia on December 1; D A 139.

1 For 'nephew' see above, 895 n. 1. Berengar was a distant cousin of Arnulf's since both were descended from Louis the Pious (Werner 1967: table). For his own earlier ambitions on Italy see above, 888 with n. 3, 890 with n. 2; on Arnulf's return he was to become effective ruler of Italy.

2 I.e. Lombardy, as opposed to Tuscany, where the army now was.

3 On him see 894 with n. 4.

4 Late January or early February 896; Dümmler 1888: 417.

5 By the gate of St Pancras, across the Tiber.

stormed. So, while all delayed returning to their camps, the king rode around spying out the walls, and by God's will a fight broke out suddenly and unexpectedly between the besiegers and the besieged; the people converged on this from all sides, all crying that the city should be stormed, and all showing the same desire for a fight. Without delay they came to the wall, drove the defenders off by throwing stones, and a mass of men hurled itself on the gates. Some attacked the gates and their iron bars with swords and clubs; others dug through the wall; others climbed the wall with ladders. And thus by God's providence the strongest and most noble of cities was nobly stormed in triumph as the day drew towards evening, with no one from so great an army of the king's side falling, and the pope and the city freed from their enemies. For the whole of the senate of the Romans and the guild of the Greeks[6] came with banners and crosses to the Milvian Bridge in order to receive the king with the due honour of hymns and *laudes*[7] and accompany him to the city. Now the pope received the king with fatherly love before the porch in that place which is called the steps of St Peter and conducted him joyfully and with honour to the church of the holy princes of the apostles,[8] and following the example of his predecessors gave him imperial coronation by placing a crown upon his head and calling him Caesar and Augustus.[9] Many matters were dealt with there and the whole people of the Romans came to St Paul to promise fidelity to the emperor with an oath.[10] We have decided to set down the oath here, lest anyone should be ignorant of it:

6 On the senate see above, 875 n. 13; the term is here the Roman equivalent of 'leading men'. The *scholae* were 'foreigners' compounds' (Krautheimer 1980: 82). Gregorovius 1890: 215 thought that the Greek *schola* was mentioned here as representative of all such colonies; there were also colonies for the Franks and Anglo-Saxons at this time.

7 For the role of the *laudes* in Frankish rulership see Kantorowicz 1946: 71, 76-84; McCormick 1986: 362-83. A similar procession of 'representative Rome' to meet Charles the Great outside the city is recorded before Charles's coronation in 800; *ARF* 800 (Scholz 1972: 80).

8 St Peter; the old basilica was dedicated to both Peter and Paul, to whom the foundation of the Roman bishopric was traditionally ascribed.

9 Before February 27, when Arnulf issued a diploma as emperor (D A140).

10 The text of the oath which follows is based on that laid down in the *Constitutio Romana*, but without reference to subsequent papal elections and adapted specifically to meet the threat from Lambert and Angeltrude.

I swear by all these God's mysteries[11] that saving my honour and my law and the fidelity due to the lord Pope Formosus I am and will be all the days of my life a faithful man to Emperor Arnulf, and I will never associate myself with any man in treachery against him, and I will never give any assistance to Lambert, the son of Angeltrude, or to her herself, his mother, in gaining any secular honour, and I will not hand over this city of Rome to Lambert himself or his mother Angeltrude or their men through any kind of trick or quibble.[12]

After these things Constantine and Stephen,[13] who were great among the senators, were accused of high treason, because they had previously conspired with Angeltrude to capture the city. Without delay the king ordered them to be taken prisoner and brought back with him to Bavaria. He left the guarding of the city on his behalf to a certain vassal, Farold.[14] He himself departed from the city on the fifteenth day after his arrival;[15] having at last learnt that Angeltrude was staying in the city of Spoleto, he decided to go there and attack the town. But before he arrived at his destination he was held back by a severe illness in his head,[16] and broke off the plan unfinished and hurried back as fast as possible through the valley of the Trent and returned to Bavaria in May,[17] leaving his little son called Ratold, who had been born to him by a concubine, at Milan to receive the fidelity of the Italian people.[18] But shortly after this even the son whom he had left in Italy returned to him across Lake Como. For after the death of Waltfred,[19] margrave of Friuli, who had held Verona with great fidelity for the emperor,

---

11 The oaths were presumably taken on bread consecrated for the Eucharist.

12 These oaths were not effective for long, as Lambert and Angeltrude entered Rome at the beginning of 897 after Arnulf's retreat from Italy; Dümmler 1888: 426.

13 Nothing is known otherwise of the careers of these 'senators' (for the term see 875 n. 13).

14 Otherwise unknown.

15 He was still there on March 1 (D A 141).

16 'Paralysis', according to Regino 896 (Kurze 1890: 144), perhaps a stroke. See the note on Charles III's illness, 887(II) n. 2.

17 He was at Piacenza on April 25 and near Milan on April 27; the next diploma is dated from Regensburg on July 8 (DD A 142-4).

18 For Ratold see 889 with n. 4; this is the last that is heard of him.

19 On him see Hlawitschka 1960: 279-82; he had previously been a supporter of Berengar, but was presumably installed by Arnulf as margrave after Berengar's defection.

Berengar straightaway invaded the kingdom of Italy[20] and took it into his possession in co-rulership with Lambert as if by hereditary right as far as the River Adda.[21] Maginfred, count of Milan, was executed by Lambert, Wido's son, and his son and son-in-law were blinded.[22]

At Rome Pope Formosus died on the holy day of Easter [April 4]; in his place Boniface was consecrated, who was attacked by gout and is said to have survived for barely two weeks. In his place a pope called Stephen [VI] succeeded, a man of notorious reputation, who in unheard-of fashion turned out his predecessor, Formosus, from his grave, had him deposed by proxy and buried outside the usual place where popes are buried.[23]

The Greeks made peace that same year with the Avars, who are called Hungarians; their fellow-citizens[24] the Bulgars took this very badly and led a hostile expedition against them and laid waste all their lands as far as the gates of Constantinople. In order to avenge this the Greeks cunningly sent their ships to the Avars and transported them beyond the Danube to the kingdom of the Bulgarians. Once they had been set down there they attacked the Bulgarian people with a great army and put a great part of them to death. Hearing this, the Bulgarians who were engaged in the expedition returned in great

20 'Invaded' in the sense that he intruded himself in the office, not that he had previously been outside the kingdom.

21 *quasi hereditario iure contra Lantbertum in participationem recepit*, i.e. as in 890 he retained Friuli. According to the *Gesta Berengarii* III, verses 235-44 (Dümmler 1871: 122-3), Berengar and Lambert agreed at Pavia to divide the Lombard kingdom. Berengar became sole ruler in Italy only after Lambert's death in a hunting accident on October 15 898.

22 A former supporter of Wido's, he had surrendered Milan to Arnulf in 894; Hlawitschka 1960: 226-9. His son was called Hugh, according to Liutprand of Cremona, Antapodosis I, 42 (Becker 1915: 30-1); his son-in-law cannot be identified. For blinding as a political punishment see e.g. the fate of Rastiz (above, 870) and Hugh (above, 885[I]) and in general Nelson 1991: 181 n. 5.

23 On Formosus's career cf. *AB* 878 (Nelson 1991: 193) and Zimmermann 1968: 49-55. As bishop of Porto he had been in opposition to John VIII, and had been deposed and forced under oath to renounce any ambition to higher office in the church, but had been released from his oath and restored to Porto by Marinus. His election, like that of Marinus, thus conflicted with the canonical prohibition against the translation of bishops (see above, 882 n. 16). There were evidently links between the internal Roman struggles of the 880s and 890s and the attempts of the Spoletine rulers to secure the emperorship, but the details are unclear; cf. Arnaldi 1951 and Zimmermann 1968: 47-60.

24 *Concives*; what the annalist means by this expression is by no means clear. For the Hungarians as Avars see above, 892 with n. 6. 'That same year' should not be taken literally, but refers to the period between c. 893 and 895; cf. Hellmann 1976: 894-5.

haste to liberate their countrymen from the enemy's attack, and after
joining battle were defeated straightaway. When they tried once again
to recover, they were once again defeated. In the end, miserable and
uncertain what source of remedy or help they could find, they all came
to the feet of their old king, Michael, who had first converted them to
the truth of the Christian religion, begging that he should advise them
how to evade the present danger. He said that they should first order
a fast for three days and do penance for the injury they had done to
Christians,[25] and then seek help from God. After doing this they began
a hard battle; both sides fought very fiercely, but in the end, with God's
mercy, victory, although a bloody one, fell to the Christians. For who
could count or set out the losses of the heathen Avars in so many
battles, when the Bulgarians, who were victorious, were found to have
lost twenty thousand horsemen? As the fighting mounted up in these
regions, the emperor commended Pannonia with the town of the
marshes to his *dux* Brazlavo, for that time, to guard it.[26]

Leo, the emperor of the Greeks, sent a certain Bishop Lazarus to
Caesar Augustus with gifts. He received him graciously at the town of
Regensburg, kept him with him for a few days, and then sent him back
to his own lands, loaded with honours.[27]

897

Caesar celebrated Christmas at the royal *curtis* of Ötting. There came
to him there ambassadors of the Moravians, who asked that, to
strengthen peace, exiles from their country should not be received.[1] As
soon as the king heard them, he absolved them, and gave them leave
to depart without delay. He himself held a general assembly at the

---

25 Either a reference to their campaign against their Greek *concives* or toan
   internal Bulgarian reaction against Christianity.

26 For Brazlavo see 884(II) with n. 13; the command here granted was in Lower
   Pannonia, cf. Mitterauer 1963: 167, Reindel 1953: 9. For the 'town of the
   marshes' (*Mosapurc*), the centre of Arnulf's earlier power, see above, 882 n. 3
   and 890 n. 1.

27 See above, 894, with n. 18. Leo VI (886-912) was perhaps trying to secure
   Frankish support against the Bulgars. Arnulf was at Regensburg in mid-July
   and early August, and again in late November (DD A 144-5, 148).

 1 On the civil war in the Moravian empire see below, 898.

 2 Arnulf's itinerary is unknown between January 30, when he was at Regensburg
   (DD A 150-1) and May 5, when he was at Velden, north-east of Nürnberg (D
   A 152). His going in effect into hiding was a significant sign of decline in royal
   authority; compare the end of Carloman's reign, 879 with n. 5.

town of Regensburg, and because of his illness decided to spend the winter in Bavaria in hidden places.[2]

A great famine spread through the whole of Bavaria, so that many died of hunger.

At the end of May there was an assembly held in the city of Worms.[3] There among other things Zwentibald, the emperor's son, came to him. He received him graciously, reconciled some of his leading men to him, who in the previous year had been deprived of their offices,[4] and after the remaining business had been dealt with between them as far as possible he was given friendly leave to return to his own lands.

After holding a general assembly at the *curtis* of Tribur,[5] the king went to the monastery of Fulda to pray. After he had done this he came to the *curtis* of Salz and there ambassadors of the Sorbs came to him with gifts, whom he absolved and gave leave to depart when he had heard them.[6] After these things had been done it came about that the *duces* of the Bohemian people came to Emperor Arnulf, who at that time was staying in the city of Regensburg, offering him royal gifts and begging for his help and that of his men against their enemies, that is the Moravians, by whom they had often been terribly oppressed, as they themselves testified. The king and emperor received these *duces* in friendship, swelled their breasts with words of consolation and allowed them to return joyfully to their own country, loaded with gifts.[7] He stayed the whole of the autumn of that year in places near to the northern banks of the Danube and Regen, in the intention of being ready with his faithful men, should it be necessary to give help to the above-mentioned people.

3 Arnulf issued a diploma there on June 8 (D A 153).

4 The leading men were Stephen, Odacer, Gerard and Matfrid; at this point Arnulf also arranged a marriage between Zwentibold and the Liudolfing Oda, daughter of Otto of Saxony. See Regino 897 (Kurze 1890: 144–5) and for commentary Hlawitschka 1968: 164–71.

5 Arnulf is found at Tribur on July 14 (D A 156); the purpose of the assembly is unknown.

6 Brankačk and Mětšk 1977: 69–70 suggest that the Sorbs had previously been under Moravian domination; like the Bohemians mentioned shortly, they were now reverting to east Frankish overlordship.

7 Evidently the earlier rapprochement (see above, 895 n. 10) had had little effect. The reports here of Arnulf's movements cannot be verified from the diploma evidence, as there is a gap in this between August 7 897 and May 15 898.

898

But afterwards in the year of the incarnation of the Lord 898 there was
a terrible dissension and feud which arose between two brothers of the
Moravian people, Moimir and Zwentopulk, and their followers, so that
if either had been able to pursue and capture the other with his men he
would have put him to death. Then the king and emperor, knowing
about these things, sent his leading Bavarians, that is his margraves
Liutpold and Count Arbo[1] together with other faithful men, to the
party which looked to him as their hope and refuge to be an aid to their
liberation and protection. And they, as far as they could, laid low their
enemies with fire and sword, and plundered and slaughtered them.
The calumniator, betrayer, and origin of this dissension and breach of
the peace turned out to be Count Arbo, at the instigation of his son
Isanrich. For this reason he lost his prefecture for a time, but received
it back again not long afterwards.[2] After this a certain man, Erambert
by name, who had once been a prince among the other leading men of
the Bavarian people,[3] and afterwards had been a rebel against the king
and his people, was taken captive by Priznolav, a certain *dux* of the
Slavs, who was known to be faithful to the emperor, and was brought
by the strong Count Liutpold bound with a chain and other fetters
before the king at Ranshofen at the Christmas at the end of the present
year.[4]

899

An expedition was again ordained for the winter and the leading men[1]
of the Bavarians with their men invaded the lands of the Moravians in
strength and intending war, and with a great force laid waste their
settlements and collected booty and returned home in possession of it.

Then a scandal, and worse, a crime, unheard of for many years, was
published about Queen Uota: that she had yielded her body to a lustful

1 On these two see above, 895 with n. 1, 893 with n. 1.
2 Wolfram 1987: 306 suggests that these events are connected with power-
  struggles between Arbo and Liutpold.
3 On Erembert see above, 879 with n. 5.
4 An indication that the annals at this point were being written contemporaneously with events. Nothing more is known about Priznolav; possibly he was
  related to Brazlavo (above, 896 with n. 26). Arnulf's diplomata show him at
  Regensburg, not Ranshofen, on December 13 and February 5 (DD A 170, 172).
1 *Principes*; see 852 n. 1.

and wicked union. She cleared herself of the accusation at Regensburg in the month of June with seventy-two oath-helpers[2] before the judgement of the leading men who were present. At that same time, and in the same great public meeting held in the great town of Regensburg the king was attacked by paralysis and fell ill; this was because a poison had been administered to the king by men and women so that he should become paralysed by it. One of these was called Graman, who was convicted of high treason and beheaded at Ötting; another fled into hiding in Italy, and a third was a woman called Ruodpurc, who was found by strict investigation to have been the instigator of the crime, and perished on the gallows at Aibling.

Not long after this the Bavarians again confidently invaded the lands of the Moravians and plundered and laid waste wherever they could, and rescued the boy Zwentopulk, the son of the old *dux* Zwentopulk, from the dungeon of the city in which he was held with his men, set fire to the city, and brought him out of pity back into their own country. In the meantime Isanrich continued to rebel against the king.[3] The king was enraged and ordered that there should be an attack (by ship, because at that time he was tired and sick in body) on the city of Mautern, in which Isanrich was staying. He resisted; but the king and his men fought fiercely and manfully and stormed the city. At length Isanrich himself was forced to come out with his wife and possessions and present himself before the emperor. The king gave him over to custodians to be guarded until he could be brought forward at Regensburg. But he, fearing that he would be punished, fled and took refuge with the Moravians. So, helped as before by their support, he seized a part of the kingdom and kept control of it.

Egilmar, bishop of Passau, died, and in his place a certain Aleman, Wiching, succeeded with the king's agreement but against the institutions of the fathers, for he had previously been sent by the pope

2 Arnulf was at Regensburg on May 1 (D A 175), and on July 2 issued a diploma for Ötting in which Uota appears as an intervenor (D A 176), so that she had presumably cleared herself by then. The accusation, like Arnulf's decision to spend the winter of 896/7 'in hidden places', and the witchcraft scandal which follows in the text, is to be taken as a sign of decline in royal authority; there is a significant parallel with accusations made against Charles III's wife Richgardis in the last year of his reign (Keller 1966: 354 n. 62, who points to other examples including Judith and Bernard of Septimania, and Bertilla, the wife of Berengar I). The figure of seventy-two oath-helpers is extraordinarily high, comparable with that required (largely theoretically) by canon law for accusations against bishops.

3 See 898 with n. 2.

to the Moravians as a bishop.[4] But not long afterwards he was deposed
by the canonical judgement of Archbishop Theotmar [of Salzburg]
and his suffragans against the king's will and immediately Rihhar was
ordained bishop of that see.[5]

900

The emperor ended his life at Regensburg[1] and was buried by his men
with honour in the monastery of St Emmeram, martyr of Christ. His
son Louis, who was then the sole small son born to him of his lawful
wife, succeeded him.[2] His brother by a concubine, Zwentibald by name,
continued to hold on to the Gallican kingdom [Lotharingia] and to
attack the lands of the church with immoderate cruelty. His worst
crime was to strike Ratbod, archbishop of Trier, on the head with his
own pastoral staff, contrary to the honour due a bishop. He was
deserted by all his men, both bishops and counts, and, rashly taking up
arms against them with a few supporters in an attempt to recover his
position, ended his life and his reign.[3]

The Bavarians proceeded through Bohemia, and, taking the
Bohemians with them, invaded the kingdom of the Moravians and
destroyed everything with fire for three weeks on end. Then they
returned home in complete safety.

Meanwhile the Avars, who are called Hungarians, laid waste the whole
of Italy, so that after they had killed many bishops the Italians tried to

---

4 Wiching had acted as Arnulf's chancellor from 893 onwards (Fleckenstein
   1959: 204); before that he had been consecrated bishop of Neutra and had acted
   as hostile assistant, rival and Frankish minder to Methodius in Moravia (Vlasto
   1970: 73-82; Dvornik 1970: 160-92). See 882 n. 16 on the canonical prohibition
   against the translation of bishops.

5 Egilmar held office from 874x887-99; Rihhar from 899 to 902.

1 December 8 899; BM 1955b. For St Emmeram as a burial place of the east
   Frankish rulers see 876 n. 2.

2 At an assembly at Forchheim on February 4 900 Louis was crowned king; cf.
   Regino 900 (Kurze 1890: 147-8).

3 Zwentibold had broken with his main supporter Reginar in 898; the latter had
   joined others in inviting Charles the Simple (following the death of Odo, sole
   ruler in west Francia, on January 3 898) to take over rule in Lotharingia. In 899
   negotiations took place at St Goar on the Rhine between representatives of
   Charles, Zwentibald and Arnulf; evidently a private agreement was reached
   between Arnulf's representatives (Hatto of Mainz and the 'Conradines' Conrad
   and Gebhard) and Charles's that Louis the Child should succeed in Lotharingia.
   Regino 898, 899, 900 (Kurze 1890: 145-6, 146-7, 148); AV 898 (von Simson
   1909: 80); Hlawitschka 1968: 174-80; Beumann 1966/7.

fight against them and twenty thousand men fell in one battle on one day.[4] They came back by the same way by which they had come, and returned home after destroying a great part of Pannonia. They sent ambassadors treacherously to the Bavarians offering peace so that they could spy out the land. Which, alas! first brought evil and loss not seen in all previous times to the Bavarian kingdom. For the Hungarians came unexpectedly in force with a great army across the Enns and invaded the kingdom of Bavaria with war, so that in a single day they laid waste by killing and destroying everything with fire and sword an area fifty miles long and fifty miles broad. When the Bavarians further away learned of this they were moved by grief and made plans to go against them, but the Hungarians had forseen this and returned whence they had come to their lands in Pannonia with those they had taken captive. At the same time, however, a part of their army broke out along the northern bank of the Danube and devastated that region. When Count Liutpold heard of this he felt it was impossible to tolerate it, and taking with him some of the leading men of the Bavarians including only one bishop, of Passau,[5] set out across the Danube to pursue them. There they joined battle with them, fighting nobly, and triumphing more nobly still.[6] For in the first onslaught of the battle God's grace so favoured the Christians that twelve hundred of the pagans were slain, and those who fled into the Danube were founded to have perished. They scarcely found one Christian dead among those who were armed. They came together at the place where heaven had granted them victory and with a great shout gave their thanks to God, who had saved those who had placed their hopes in Him not through the multitude of fighters but through his pious mercies. Then they returned to their fellows, rejoicing after so great a victory, and quickly and immediately built a wall around a strong town[7] on the banks of the Enns for the defence of the region. Having done this, each returned to his home.

---

4 Berengar had raised a large army to drive the Hungarians out of Italy; the Hungarians asked for an armistice, and when this was not granted made a desperate surprise attack on Berengar's forces on September 24 899; Liudprand, *Antapodosis* II, 13 (Becker 1915: 43-4).

5 Rihhar; see above, 899 with n. 4, and note the implication that the participation of Bavarian bishops on campaigns was normal. At the disaster at Preßburg in 907, at which an army led by Liutpold against the Hungarians was annihilated, three bishops were killed: Reindel 1953: 62-70.

6 Probably on November 20; Dümmler 1888: 515.

7 Ennsburg, near Lorch, on the Danube.

901

A general assembly was held in the city of Regensburg.[1] There among other things there came embassies from the Moravians seeking peace; this was soon agreed on the terms they wished and confirmed with an oath. On this account Bishop Rihhar [of Passau] and Count Udalrich[2] were sent to Moravia, who bound the *dux* and all his leading men with oaths to keep the peace on the same terms as it had been made in Bavaria.[3]

In the meantime, however, the Hungarians laid waste Carinthia and invaded the southern part of their [the Moravians'] kingdom.

The king proceeded through Alemannia, settling affairs there, and made for Franconia to celebrate Easter [April 12].[4]

1 Early in January; a diploma of Louis's for St Florian issued there is dated January 19 (D LC 9).

2 Possibly a count in the Zürichgau; Borgolte 1986: 268-70.

3 The eastern Franks had evidently finally decided that the Hungarians were a greater threat than the Moravians; but their decision came too late. By 906 at the latest the Moravian empire had effectively ceased to exist as a political entity and hence as a potential ally.

4 There are no diplomata to confirm or deny this itinerary. Louis had been in Alemannia before the meeting at Regensburg, issuing diplomata at Strasbourg on October 31 900 and at Bodman on January 1 901 (DD LC 7-8). Note the way the text refers to him as if he were a fully adult ruler.

BIBLIOGRAPHY

Primary sources

A Narrative, annalistic, biographical and hagiographical texts

1 Andreas of Bergamo, *Historia*
   Ed. Waitz 1878b: 220-30. Composed shortly after 877, it is a brief continuation of Paul the Deacon's *Historia Langobardorum* down to the late 870s, with useful information on the politics of the succession to Louis II.

2 *Anglo-Saxon Chronicle*
   Trans. Whitelock 1979. Composed in the early 890s, it shows little interest in continental affairs, but does have an account of Charles III's fall in 887-88.

3 *Annales Alamannici*
   Ed. Pertz, *MGH SS* 1: 22-31, 40-4, 47-56 and Lendi 1971: 146-93. A set of related texts rather than a single work, compiled at the Reichenau and later St Gallen, and reworked in a manuscript now at Monza; cf. Lendi 1971 and Löwe 1990: 787-9.

4 *Annals of St-Bertin (Annales Bertiniani)*
   Trans. Nelson 1991; a very full and frank account of Frankish and especially west Frankish affairs from 830 to 882.

5 *Annals of Corvey (Annales Corbeienses)*
   Ed. Prinz 1982. Brief contemporary notices from the Westfalian monasteries of Corvey and Werden.

6 *Annals of Hildesheim (Annales Hildesheimenses)*
   Ed. Waitz 1878a. A composite work put together in the eleventh century, whose ninth-century entries are drawn from now lost Hersfeld annals with a few additions drawn from Hildesheim information.

7 *Annals of St-Vaast (Annales Vedastini)*
   Ed. von Simson 1909: 40-82. Written at the monastery of St-Vaast, Arras, they give a contemporary account of events with a strong Lotharingian–west Frankish focus from 873 to 900. An English translation by S. Coupland is forthcoming in the MUP series.

8 *Annals of Salzburg (Annales Iuvavenses)*
   Ed. Bresslau, *MGH SS* 30: 727-44. Now known only in fragmentary form from medieval and early modern transcripts, they offer information on south-eastern affairs not found elsewhere.

9 *Annals of Xanten (Annales Xantenses)*

Ed. von Simson 1909: 7-33. Written probably at Lorsch by the royal chaplain Gerward and continued for the period 852-73 at Cologne by an unknown writer, they give an independent account of events between 832 and 873. An English translation by S. Coupland is forthcoming.

10 Astronomer, *Vita Hludovici Pii*
Ed. Pertz, *MGH SS* 2: 607-48. An anonymous biography of Louis the Pious, written shortly after his death. A new edition by E. Tremp is to appear shortly; on the origins of the work see Tremp 1991.

11 Einhard, *Vita Karoli Magni*
Ed. Holder-Egger 1911. Biography of Charles the Great written in the early 830s. There are various English translations; Thorpe 1968, the most readily available, is unfortunately not the best.

12 *Continuatio Erchanberti*
Ed. Pertz, *MGH SS* 2: 329-30. Brief notices of east Frankish affairs (including the division of 865), probably by Notker the Stammerer.

13 Flodoard, *Historia Remensis Ecclesiae*
Ed. Waitz and Heller, *MGH SS* 13: 405-599. Written from the Rheims archives in the mid-tenth century; important above all for the large number of extracts it contains from lost letters by and to the Rheims archbishops Hincmar and Fulco.

14 *Gesta Berengarii imperatoris*
Ed. Dümmler 1871: 77-133 and also by P. Winterfeld in *MGH Poetae* 4: 354-403. A difficult and often maddeningly vague epic poem on Berengar's career up to 915 which throws some light on the politics of the 890s.

15 *Liber Pontificalis*
Ed. Duchesne 1892. Contemporary lives of the ninth-century popes up to and including Hadrian II; a fragmentary life of Stephen V has also survived.

16 Liutprand of Cremona, *Antapodosis*
Ed. Becker 1915: 1-158. An account of highly selected Italian and European affairs from the late Carolingian era down to the 960s, book I offers Italian politics of the 890s as filtered through the mind of a great moralist and *raconteur*; occasionally useful as confirmation of more sober sources.

17 Nithard, *Historiarum Libri IV*
Ed. Lauer 1926. The fullest account of the 'civil war' of 840-4, written by a participant who supported Charles the Bald; cf. Nelson 1985 on its composition. English translation in Scholz 1972.

18 Notker the Stammerer, *Gesta Karoli Magni Imperatoris*
Ed. Haefele 1959. Charles the Great as seen nostalgically from the end of the ninth century, with much incidental information about east Frankish politics; see Goetz 1981. The English translation and commentary in Thorpe 1968 should be used with some caution.

19 Regino of Prüm, *Chronicon*
Ed. Kurze 1890. Universal chronicle, largely independent from 814

onwards and a full though idiosyncratic and chronologically careless account of events from about 860 onwards, written in Lotharingia in the early years of the tenth century.

20 Rimbert, *Vita Anskarii*
Ed. Waitz 1884; English translation in Robinson 1921. Life of Ansgar, missionary to the Danes and bishop of Hamburg-Bremen; important for information on Franco-Danish relations in the ninth century.

21 *Royal Frankish Annals (Annales Regni Francorum)*
Ed. Kurze 1895; English translation in Scholz 1972. 'Courtly' annals compiled in the late eighth century and continued down to 830 by writers closely associated with the royal chapel; at the end of Charles the Great's reign a revision of the earlier text was carried out and this survives in a number of manuscripts (the so-called 'E'-text, long falsely ascribed to Einhard).

B Letters, diplomata, legal and poetic texts

(i) Letters

The surviving letters of the period of interest for east Frankish affairs have almost all been edited in *MGH Epp.* 4–8. *MGH Epp.* 4 contains Einhard's letters; *MGH Epp.* 5 the surviving fragments of Hrabanus Maurus's correspondence; *MGH Epp.* 6 and 7 are important for the correspondence of the popes from Nicholas I to Formosus, especially Nicholas I, John VIII and Stephen V; and *MGH Epp.* 8, as yet incomplete, contains Hincmar of Rheims's correspondence.

(ii) Diplomata

Royal diplomata offer information above all about the king's itinerary and entourage. The diplomata of Louis the German, Louis the Younger and Carloman were edited by Kehr 1934; those of Charles III by Kehr 1936-37; and those of Arnulf by Kehr 1940. For the early years of the east Frankish kingdom the diplomata of Lothar I and Lothar II are also of significance; they were edited by Schieffer 1966.

(iii) Legal Texts

The ecclesiastical legislation for our period has been edited only in part, in Hartmann 1984. For the period after 859 it must be studied in Mansi 1757-98 though many of the more important texts were edited together with the 'capitulary' legislation of the Frankish rulers in Boretius and Krause 1893-97.

(iv) Poetry

Apart from its intrinsic interest, the Latin poetry of the Carolingian period throws occasional light on the *histoire événementielle* of the period. It has been edited principally in *MGH Poetae* 1-4 and 6; for our period vols. 4 and 6 are of most significance.

Secondary works and editions of primary sources

Althoff, G. 1988. 'Zur Bedeutung der Bündnisse Svatopluks von Mähren mit Franken', in Trost 1988, pp. 13-22.

Althoff, G. 1990. *Verwandte, Freunde und Getreue*, Darmstadt.

Arnaldi, G. 1951. 'Papa Formoso e gli imperatori della casa di Spoleto', *Annale della facultà di lettere, Napoli* 1, pp. 85-104.

Arnaldi, G. 1990. *Natale 875*, Rome.

Bachrach, B. S. 1970. 'Charles Martel, mounted shock combat, the stirrup, and feudalism', *Studies in Medieval and Renaissance History* 7, pp. 49-75.

Bartha, A. 1975. *Hungarian Society in the Ninth and Tenth Centuries*, Budapest.

Bautier, R.-H. 1973. 'Aux origines du royaume de Provence. De la sédition avortée de Boson à la royauté légitime de Louis', *Provence Historique* 23, pp. 41-68.

Becker, J. ed. 1915. *Die Werke Liudprands von Cremona, MGH SRG*, Hanover.

Beeson, C. H. 1926. 'The vocabulary of the Annales Fuldenses', *Speculum* 1, pp. 31-7.

Beumann, H. 1966/7. 'König Zwentibalds Kurswechsel 898', *Rheinische Vierteljahrsblätter* 31, pp. 17-41.

Bischoff, B. 1980. *Die südostdeutschen Schreibschulen in der Karolingerzeit, Teil 2: Die vorwiegend österreichischen Diözesen*, Munich.

Boba, I. 1971. *Moravia's History Reconsidered. A Reinterpretation of Medieval Sources*, The Hague.

Boba, I. 1986. 'Die Lage von Moravien nach den mittelalterlichen Quellen aus Bayern', *Mitteilungen der Gesellschaft für Salzburger Landeskunde* 126, pp. 59-70.

Boretius, A. and Krause, V. eds. 1893-97. *Capitularia regum Francorum*, 2 vols., *MGH Capit.*, Hanover.

Borgolte, M. 1977. 'Karl III. und Neuendingen', *Zeitschrift für die Geschichte des Oberrheins*, neue Folge 125, pp. 21-55.

Borgolte, M. 1986. *Die Grafen Alemanniens im merowingischer und karolingischer Zeit. Eine Prosopographie*, Sigmaringen.

Boshof, E. 1976. 'Untersuchungen zur Armenfürsorge im fränkischen Reich des 9. Jahrhunderts', *AKG* 58, pp. 265-339.

Bouchard, C. 1988. 'The Bosonids, or rising to power in the late Carolingian age', *French Historical Studies* 15, pp. 407-31.

Bowlus, C. R. 1973. 'Die Wilheminer und die Mährer', *Zeitschrift für bayerische Landesgeschichte* 36, pp. 759-75.

Bowlus, C. R. 1985. 'Prosopographical evidence concerning Moravia's location', *Medieval Prosopography* 6, pp. 1-22.

Bowlus, C. R. 1987. 'Imre Boba's reconsideration of Moravia's early history and Arnulf of Carinthia's Ostpolitik', Speculum 67, pp. 552-74.

Brankačk, F. and Mětšk, J. 1977. Geschichte der Sorben, vol. 1, Bautzen.

Bresslau, H. 1923. Die ältere Salzburger Annalistik, Abhandlungen der Preußischen Akademie der Wissenschaften, phil.-hist. Klasse 2, Berlin.

Bresslau, H. 1926. Annales Iuvavenses maiores, MGH SS 30/2, Hanover, pp. 727-44.

Brunner, K. 1973. 'Die fränkischen Fürstentitel im neunten und zehnten Jahrhundert', in H. Wolfram ed., Intitulatio II, Vienna, pp. 179-340.

Chroust, A. 1890. 'Topographische Erklärungen zu einigen Stellen in den Monumenta Germaniae', NA 16, pp. 585-91.

D'Haenens, A. 1969. Les Invasions normandes en Belgique au 9ᵉ siècle, Louvain.

De Vajay, S. 1968. Der Eintritt der ungarischen Stammesbundes in die europäische Geschichte (852-933), Mainz.

Delogu, P. 1968. 'Vescovi, conti e sovrani nella crisi del Regno Italico', Annali dela scuola speciale per arcivisti e bibliotecari dell'università di Roma 7, pp. 3-72.

Dienemann-Dietrich, I. 1955. 'Der fränkische Adel in Alemannien im 8. Jahrhundert', Vorträge und Forschungen 1, Lindau, pp. 149-92.

Dopsch, H. 1980. Geschichte Salzburgs, vol. 1, Salzburg.

Dopsch, H. 1986. 'Slawenmission und päpstliche Politik zu den Hintergründen des Methodius-Konfliktes', Mitteilungen der Gesellschaft für Salzburger Landeskunde 126, pp. 303-40.

Duchesne, L. ed. 1892. Le Liber Pontificalis, vol. 2, Paris.

Dümmler, E. 1857. Das Formelbuch des Bischofs Salomo III. von Konstanz aus dem neunten Jahrhundert, Leipzig.

Dümmler, E. 1871. Gesta Berengarii Imperatoris, Berlin.

Dümmler, E. 1887a, 1887b, 1888. Jahrbücher des ostfränkischen Reiches, 2nd edn, 3 vols., Leipzig.

Dvornik, F. 1926. Les Slaves, Byzance et Rome au IXe siècle, Paris.

Dvornik, F. 1970. Byzantine Missions among the Slavs. SS. Constantine-Cyril and Methodius, New Brunswick, NJ.

Dvornik, F. 1974. The Making of Central and Eastern Europe, 2nd edn, Gulf Breeze, FL.

Eggert, W. 1973. Das ostfränkisch-deutsche Reich in der Auffassung seiner Zeitgenossen, Berlin (E).

Erler, A. 1971. 'Handschlag', Handwörterbuch zur deutschen Rechtsgeschichte, ed. A. Erler and E. Kaufmann, Berlin, p. 1974.

Ewig, E. 1962. 'Kaiser Lothars Urenkel, Ludwig von Vienne, der präsumtive Nachfolger Kaiser Karls III.', in V. H. Elbern ed., Das erste Jahrtausend, vol. 1, Düsseldorf, pp. 336-43.

Ewig, E. 1981. 'Überlegungen zu den merowingischen und karolingischen Teilungen', *Settimane* 28, pp. 225-60.

Fasoli, G. 1945. *Le incursioni ungare in Europa nel secolo X*, Florence.

Finsterwalder, W. 1922. 'Beiträge zu Rudolf von Fulda', unpublished Ph. D. thesis, Königsberg.

Fisher, P. and Davidson, H. E. 1979, 1980. *Saxo Grammaticus. The History of the Danes. 1. Translation. 2. Commentary*, Cambridge.

Fleckenstein, J. 1957. 'Über die Herkunft der Welfen und ihre Anfänge in Süddeutschland', in Tellenbach 1957a, pp. 71-136.

Fleckenstein, J. 1959. *Die Hofkapelle der deutschen Könige, I. Teil: Grundlegung. Die karolingische Hofkapelle*, Stuttgart.

Foote, P. G. and Wilson, D. M. 1980. *The Viking Achievement*. London.

Fouracre, P. 1985. 'The context of the OHG *Ludwigslied*', *Medium Aevum* 54, pp. 87-103.

Freher, M. 1600. *Germanicarum rerum scriptores aliquot insignes*, vol. 1, Frankfurt.

Fried, J. 1976. 'Boso von Vienne oder Ludwig der Stammler: Der Kaiserkandidat Papst Johannes VIII.', *DA* 32, pp. 193-208.

Fried, J. 1984. *König Ludwig der Jüngere in seiner Zeit*, Lorsch.

Friedmann, B. 1986. *Untersuchungen zur Geschichte des abodritischen Fürstentums bis zum Ende des 10. Jahrhunderts*, Berlin.

Fritze, W. H. 1960. 'Probleme der abodritischen Stammes- und Reichsverfassung und ihrer Entwicklung vom Stammesstaat zum Herrschaftsstaat', in *Siedlung und Verfassung der Slaven zwischen Elbe, Saale und Oder*, ed. H. Ludat, Gießen, pp. 141-219.

Fuchs, F. 1992. 'Das Grab der Königin Hemma († 876) zu St. Emmeram in Regensburg', in *Regensburg und Ostbayern. Max Piendl zum Gedächtnis*, ed. F. Karg, Kallmünz, pp. 1-12.

Ganshof, F. L. 1968. *Frankish Institutions under Charlemagne*, Providence, RI.

Ganshof, F. L. 1971. 'On the genesis and significance of the Treaty of Verdun (843)', in *The Carolingians and the Frankish Monarchy*, trans. Janet Sondheimer, London, pp. 273-88.

Ganz, D. 1990. 'The debate on Predestination', in Gibson and Nelson 1990, pp. 283-302.

Geldner, F. 1971. *Neue Beiträge zur Geschichte der 'alten Babenberger'*, Bamberg.

Gensicke, H. 1974. 'Samuel, Bischof von Worms 838-856', in *Die Reichsabtei Lorsch*, vol. 1, Darmstadt, pp. 253-6.

Gibson, M. and Nelson, J. eds. 1990. *Charles the Bald. Court and Kingdom*, 2nd rev. edn, London.

Goetz, H.-W. 1981. *Strukturen der spätkarolingischen Epoche im Spiegel der Vorstellungen eines zeitgenössischen Mönchs. Eine Interpretation der 'Gesta Karoli' Notkers von St. Gallen*, Cologne.

Goetz, H.-W. 1987. 'Regnum: Zum politischen Denken der Karolingerzeit', *ZRGGA* 104, pp. 110-90.

Gottlob, T. 1928. *Der abendländische Chorepiskopat*, Bonn.

Graus, F. 1980. *Die Nationenbildung der Westslawen im Mittelalter*, Sigmaringen.

Gregorovius, F. 1890. *Geschichte der Stadt Rom im Mittelalter. Vom V. bis zum XVI. Jahrhundert*, vol. 3, 4th rev. edn, Stuttgart.

Haefele, H. F. ed. 1959. *Notker der Stammler, Taten Kaiser Karls des Großen*, MGH SRG NS, Berlin.

Halphen, L. 1907. *Études sur l'administration de Rome au moyen âge*, Paris.

Harthausen, H. 1966. *Die Normanneneinfälle im Elb- und Wesermündungsgebiet mit besonderer Berücksichtigung der Schlacht von 880*, Hildesheim.

Hartmann, W. 1977. *Das Konzil von Worms 868. Überlieferung und Bedeutung*, Göttingen.

Hartmann, W. 1983. 'Eine kleine Sammlung von Bußtexten aus dem 9. Jahrhundert', *DA* 39, pp. 207-13.

Hartmann, W. ed. 1984. *Die Konzilien der karolingischen Teilreiche 843-859*, MGH Conc. 3, Hanover.

Hartmann, W. 1989. *Die Synoden der Karolingerzeit im Frankenreich und in Italien*, Paderborn.

Havlík, L. *et al.* eds. 1966, 1967, 1969, 1971, 1978. *Magnae Moraviae Fontes Historici*, Brno.

Heidingsfelder, F. 1938. *Die Regesten der Bischöfe von Eichstätt*, Erlangen.

Hellmann, M. 1973, 'Bemerkungen zum Aussagewert der Fuldaer Annalen und anderer Quellen über slavische Verfassungszustände', in *Festschrift für Walter Schlesinger*, vol. 1, Cologne, pp. 50-62.

Hellmann, M. 1976. 'Die politisch-kirchliche Grundlegung der Osthälfte Europas', in *Handbuch der europäischen Geschichte I*, ed. T. Schieffer, Stuttgart, pp. 857-938.

Hellmann, S. 1908. 'Die Entstehung und Ueberlieferung der Annales Fuldenses. I', *NA* 33, pp. 695-742.

Hellmann, S. 1909. 'Die Entstehung und Ueberlieferung der Annales Fuldenses. II', *NA* 34, pp. 15-66.

Hellmann, S. 1912. 'Die Annales Fuldenses', *NA* 37, pp. 53-65.

Hellmann, S. 1913. 'Einhard, Rudolf, Meginhard. Ein Beitrag zur Frage der *Annales Fuldenses*', *HJb* 34, pp. 40-64.

Herrmann, E. 1965. *Slawisch-Germanische Beziehungen im süudostdeutschen Raum von der spätantike bis zum Ungarnsturm. Ein Quellenbuch mit Erläuterungen*, Munich.

Herrmann, J. *et al.* 1972. *Die Slawen im Deutschland*, 2nd edn, Berlin (E).

Heuwieser, M. 1939. *Geschichte des Bistums Passau*, vol. 1, Passau.

Hirsch, P. 1910. *Die Erhebung Berengars von Friaul zum König in Italien*, Strasbourg.

Hirsch, P. and Lohmann, H.-E. eds. 1935. *Die Sachsengeschichte des Widukind von Korvei, MGH SRG*, Hanover.

Hlawitschka, E. 1960. *Franken, Alemannen, Bayern und Burgunder in Oberitalien (774-962)*, Freiburg im Breisgau.

Hlawitschka, E. 1968. *Lothringen und das Reich an der Schwelle der deutschen Geschichte*, Stuttgart.

Hlawitschka, E. 1969. Response to Schlesinger 1969, *HZ* 208, pp. 777-82.

Hlawitschka, E. 1974. 'Zur Herkunft der Liudolfinger', *Rheinische Vierteljahresblätter* 38, pp. 92-165.

Hlawitschka, E. 1978. 'Nachfolgeprojekte aus der Spätzeit Kaiser Karls III.', *DA* 34, pp. 19-50.

Hlawitschka, E. 1983. 'Die Widonen im Dukat von Spoleto', *QFIAB* 63, pp. 20-92.

Hoffmann, H. 1958. *Untersuchungen zur karolingischen Annalistik*, Bonn.

Hofmeister, A. 1907. 'Markgrafen und Markgrafschaften im Italischen Königreich in der Zeit von Karl dem Großen bis auf Otto den Großen 774-962', *MIÖG* Ergänzungsband 7, pp. 215-435.

Holder-Egger, O. ed. 1911. *Einhardi Vita Karoli, MGH SRG*, Hanover.

Jaffé, P. 1885, 1888. *Regesta Pontificum Romanorum ab condita ecclesia ad annum post Christum natum MCXCVIII*, 2nd edn, ed. W. Wattenbach *et al.*, Leipzig.

Janssen, M. 1912. 'Zu den *Annales Fuldenses*', *HJb* 33, pp. 101-3.

Kahl, H.-D. 1971. '*Schwerin, Svarinsburg* und die *Sclavorum civitas* des Prudentius von Troyes', in K. Zernack ed., *Beiträge zur Stadt- und Regionalgeschichte Ost- und Nordeuropas. Herbert Ludat zum 60. Geburtstag*, Wiesbaden, pp. 49-134.

Kantorowicz, E. H. 1946. *Laudes Regiae. A Study in Liturgical Acclamations and Mediaeval Ruler Worship*, Berkeley, CA.

Kehr, P. ed. 1934. *Die Urkunden Ludwigs des Deutschen, Karlmanns und Ludwigs des Jüngeren, MGH Diplomata regum Germaniae ex stirpe Karolinorum* 1, Berlin.

Kehr, P. ed. 1936-37. *Die Urkunden Karls III, MGH Diplomata regum Germaniae ex stirpe Karolinorum* 2, Berlin.

Kehr, P. ed. 1940. *Die Urkunden Arnulfs, MGH Diplomata regum Germaniae ex Stirpe Karolinorum* 3, Berlin.

Keller, H. 1966. 'Zum Sturz Karls III', *DA* 34, pp. 333-84.

Keller, H. 1967. 'Zur Struktur der Königsherrschaft im karolinigshcen und nachkarolingischen Italien. Der "consiliarius regis" in den italienischen Königsdiplomen des 9. und 10. Jahrhunderts', *QFIAB* 47, pp. 123-223.

Kottje, R. 1975. 'König Ludwig der Deutsche und die Fastenzeit', *Mysterium der Gnade. Festschrift Johann Auer*, ed. H. Roßmann and J. Ratzinger, Regensburg, pp. 307-11.

Kottje, R. 1982/3. 'Hrabanus Maurus', in K. Ruh ed., *Die deutsche Literatur des Mittelalters. Verfasserlexikon*, vol. 4, Berlin, pp. 166-95.

Kottje, R. and Zimmermann, H. eds. 1982. *Hrabanus Maurus. Lehrer, Abt und Bischof*, Wiesbaden.

Krautheimer, R. 1980. *Rome: Profile of a City, 312-1308*, Princeton, NJ.

Krüger, S. 1950. *Studien zur sächsischen Grafschaftsverfassung im 9. Jahrhundert*, Göttingen.

Krusch, B. ed. 1933. *Die Übertragung des Hl. Alexander von Rom nach Wildeshausen durch den Enkel Widukinds 851*, Nachrichten von der Gesellschaften der Wiessenschaften zu Göttingen, phil.-hist. Klasse II 13, Göttingen, pp. 405-36.

Kudorfer, D. 1970. 'Das Ries zur Karolingerzeit', *Zeitschrift für bayerische Landesgeschichte 33*, pp. 470-541.

Kurze, F. ed. 1890. *Reginonis abbatis Prumiensis Chronicon cum continuatione Treverensi, MGH SRG*, Hanover.

Kurze, F. ed. 1891. *Annales Fuldenses, MGH SRG*, Hanover.

Kurze, F. 1892. 'Ueber die Annales Fuldenses', *NA* 17, pp. 83-158.

Kurze, F. ed. 1895. *Annales regni Francorum inde ab a. 741 usque ad a. 829, qui dicuntur Annales Laurissenses maiores et Einhardi, MGH SRG*, Hanover.

Kurze, F. 1911. 'Die Annales Fuldenses. (Entgegnung)', *NA* 36, pp. 343-93.

Kurze, F. 1912. 'Die Annales Fuldenses. (Duplik)', *NA* 37, pp. 778-85.

Lauer, P. ed. 1926. *Nithard. Histoire des fils de Louis le Pieux*, Paris.

Lehn, J. 1987. 'Die Synoden zu Mainz (888) und Tribur (895). Ihre Bedeutung für das Verhältnis Arnulfs von Kärnten zum ostfränkischen Episkopat im ausgehenden 9. Jahrhundert', *Jahrbuch für westdeutsche Landesgeschichte* 14, pp. 43-62.

Lendi, W. 1971. *Untersuchungen zur frühalemannischen Annalistik. Die Murbacher Annalen. Mit Edition*, Freiburg (Schweiz).

Levison, W. and Löwe, H. eds. 1953. W. Wattenbach, *Deutschlands Geschichtsquellen im Mittelalter. Vorzeit und Karolinger, II. Heft: Die Karolinger vom Anfang des 8. Jahrhunderts bis zum Tode Karls des Großen*, Weimar.

Lintzel, M. 1929. 'Der Ursprung der deutschen Pfalzgrafschaften', *Zeitschrift der Savigny-Stiftung für Rechtsgeschichte* 49, pp. 233-63.

Lot, F. and Halphen, L. 1909. *Le Règne de Charles le Chauve, I. 840-851*, Paris.

Löwe, H. 1986. 'Ermenrich von Passau, Gegner des Methodius. Versuch eines Persönlichkeitsbildes', *Mitteilungen der Gesellschaft für Salzburger Landeskunde* 126, pp. 221-41.

Löwe, H. ed. 1990. W. Wattenbach, *Deutschlands Geschichtsquellen im Mittelalter. Vorzeit und Karolinger, VI Heft*: ... *Das ostfränkische Reich*, Weimar.

MacCartney, C. A. 1953. *The Medieval Hungarian Historians. A Critical and Analytical Guide*, Cambridge.

McCormick, M. 1975. *Les 'Annales' du haut moyen âge*, Typologie des sources du haut moyen âge occidental 14, Turnhout.

McCormick, M. 1986. *Eternal Victory. Triumphal Rulership in Late Antiquity, Byzantium, and the Early Medieval West*, Cambridge.

Mansi, J.-D. 1757-98. *Sacrorum Conciliorum Nova et Amplissima Collectio*, 36 vols., Venice.

Marenbon, J. 1990. 'John Scottus and Carolingian theology: from the *De Praedestionatione*, its background and its critics, to the *Periphyseon*', in Gibson and Nelson eds. 1990, pp. 303-25.

Märtl, C. ed. 1986. *Die falschen Investiturprivilegien*, *MGH Fontes Iuris Germanici Antiqui*, Hanover.

Meyer-Gebel, M. 1987. 'Zur annalistischen Arbeitsweise Hinkmars von Reims', *Francia* 15, pp. 75-108.

Mitterauer, M. 1963. *Karolingische Markgrafen im Südosten. Fränkische Reichsaristokratie und bayerischer Stammesadel im österreichischen Raum*, Vienna.

Mühlbacher, E. *et al.* eds. 1908. J. F. Böhmer, *Regesta Imperii 1. Die Regesten des Karolingerreichs*, 2nd edn, Innsbruck.

Müller-Mertens, E. 1972. 'Der Stellingaaufstand. Seine Träger und die Frage der politischen Macht', *Zeitschrift für Geschichtswissenschaft* 20, pp. 818-42.

Nelson, J. L. 1985. 'Public *Histories* and private history in the work of Nithard', *Speculum* 60, pp. 251-93.

Nelson, J. L. 1988. 'A tale of two princes: politics, text and ideology in a Carolingian annal', *Studies in Medieval and Renaissance History* 10, pp. 105-41.

Nelson, J. L. 1990a. 'Hincmar of Reims on king-making: the evidence of the Annals of St. Bertin', in J. M. Bak ed., *Coronations*, Berkeley and Los Angeles, CA, pp. 16-34.

Nelson, J. L. 1990b. 'Women and the Word', *Studies in Church History* 27, pp. 53-78.

Nelson, J. L. 1991. *The Annals of St-Bertin*, Manchester.

Nineham, D. 1989. 'Gottschalk of Orbais', *JEccH* 40, pp. 1-18.

Noble, T. F. X. 1984. *The Republic of St. Peter. The Birth of the Papal State, 687-825*, Philadelphia, PA.

Oesterle, H.-J. 1979. 'Die sogenannte Kopfoperation Karls III., 887', *Archiv für Kulturgeschichte* 61, pp. 445-51.

Oexle, O. G. 1967. 'Die Karolinger und die Stadt des heilige Arnulf', *FMS* 1, pp. 250-364.

Parisot, R. 1899. *Le Royaume de Lorraine sous les Carolingiens, 843-923*, Paris.

Perz, G. H. ed. 1826. *Annales Alamannici, MGH SS* 1, pp. 22-31, 40-4, 47-56.

Perz, G. H. ed. 1829a. *Astronomi Vita Hludowici Pii, MGH SS* 2, pp. 607-48.

Pertz, G. H. ed. 1829b. *Continuatio Erchanberti, MGH SS* 2, pp. 329-30.

Pithou, P. 1588. *Annalium et historiae Francorum ab anno 708 ad annum 990 scriptores coetanii XII*, Paris.

Poupardin, R. 1901. *Le Royaume de Provence sous les Carolingiens (855-933?)*, Paris.

Poupardin, R. 1907. *Le Royaume de Bourgogne (888-1038)*, Paris.

Preidel, H. 1968. *Das Großmährische Reich im Spiegel der Bodenfunde*, Munich.

Prinz, F. 1971. *Klerus und Krieg im frühen Mittelalter*, Stuttgart.

Prinz, J. 1977. 'Der Feldzug Karls des Kahlen an dem Rhein im September 876', *DA* 33, pp. 543-5.

Prinz, J. 1982. *Die Corveyer Annalen. Textbearbeitung und Kommentar*, Münster.

Rau, R. 1960. *Quellen zur karolingischen Reichsgeschichte*, vol. 3, Darmstadt.

Rehdantz, C. 1852. *Die Jahrbücher von Fulda und Xanten*, Geschichtsschreiber der deutschen Vorzeit 23, Leipzig.

Reindel, K. 1953. *Die bayerischen Luitpoldinger 893-989. Sammlung und Erläuterung der Quellen*, Munich.

Rethfeld, A. 1886. *Über den Ursprung des zweiten, dritten und vierten Teils der sogenannten Fuldischen Annalen*, Diss. Halle.

Reuter, T. 1985. 'Plunder and tribute in the Carolingian Empire', *Transactions of the Royal Historical Society* fifth series 35, pp. 75-94.

Reuter, T. 1991. *Germany in the Early Middle Ages, c. 800-1056*, London.

Rexroth, K.-H. 1978. 'Volkssprache und werdendes Volksbewußtsein im ostfränkischen Reich', in H. Beumann and W. Schröder eds., *Aspekte der Nationenbildung im Mittelalter*, Nationes 1, Sigmaringen, pp. 275-315.

Robinson, A. 1921. *Anskar, the Apostle of the North*, London.

Sandmann, M. 1978. 'Die Folge der Äbte', in Schmid *et al.* 1978a, pp. 178-204.

Sandmann, M. 1980. 'Hrabanus als Mönch, Abt und Erzbischof', in W. Browe ed., *Hrabanus Maurus und seine Schule*, Fulda, pp. 13-47.

Schiaparelli, L. 1902. *I diplomi di Berengario I*, Rome.

Schiaparelli, L. 1905. 'I diplomi dei re d'Italia. Richerche storico-diplomatiche. Parte II. I diplomi di Guido e di Lamberto', *Bolletino dell'istituto storico italiano per il medio evo* 26, pp. 7-104.

Schieffer, T. ed. 1966. *Die Urkunden Lothars I. und Lothars II., MGH Die Urkunden der Karolinger* 4, Berlin.

Schlachter, W. 1914. *Zur Latinität der Annales Fuldenses*, Diss. Greifswald.

Schlesinger, W. 1961 (1960). 'Die Verfassung der Sorben', reprinted with additions and corrections in *Mitteldeutsche Beiträge zur deutschen Verfassungsgeschichte des Mittelalters*, Göttingen, pp. 7-47, 471.

Schlesinger, W. 1963 (1960). 'Die Grundlegung der deutschen Einheit im frühen Mittelalter', in *Beiträge zur deutschen Verfassungsgeschichte des Mittelalters*, 1: *Germanen, Franken, Deutsche*, Göttingen.

Schlesinger, W. 1969. Review of Hlawitschka 1968 and reply to Hlawitschka's response, *HZ* 208, pp. 379-89, 783-5.

Schmid, A. 1976. 'Die Herrschergräber in St. Emmeram zu Regensburg', *DA* 32, pp. 333-69.

Schmid, K. 1957. 'Königtum, Adel und Klöster zwischen Bodensee und Schwarzwald', in Tellenbach 1957a, pp. 225-334.

Schmid, K. 1959. *Kloster Hirsau und seine Stifter*, Freiburg im Breisgau.

Schmid, K. *et al.* 1978a, 1978b, 1978c, 1978d, 1978e. *Die Klostergemeinschaft von Fulda im früheren Mittelalter*, 3 vols. in 5, Munich.

Schmid, P. 1977. *Regensburg. Stadt der Könige und Herzöge im Mittelalter*, Kallmünz.

Schneider, R. 1964. *Brüdergemeine und Schwurfreundschaft*, Lübeck.

Schneider, R. 1977. 'Mittelalterliche Verträge auf Brücken und Flüssen (und zur Problematik von Grenzgewässern)', *AfD* 23, pp. 1-24.

Scholz, B. 1972. *Carolingian Chronicles*, Ann Arbor, MI.

Schramm, P. E. 1968a, 1968b, 1969, 1970, 1971. *Kaiser, Könige und Päpste. Gesammelte Aufsätze*, 4 vols. in 5, Stuttgart.

Schwarzmaier, H. 1972. 'Ein Brief des Markgrafen Aribo an König Arnulf über die Verhältnisse in Mähren', *Frühmittelalterliche Studien* 6, pp. 55-66.

Silagi, G. 1988. 'Die Ungarnstürme in der ungarischen Geschichtsschreibung: Anonymus und Simon von Kéza', *Settimane* 35, pp. 245-72.

von Simson, B. 1875, 1876. *Jahrbücher des fränkischen Reiches unter Ludwig dem Frommen*, 2 vols., Leipzig.

von Simson, B. ed. 1905. *Annales Mettenses Priores*, MGH SRG, Hanover.

von Simson, B. ed. 1909. *Annales Xantenses et Annales Vedastini*, MGH SRG, Hanover.

Sláma, J. 1973. 'Civitas Wiztrachi ducis', *Historische Geographie. Beiträge zur Problematik der mittelalterlichen Siedlung und der Wege* 11, pp. 3-30.

Smalley, B. 1970. 'Sallust in the Middle Ages', in R. R. Bolgar ed., *Classical Influences on European Culture A.D. 500-1500*, Cambridge, pp. 165-75.

Sós, A. C. 1973. *Die slawische Bevölkerung Westungarns im 9. Jahrhundert*, Munich.

Stengel, E. E. 1914. 'Die Urkundenfälschungen des Rudolf von Fulda', *Archiv für Urkundenforschung* 5, pp. 41-152.

Stengel, E. E. 1965. 'Kaisertitel und Suveranitätsidee', *Zum Kaisergedanken im Mittelalter*, Cologne, pp. 239-86.

Tellenbach, G. 1939. *Die Entstehung des deutschen Reiches*, Weimar.

Tellenbach, G. ed. 1957a. *Studien und Vorarbeiten zur Geschichte des großfränkischen und frühdeutschen Adels*, Freiburg im Breisgau.

Tellenbach, G. 1957b. 'Zur ältesten Geschichte der Welfen in Süddeutschland', in Tellenbach 1957a, pp. 335-40.

Tellenbach, G. 1979. 'Die geistigen und politischen Grundlagen der karolingischen Thronfolge. Zugleich eine Studie über kollektive Willensbildung und kollektives Handeln im neunten Jahrhundert', *FMS* 13, pp. 184-302.

Thorpe, L. 1968. *Two Lives of Charlemagne*, Harmondsworth.

Tremp, E. 1991. *Die Überlieferung der Vita Hludowici imperatoris des Astronomus, MGH Studien und Texte* 1, Hanover.

Toubert, P. 1973. *Les Structures du Latium médiévale*, 2 vols., Paris.

Trost, K. *et al.* ed. 1988. *Symposium Methodianum. Beiträge der Internationale Tagung in Regensburg (17. bis 24. April 1985) zum Gedenken an den 1100. Todestag des hl. Method*, Neuried.

Turek, R. 1974. *Böhmen im Morgengrauen der Geschichte. Von den Anfängen der slawischen Besiedlung bis zum Eintritt in die europäische Kulturgemeinschaft (6. bis Ende des 10. Jahrhunderts)*, Wiesbaden.

Untermann, M. 1983. 'Zur Kölner Domweihe von 870', *Rheinische Vierteljahresblätter* 47, pp. 335-42.

Vlasto, A. P. 1970. *The Entry of the Slavs into Christendom*, Cambridge.

Vogel, W. 1906. *Die Normannen und das fränkische Reich bis zur Gründung der Normandie (799-911)*, Heidelberg.

Voss, I. 1987. *Herrschertreffen im frühen und hohen Mittelalter*, Cologne.

Wagner, N. 1980. 'Der Name der Stellinga', *Beiträge zur Namensforschung* 15, pp. 128-33.

Waitz, G. ed. 1878a. *Annales Hildesheimenses, MGH SRG*, Hanover.

Waitz, G. ed. 1878b. *Scriptores rerum Langobardicarum et Italicarum saeculo VI-IX, MGH SRL*, Hanover.

Waitz, G. 1880, 1882, 1883, 1885, 1893, 1896, 1876, 1878c. *Deutsche Verfassungsgeschichte*, 8 vols., vols. 1-3 3rd edn, vols. 4-6 2nd edn, Berlin.

Waitz, G. ed. 1884. *Vita Anskarii auctore Rimberto, MGH SRG*, Hanover.

Waitz, G. and Heller, J. eds. 1881. *Flodoardi Historia Remensis Ecclesiae, MGH SS* 13, pp. 405-599.

Waquet, H. ed. 1942. *Abbon. Le Siège de Paris par les Normands*, Paris.

Wattenbach, W. 1889. Rev. edn of Rehdantz 1852, Leipzig.

Wehlt, H.-P. 1970. *Reichsabtei und König dargestellt am Beispiel der Abtei Lorsch mit Ausblicken auf Hersfeld, Stablo und Fulda*, Göttingen.

Weinfurter, S. and Engels, O. 1982. *Series episcoporum ecclesiae catholicae occidentalis. Series V: Germania, Tomus I: Archiepiscopatus Coloniensis*, Stuttgart.

Weinfurter, S. and Engels, O. 1984. *Series episcoporum ecclesiae catholicae occidentalis. Series V: Germania, Tomus II: Archiepiscopatus Hammaburgensis sive Bremensis*, Stuttgart.

Wendehorst, A. 1962. *Das Bistum Würzburg. Teil 1. Die Bischofsreihe bis 1254* (Germania Sacra, neue Folge 1: Die Bistümer der Kirchenprovinz Mainz), Berlin.

Werner, K.-F. 1959. 'Untersuchungen zur Frühzeit des französischen Fürstentums (9.-10. Jht.), IV', *Die Welt als Geschichte* 19, pp. 146-93.

Werner, K.-F. 1967. 'Die Nachkommen Karls des Großen', in W. Braunfels ed., *Karl der Große, IV. Das Nachleben*, Düsseldorf, pp. 403-79 and table.

Werner, K.-F. 1979. 'Gauzlin von Saint-Denis und die westfränkische Reichsteilung von Amiens (880)', *DA* 35, pp. 395-462.

Werner, K.-F. 1981. 'La genèse des duchés en France et en Allemagne', *Settimane* 28, pp. 175-207.

Whitelock, D. ed. 1979. *English Historical Documents*, vol. 1, 2nd edn London.

Wibel, H. 1902. *Beiträge zur Kritik der Annales Regni Francorum*, Strasbourg.

Wickham, C. 1981. *Early Medieval Italy, 400-1000*, London.

Winterfeld, P. *Gesta Berengarii imperatoris, MGH Poetae* 4/1, pp. 354-403.

Wolfram, H. 1979. *Conversio Bagoariorum et Carantonorum*, Vienna.

Wolfram, H. 1987. *Die Geburt Mitteleuropas*, Vienna and Berlin.

Wood, I. N. 1987. 'Christians and pagans in ninth-century Scandinavia', in B. Sawyer, P. Sawyer and I. Wood eds., *The Christianization of Scandinavia*, Alingsås, pp. 36-67.

Yeandle, D. N. 1989. 'The *Ludwigslied*: King, Church and context', in J. Flood and D. N. Yeandle eds., *'mit regulu bituungan'. Neue Arbeiten zur althochdeutschen Poesie und Sprache*, Göppingen.

Zatschek, H. 1935. 'Die Reichsteilungen unter Kaiser Ludwig dem Frommen', *MIÖG* 49, pp. 186-224.

Zielinski, H. 1991. 'Reisegeschwindigkeit und Nachrichtenübermittlung als Probem der Regestenarbeit am Beispiel eines undatierten Kapitulars Lothars I. von 847 Früjahr (846 Herbst?)', in P.-J. Heinig ed., *Diplomatische und chronologische Studien aus der Arbeit an den Regesta Imperii*, Cologne, pp. 37-49.

Zimmermann, H. 1968. *Papstabsetzungen des Mittelalters*, Cologne.

Zimmermann, H. 1974. 'Imperatores Italiae', in H. Beumann ed., *Historische Forschungen für Walter Schlesinger*, Cologne, pp. 379-99.

INDEX

Notes: (i) homonyms are listed thus: clerical personnel precede lay, lay persons are ordered chronologically and generational seniority is followed within families; (ii) an asterisk indicates that a person can be found on one of the genealogical tables; (iii) places can be identified using the notes and the maps; (iv) a hyphen between page-numbers does *not* necessarily indicate continuous treatment of the subject in the text.